WHAT THE

Stories of Hawaii

by JACK LONDON

Edited by

A. GROVE DAY

MUTUAL PUBLISHING

Library of Congress Catalogue Card Number: 65-11682

ISBN 0-935180-08-7

Reprinted 1986, 1990, 1994, 1998, 2001

Cover photographs from the Baker-Van Dyke Collection.
Cover design by Bill Fong, the Art Directors.

Mutual Publishing
1215 Center Street, Suite 210
Honolulu, Hawaii 96816
Telephone (808) 732-1709
Fax (808) 734-4094
e-mail: mutual@lava.net
www.mutualpublishing.com

Printed in Australia

CONTENTS

STORIES OF HAWAII

INTRODUCTION

"THEY DON'T KNOW WHAT THEY'VE GOT!" JOHN GRIFFITH London exclaimed about the American people when he landed in the Territory of Hawaii in 1907, on the first leg of a yachting trip through the Pacific.

His observations on the future fiftieth state, experienced during a five-month tour in that year, as well as during longer stays in 1915 and 1916, were passed on to his world-wide reading public in many articles and several books. His finest novel, the semiautobiographical *Martin Eden,* was written on the *Snark* cruise. A number of other great stories were likewise written in Hawaii, as well as the two popular novels about dogs, *Jerry of the Islands* and *Michael, Brother of Jerry.*

Two volumes of short stories that should be more widely known were written about the Hawaiian Islands and their people. London showed a great *aloha* for the Paradise of the Pacific over a period of thirteen years, and was proud to call himself a *kamaaina,* or old-timer, there in the islands where he had explored and had pioneered in surfboard-riding off Waikiki. And when on November 22, 1916, he was found dying in his home in the Valley of the Moon in California from uremic poisoning, he had been working on a novelette about race relations in Hawaii.

Born in San Francisco on January 12, 1876, son of John and Flora London, Jack went through early adventures as oyster pirate, sailor on a sealing ship, hobo, student for one semester at the University of California, and prospector in the Alaskan gold rush. Drawing on his experiences in the Klondike, he began to write vigorous stories such as *The Call of the Wild,* which brought him popularity when it appeared in 1903.

London first glimpsed the Big Island of Hawaii in the 1890's from the decks of the sealing ship *Sophie Sutherland.* He spent a day swimming at Waikiki in mid-January, 1904, on his way to the Orient in the *Manchuria* as correspondent in the Russo-Japanese War, and briefly stopped in Honolulu when returning in the *Korea* six months later. But the voyage that was to take him around the Pacific on his own specially built yacht had its origin during chats around a swimming pool at Glen Ellen, near Sonoma, California. Jack remarked that he would like to emulate Captain Joshua Slocum, who had girdled the globe on his tiny yacht *Spray.* The result of this idea was the "inconceivable and monstrous" adventures chronicled in London's volume *The Cruise of the "Snark"* (Macmillan, 1911). This South Sea voyage ended after two years when its owner became seriously ill from an affliction that London believed came from exposure of a blond skin to tropical sunlight.

This entertaining volume is composed of a series of articles written to help defray the enormous expense of the cruise. More than a third of its pages describe the troubles and misunderstandings that arose when the author began planning his dream cruise, or deal with the rough traverse to Hawaii and experiences ashore in those islands.

Everything went wrong that could go wrong; even the San Francisco earthquake of 1906 conspired to delay the completion of the forty-three-foot ketch that was built at enormous expense to meet Jack's specifications. Thousands of people, yearning to escape to the alluring South Seas, applied to be unpaid members of the *Snark's* minuscule crew. Sight unseen, Jack selected one young man to be cook on the voyage; his name was Martin Johnson, and he later wrote a book, *Through the South Seas with Jack London* (Dodd, Mead, 1913) and became a famed African explorer.

The total roster of the *Snark*, as it headed out beyond the Golden Gate on April 23, 1907, consisted of Jack London; his recently wedded second wife, Charmian Kittredge London; her aunt's husband Roscoe Eames, who vied with London for the title of "captain" but who, it turned out, did not know how to navigate; Martin Johnson, cook; Herbert Stolz, young Stanford University student, engineer; and Tochigi, Japanese cabin boy.

The *Snark* was a boojum. The vessel leaked; the engine did not work; the design made it impossible for the ship to come about, and it often wallowed in the trough of a sea; the gasoline tanks leaked and fumes made it impossible to stay below or even to strike a match. Everybody was seasick for several days. Moreover, Charmian had decided that this was a good time to cure Jack of his habit of chain smoking, and had persuaded Bert Stolz to throw overboard all supplies of tobacco. London was forced to teach himself navigation, and in mid-ocean had to sit down and solve the riddles of sextant and log tables. Small Charmian often took her trick at the helm for eight hours in the dark, while the five men tried to get some sleep on a pitching small craft somewhere in the Pacific.

Through luck or skill, the *Snark* arrived off Honolulu on May 21. Newspapers brought aboard by the men of the customhouse tug told the amateur sailors that, considering the time that had elapsed since they left San Francisco, all hopes had been given up, for the *Snark* had evidently gone down with all hands!

Safely moored at Pearl Harbor, the *Snark* was repaired and the Londons immediately began enjoying their stay in Hawaii. They shared their time between the Thomas W. Hobron bungalow on a peninsula near Pearl City and quarters on the grounds of the Seaside Hotel at Waikiki. On the beach they set up housekeeping in a "brown-tent cottage" under a coconut palm at a site on the Diamond Head edge of what is now the Royal Hawaiian Hotel property, not far from the old Outrigger Canoe Club, which then did not exist. The main landmark was the Seaside Hotel, managed by Fred Church, an old Yukon friend of Jack's.

Although enjoying the society life of Honolulu, they found that most of their pleasure came from swimming and chatting with bronzed Polynesians and others on the beach. Jack, always daring and willing to try any game, became fascinated with the art of riding a surfboard, and after a lesson or two from Alexander Hume Ford and George Freeth, he became expert enough to write his article "A Royal Sport: Surfing at Waikiki." But exposure of his body for four hours to the burning rays of the subtropical sun and the brine of the swells offshore resulted in a painful, skin-peeling case of sunburn that kept him incapacitated for days.

The Londons were invited to a reception given for visiting congressmen by Prince Jonah Kuhio Kalanianaole, Hawaii's delegate to Washington, and his wife, Princess Elizabeth, at their Waikiki home. The deposed Queen Liliuokalani emerged from her seclusion to meet the visitors gracefully on this occasion.

On one of their hikes, Jack and Charmian climbed up Diamond Head and viewed the interior of this crater. They joined in the sentimental rite of bidding farewell to travelers on a transport steamer at the wharf, with everyone wearing flower leis and the Royal Hawaiian Band playing *"Aloha Oe."* The couple enjoyed a "calabash luau" at Pearl Lochs, were driven around Oahu by carriage, visited the Honolulu Aquarium, and were welcomed to Ainahau, garden residence of A. S. Cleghorn, who had married King Kalakaua's sister Likelike and fathered the little heiress apparent, Princess Kaiulani, who had died at the age of twenty-four. They breakfasted with Sanford B. Dole, for a decade the political head of Hawaii, and Jack, the theoretical revolutionist, talked with the leader of a real if bloodless revolution that had deposed the old Hawaiian monarchy.

On the first of July the Londons embarked on the *Noeau* for a five-day visit to the leper settlement of Kalaupapa on Molokai, and were surprised to find that the people there were well treated and on the whole happy. The Londons left the peninsula by ascending the almost vertical 2300-foot cliff trail, and departed from Molokai from the port of Kaunakakai on the little *Iwalani*.

Jack and Charmian soon after visited Maui and rode with the Polish adventurer Louis von Tempsky on a cattle ranch on the slopes of the gigantic crater of Haleakala. The party included not only the Londons but Lorrin A. Thurston, publisher of the Honolulu *Advertiser*, and his wife. Thurston became so seasick on the interisland steamer *Claudine* that in compassion the group disembarked at Lahaina, the famed old whaling port, instead of at Wailuku. They put up at the Pioneer Inn, which had been built about seven years before. The mosquitoes were so bad that in the night Jack fled his room and was found at dawn lying on the boards of the upstairs front veranda.

Welcomed at Haleakala Ranch, the group set off after two days to penetrate "The House of the Sun," largest volcanic crater on earth. London was amazed that so few of his fellow Americans were aware that one of the greatest scenic vistas of our world was so accessible to them and yet so relatively unknown. The party of four visitors was accompanied by Von Tempsky and his two daughters—Armine, fourteen, and Gwen, fifteen—and two cowboys. They explored the slopes of the ten-thousand-foot mountain and then descended into the crater and camped among the brightly colored cinder cones. This titanic desert in the sky they traversed, emerging after several days through the Kaupo Gap. The return trip went by way of Hana and the north side of the island of Maui, then through the sugar lands of the torrential Nahiku Ditch country, and it required several days on horseback. The trail spanned hair-raising gorges on narrow wooden flumes, where the bravest cowboy of the ranch sheepishly dismounted and led his horse across.

The young girls, reared on horseback, took a great liking to the Londons, and pelted Jack with wild raspberries at a stopping place called Ukulele on the slopes of Haleakala, or splashed him with mud from their galloping horses. In later years Armine, author of a fine autobiography (*Born in Paradise,* Duell, Sloan and Pearce, 1940), attributed to Jack London her first encouragement in the writer's craft.

The *Snark,* refitted and supplied with a new crew except for the faithful Martin Johnson, sailed from Oahu on August 15 to take the Londons to Hawaii, biggest of the island group. The couple disembarked on the sleepy Kona Coast, while the yacht went round the south end of the island and up to the port of Hilo.

After touring Kona, the Londons visited the world-famed Parker Ranch and rode with the Hawaiian cowboys there, and on the way to Hilo explored the sugar plantations of the Hamakua Coast (where they experienced a "mild" earthquake). From Hilo, like thousands of visitors before and after them, they ascended the volcanic region of Kilauea and stopped at Volcano House (whose owner, George Lycurgus, was misnamed "Mr. Demosthenes" in Charmian's journal). They gazed into the bubbling fire pit of Halemaumau, which Jack admiringly characterized as "a hell of a hole." And the manager of the Waipalia sugar mill invited the party to a thrilling ride down the steep water flumes on mats of sugarcane stalks.

Regretfully, the Londons left on October 7 for the Marquesas and for other adventures that would take two years and result in half a dozen other books on the South Seas. But they were destined to return several times before Jack's death at the age of forty.

London's lifelong habit of turning out a thousand words a day of printable manuscript persisted throughout his cruise. Off San Francisco, as soon as the *Snark* became partly manageable, the author began work on *Martin Eden.* At Pearl Harbor, although dejected by a sheaf of rejections of another great book, *The Iron Heel,* he wrote one of his finest short stories, "To Build a Fire." It is ironic to think of London, sitting under the tropical sun of Hawaii, writing a story about a man in Alaska who falls through the ice and freezes to death.

His host Lorrin A. Thurston noted in his memoirs that while the Londons were house guests at a cottage on Tantalus, a hill behind Honolulu, London would get out his basket of notes and begin writing in longhand. "The rest of us would be laughing and talking in the room but London was absolutely oblivious to everything. He studiously and laboriously concentrated on his work until eleven or twelve o'clock when he suddenly would throw down his pencil and say with a sigh, 'Well, my job's done for today!' After he had written a thousand words, nothing could induce him to write another word until the morrow."

The *Snark* chapters recording this first stay in Hawaii were supplemented by six short stories collected in *The House of Pride* (Macmillan, 1912). Three of them mentioned the dread subject of leprosy, a word so fearful that as late as 1949 the Territorial Legislature passed a law that henceforth it should be known in Hawaii only under the name of "Hansen's disease."

London was fascinated by the isolation colony on Molokai for victims of the disease and their helpers, and spent five days there. He was amazed to find that the eight hundred inhabitants of the village were quite human and, on the whole, well adjusted. His description of participating in a Fourth of July picnic reveals that his conception of Molokai as "the pit of hell, the most cursed place on earth" had been modified greatly. Those who later accused Jack of misrepresenting conditions could have read in his chapter: "All the foregoing is by way of preamble to the statement that the horrors of Molokai, as they have been painted in the past, do not exist. The Settlement has been written up repeatedly by sensationalists, and usually by sensationalists who have never laid eyes on it. Of course, leprosy is leprosy, and it is a terrible thing; but so much that is lurid has been written about Molokai that neither the lepers, nor those who devote their lives to them, have received a fair deal."

It is true, however, that of the six stories in *The House of Pride*, three concern the leper problem. Like Robert Louis Stevenson before him and James A. Michener after him,

London was accused of exploiting a minor feature of the Hawaiian scene to terrify prospective visitors.

After his departure, the publication of the three stories aroused a tempest in the Honolulu newspapers. He was accused of making the world think that everybody in Hawaii was a gruesome leper. One letter signed "Bystander" termed London "a dirty little sneak, a sneak of the first water, a thoroughly untrustworthy man, an ungrateful and untruthful bounder."

In an exchange of lengthy letters between London and his friend Thurston, editor of the *Advertiser,* the two men aired their opinions concerning Hawaii's "peculiar institution" and its reception of criticism. "I think Hawaii is too touchy on matters of truth" London remarked; "and while she complacently in her newspapers exploits the weaknesses and afflictions of other lands, gets unduly excited when her own are exploited. Furthermore, the several purely fictional stories on leprosy written by me have not shaken the world at all, Hawaii's fevered imagination to the contrary. . . . Stevenson's Father Damien letter has more effect in a minute, and will go on having more effect in a minute, than all the stories I have written or ever shall write."

The sensitiveness of the people of Hawaii to their valiant efforts to handle the problem of this imported disease by isolation of victims continued long after its dangers had virtually been wiped out by modern medical science, but the theme still attracts writers. One of the finest recent novels about Hawaiian history is Dr. O. A. Bushnell's *Molokai* (World, 1963.)

In *The House of Pride* appears one of the best known of the London stories, "Koolau the Leper." As with some of the other yarns, London drew upon local history and legend for its basis, but it is fiction, not fact, and the real events did not happen in just that way.

London probably first heard the tale of Koolau from his young crewman Bert Stolz on the rolling deck of the *Snark,* for Bert had been born on the island of Kauai, setting for the story, and his father had been the deputy sheriff who was killed during an attempt to capture the outlaw peaceably.

The true adventures of the real Koolau are in some ways more astounding even than the figure of London's creation. During the unsettled year of 1893, right after the overthrow of Queen Liliuokalani, the Provisional Government attempted to corral all known lepers and treat them at the Molokai center, since isolation was the only known palliative at the time. The thirty-one-year-old cowboy Koolau helped to round them up on Kauai, and then, discovering that he himself was stricken, agreed to go with the group by ship if his healthy wife, Piilani, could go along to attend him. But at the last minute she was held ashore on a baseless charge, and Koolau leaped overboard and swam back, to become the leader of a defiant leper band in the Kalalau Valley. He did murder Deputy Sheriff Louis H. Stolz, and did withstand a company of National Guardsmen armed with a Krupp gun. For three years Koolau, his wife Piilani, and their young son hid in the valley. Then the child, who had been infected with leprosy, died and was buried by the grieving couple. Two months later Koolau died, and was buried in a grave overlooking the valley of his exploits, in a grave hacked out beneath a cliff by Piilani with a small knife. The outlaw was dead, but his legend had just begun, and will be perpetuated for a long time by chatty tour guides.

The differences between the fiction and the true story are not important. London had created another tale on his favorite theme—the defiance of a strong man who feels that his cause is just and who will never give in unto death. The Koolau of his book is true in spirit to the desperate pariah of history who refused to yield even to a company of soldiers.

The story "Good-by, Jack" tells of a brilliant young millionaire who is also a brave man, but who at the end suffers a fear a thousand times more hideous than the fear he had endured by the narrator when he sees a writhing centipede. "I never knew!" Jack cries, when his friend says: "You, of all men, should have known." It is easy to be brave when one is sure there is no possible cause for infection by disease.

A third story, "The Sheriff of Kona," also has a brave man for protagonist. He is also a lucky man, but he, whose duty requires him to send others into exile at Molokai, is ironically stricken with "the mark of the beast." The theme here, however, although there is an exciting midnight rescue from Molokai, is that Lyte Gregory feels a profound love for Kona, but can never return to his family and his paradise above the serene Kona sea; and nobody can do anything about it.

The setting for "Aloha Oe" is the Honolulu wharf in the days when visitors could come only by sea and the departure of a steamer was a gala event. At the railing, Dorothy Sambrooke, fifteen-year-old daughter of a junketing United States senator, realizes that her friendship with Stephen Knight has blossomed into the love that comes once in a lifetime. But Steve is one-fourth Hawaiian, and "because there was tropic sunshine in his veins he could not marry her." This tale recalls a time that seems far distant. Nowadays Hawaiian ancestry is a marked social and political asset, and almost half the marriages in Hawaii are between people of different racial or national stocks.

The title story of the collection deals likewise with racial snobbishness, and the key is the commentary of Percival Ford's informant, who says: "Just because your blood is cold, well-ordered, and well-disciplined is no reason that you should frown upon Joe Garland. When Joe Garland undoes the work you do, remember that it is only old Isaac Ford on both sides, undoing with one hand what he does with the other."

The finest story in *The House of Pride*, perhaps, is "Chun Ah Chun." Like the Koolau yarn, this also was clearly derived from London's recollection of a unique character in Hawaiian history, although again the needs of fiction unified the facts and eliminated many fascinating details. The real "Ah Chun" family was actually named Ah Fong.

The main character of this story was modeled on an Asian who came early to the Melting Pot of the Pacific. Chun Ah

Fong was a young mandarin merchant who arrived in 1849—five years before the landing of the first shipload of imported Chinese field hands. He married Julia Hope Kamakia Paaika-mokalani e Kinau Beckley Fayerweather, a girl who was descended from proud Hawaiian chiefs, whose grandfather was a British sea captain, and whose father was a Yankee sugar planter. Ah Fong made a fortune in business, and with his sixteen children—four boys and twelve girls—founded the most remarkable of Honolulu's cosmopolitan families. All but one of the children lived to be adult, and most of them married well—many of them to Caucasians.

Obviously, in London's short story he is not attempting a history of this fascinating family, but is once more showing a strong character solving his main problem by pursuing his main trait. James A. Michener, in his introduction to *A Hawaiian Reader* (Appleton-Century-Crofts, 1959), exercised his critical privilege to remark that when Jack London came to Hawaii "and saw at first hand a population—the Chinese—which had many of the characteristics he had espoused in mainland America, he was completely unable to understand what he saw. In 'Chun Ah Chun' . . . he not only failed to comprehend what was happening in the Pacific; he actually denigrated an entire body of people, largely on racist grounds. . . . I have never understood how Jack London could be one man in California, and such a different man in Hawaii. . . . Yet the story 'Chun Ah Chun' does have a sly warmth and much wit and remains one of the focal works in the London repertoire."

It is true that in many places elsewhere, Jack London glorified the battling, unyielding spirit of the Caucasian race. He went so far as to exclaim, during the Russo-Japanese War in 1904: "What the devil! I am first of all a white man and only then a Socialist!" Yet a careful reading of "Chun Ah Chun" should reveal that actually the fools and knaves of the story are the Caucasian men who by one means or another are persuaded to marry into the part-Chinese clan, and that the most admirable figure in the cast is the father, who does solve his problem intelligently and gracefully, and then retires to enjoy his success and contemplate philosophically the outcome of his actions. The story is great because it deals amusingly and with keen insight into an age-old human problem and offers a plausible solution.

When the Londons again sought refuge in Hawaii, during the two years before America entered World War I, Jack was at the height of his fame. Author of some fifty books, the best known, highest paid, and most popular writer in the world, he was nevertheless still filled with a boyish enthusiasm to see new sights. Visitors were more common in 1915 and 1916 than in 1907; Hawaii National Park, including London's spectacular "House of the Sun" and other volcanoes, was established in 1916. Of the American people he said on this trip: "Because they have no other place to go, they are just beginning to realize what they've got."

"Keaka Lakana," to give him his Hawaiian name, and Charmian were again invited to participate in the social whirl. Although some people recalled that he had been too fond of writing about leprosy, and although *The House of Pride* was not available in local bookshops or prominent on family shelves, Jack had earned the right to be called a *kamaaina*, or old-timer, and was royally received. His fondness for open-throated sport dress and hatless comfort sometimes barred him from formal affairs. Once he accepted such an invitation but in fun stayed away and ordered a dress suit to be put in a cardboard box and delivered in his stead.

The Londons arrived in Honolulu on the *Matsonia* on March 2, 1915, but after a day ashore they went on a circle cruise on the same ship to the Big Island, where they witnessed an eruption in the fire pit of Halemaumau and looked up old friends. Later in the year, they took a six-week jaunt around the same island, visiting the City of Refuge at Honaunau, the Parker Ranch, the Kau region, the black-sand beach of Kalapana, the deeps of Waipio Valley, and the hills of Kohala. Julian Monsarrat, of a ranching family, and Mary

Low, related to the Parkers, filled Jack's ears with enough local commentary for a hundred stories.

Back in Waikiki, jostled by tourists—many of whom had been attracted to Hawaii by Jack's writings—the Londons rented a cottage on Beach Walk, and discovered that near where they had lived in a brown tent had been built the Outrigger Canoe Club, through the efforts of many lovers of surf sports led by Alexander Hume Ford. Here they relaxed and swam with famed Duke Paoa Kahanamoku, who in 1912 had broken the hundred-yard record at the Stockholm Olympics. "I'm glad we're here now," Jack would reflect, lying in the shade of the Outrigger veranda, "for some day Waikiki Beach is going to be the scene of one long hotel." But not even Jack London could have guessed that in 1964 the Outrigger Club itself would have to move several miles toward Diamond Head to make way for another skyscraping hotel.

Another lasting promotion by Jack's friend Ford was the establishment of the Trail and Mountain Club, which is still active in the islands. Ford was also busy publishing a magazine and promoting the idea of the Pan-Pacific Union, which held its first celebration on Balboa Day, September 25, 1916. London had helped to forward this "hands-around-the-Pacific" idea through speeches such as one he gave at the Outrigger Club in 1915, in which he said: "I believe that there should be a club here in polyglot Hawaii where we may study the tribal language." Another outcome of Ford's efforts was the Pan-Pacific Scientific Council; forty years later, in 1960, the Pacific Science Congress, as it came to be called, held another meeting in Honolulu, attended by hundreds of savants from all over the world.

The Londons in 1915 again visited Queen Liliuokalani and "Prince Cupid" Kuhio Kalanianaole, went to Maui to ride with the Von Tempskys on Haleakala, and returned to see the improvements at the settlement on Molokai. On this latter trip they reversed the route by descending the trail to the Kalaupapa Peninsula, and then took a sampan or fishing launch for a cruise along the almost inaccessible coast of windward Molokai.

The Londons returned to California in July so that Jack could attend the Bohemian Club High Jinks, but were back again at Honolulu on December 23 on the *Great Northern*. They found a comfortable cottage at 2201 Kalia Road, not far from the Halekulani Hotel. From this cottage Jack wrote a letter, on March 7, 1916, resigning from the Socialist Party. There, in a blue kimono, during the last year of his life, he wrote most of the stories reprinted in the posthumous volume *On the Makaloa Mat* (1919), as well as others not set in Hawaii. He had already written in Hawaii his two very popular "dog stories," *Jerry of the Islands* and *Michael, Brother of Jerry,* both to be published in 1917. "My Hawaiian Aloha," a few pages of which are reprinted herein, was written at Puuwaawaa Ranch, Hawaii, on April 19, 1916.

The stories appearing in *On the Makaloa Mat* should be considered in the order in which they were written. It is notable that in this book London, although he had revisited the Molokai station, carefully omitted any mention of leprosy except that in "Shin Bones" the narrator does encounter on a spooky journey in a hidden valley "an old leper in hiding." In fact, London in that story goes so far as to avoid even mentioning the name of Molokai, and the setting is an imaginary island east of Oahu called "Lakanaii."

The title story of *On the Makaloa Mat* portrays two elderly sisters, sitting at Waikiki and revealing their secrets. Both are one-fourth Hawaiian, and both married to *haoles,* white men from New England who were destined to buy lands and make fortunes. The older one, Bella, confesses that, swept up in a royal progress around the Big Island, she had for two weeks shared with Prince Lilolilo the fine-woven *makaloa* mat, taboo to all but royalty. The tone is nostalgic, recalling the days when the nobility of the islands still exerted an imperious will.

In "The Tears of Ah Kim" the main character is a fifty-year-old Chinese who has risen from tow-rope coolie on the Yangtze River to shop owner in Honolulu. The various characterizations are amusing, but perhaps the main point of the story is: Why doesn't Ah Kim weep under the beatings of his mother's bamboo stick until a certain day?

In "The Bones of Kahekili," Hardman Poole, haole ranch patriarch who has made himself a ruler of men, persuades an old Hawaiian cowboy to tell him the story of the death and burial of Chief Kahekili. (This name was that of a historic and powerful chief, ruler of all the islands except Hawaii, but he died in 1794, not in 1828, when London sets his tale.) The reminiscences of the old Hawaiian, who had been chosen as a human sacrifice, are exciting, but the theme of the story probably is found in the remarks of Hardman Poole on the nature of chiefs and chieftainship.

"Shin Bones" also reveals London's explorations into Hawaiian history and burial customs. Prince Akuli, descendant of the highest nobility, tells how he won his parents' consent to an Oxford education. At the age of fifteen he had accompanied an old retainer to a museum-like cave on the "Ironbound Coast" to collect the bones of his mother's mother. He had secretly brought back also the shin bones of Laulani, a Hawaiian Guinevere, and a spearhead made from the bones of her Lancelot. To possession at this early age of these reminders of humility, the prince owed more than to anything else.

"The Kanaka Surf" is a triangle story of three super-people —Lee and Ida Barton, who had early learned to be expert body-surfers in the biggest waves off Waikiki, and Sonny Grandison, social leader and rival for Lee's wife. In the swells far beyond hope of rescue by the alert lifeguards on the Outrigger Club veranda, Lee feigns fatal cramps to test whether he can retain his wife. A possible flaw in this story is that the couple are both such super-beings that it is hard to excuse their all too human defects, and London does not make it easier by inveighing for several pages against weaklings and envious gossips. Beneath the fiction one can sense a good deal about Jack and Charmian and their relationships with Honolulu society.

In "When Alice Told Her Soul," written when London

had barely returned from his final visit to Hawaii, he tells of Abel Ah Yoh, a polyracial Billy Sunday who converts long-memoried but tight-tongued Alice Akana. When terror finally unloosens her tongue in the filled tabernacle, "Never was a more fearful and damning community narrative enunciated in the entire Pacific, north and south, than that enunciated by Alice Akana, the penitent Phryne of Honolulu."

Underlying the rollicking comedy of this Honolulu fable, which might have been concocted by one who had listened keenly to all the local gossip, was London's growing interest in C. C. Jung's *Psychology of the Unconscious,* in his copy of which he had underlined a passage pointing out that a neurotic derives special benefit when he can at last rid his libido of its various secrets.

Modern psychology is even more prominent in the last short story ever written by this master, "The Water Baby," completed at Glen Ellen on October 2. Outwardly it is a simple reminiscence of fishing off Waihee with a seventy-year-old Hawaiian who thinks nothing of breaking off his conversation to dive down forty feet and kill a large octopus, and who otherwise passes the time by retelling the age-old story of Maui's deeds in the islands, or the tall tale of Keikiwai, the "water baby" who fools forty sharks. The narrator has been "born in the islands," but significantly his name is John Lakana—which is to say, Jack London. The two men discuss the riddles of religion and dreams, including the idea that life is all a dream—a conclusion reached in Mark Twain's posthumous novel *The Mysterious Stranger,* published that same year of 1916.

Despite the air of lazy legend-telling, the story has modern profundity. Often dismissed as a primitivist, London in his last years was aware, long before the theories of Freud and Jung were topics of cocktail chat in the 1920's, of the role of dreams and the unconscious. His tales often dredge the deep-rooted myths of our species, and the ponderings even of a lowly old Polynesian may have meanings still to be discovered by the psychologists. This tale of "The Water Baby" was labeled by London's wife a Jungian parable, "clearly a symbolic representation of the Rebirth, the return of the Mother" (*The Book of Jack London*, Century, 1921.)

Those seven months in Hawaii during London's last year were comparatively quiet, for already dread signs were appearing in the ex-sailor's robust body. He suffered insomnia, uremia, and the agonies of kidney stones. But many friends were still to be entertained. Almost daily there were luncheon parties. Once a neighbor asked Jack: "Why do you always have twelve at your table?" The answer came "Because it won't hold any more!" Before the Londons sailed from Hawaii on July 26, 1916, they gave a farewell dinner for forty people at their cottage, during which was sung the "Jack London Hula," a *mele* or chant written by Mary Low, recounting the many deeds of Keaka Lakana, *kamaaina* friend of Hawaii.

The following November 22, Jack was found in his bed at Glen Ellen, dying from uremic poisoning. Beneath the boulder on Sonoma Mountain that marks his grave was buried with him a withered ilima lei given to him in Hawaii by his ranch-owning friend Colonel Samuel Parker. Perhaps London's most touching epitaph was the expression of a Hawaiian lad who played the ukulele at a San Francisco theater: "Better than any one, he *knew* us Hawaiians. . . . Jack London, the Story Maker. . . . The news came to Honolulu—and people, they seemed to have lost a great friend—*auwe!* They could not understand. . . . They could not believe. I tell you this: Better than any one, he knew us Hawaiians."

On London's writing desk on November 22 lay a manuscript on which he had been working the previous day. His last words to the world were part of a novelette about a lovely Japanese girl reared in Hawaii. The yarn was finished by Charmian and appeared in two issues of *Cosmopolitan* in 1924. There is a noticeable break in style midway, after the wife's pen takes over, but the outcome of the story had frequently been talked over with her. As she wrote: "Jack and I enjoyed more discussion about the development of this

romance than about any of the other thirty-five-odd books
he published during our eleven years together. And so it
happens I feel unusually close to his unfinished tale. Not
entirely unfinished, happily; for he left notes, and in my
mind his intention is unforgotten."

"Eyes of Asia" tells of a baby girl who is the only person
rescued from a mysterious vessel cast up on the rocks of the
Big Island. Adopted by a wealthy American family, she bene-
fits by all the advantages of Occidental culture, and her
exotic beauty captures the hearts of many young men of
various nationalities. Cherry, as she is called—for her patrician
Japanese origin is clear—is restless and fears she may never
know love.

She then begins to feel an uncanny interest in Nomura,
one of the Japanese yard boys on the estate, whose actions
suggest that he is more aristocratic than he appears. Despite
the desperate appeals of her haole suitors, one of whom com-
mits suicide when he sees his rejection in her Oriental eyes,
the girl elopes to Japan with Nomura, leaving behind her
American heritage. Despite the many other colorful features
of this last work of London's, the theme was not a new one.
Although Jack had for years observed and admired the harmony with which people of many races lived together in
Hawaii in amity and frequently married across racial lines
with happy results, he felt to the end that instinct is stronger
than environment. The conclusion of "Eyes of Asia," a liter-
ary curiosity never printed in book form, is that blood still
calls to blood.

Much of Jack London's best writing, one must conclude,
was done in Hawaii and the Pacific. Although the stories
with a Pacific setting are often overlooked by readers of his
other works, those describing the adventures to be found
in this biggest of oceans, and particularly in the Hawaiian
Islands he loved so well, should be remembered and read.

A. GROVE DAY

University of Hawaii

The House of Pride

THE HOUSE OF PRIDE

PERCIVAL FORD WONDERED WHY HE HAD COME. HE DID NOT dance. He did not care much for army people. Yet he knew them all—gliding and revolving there on the broad *lanai* of the Seaside, the officers in their fresh-starched uniforms of white, the civilians in white and black, and the women bare of shoulders and arms. After two years in Honolulu the Twentieth was departing to its new station in Alaska, and Percival Ford, as one of the big men of the Islands, could not help knowing the officers and their women.

But between knowing and liking was a vast gulf. The army women frightened him just a little. They were in ways quite different from the women he liked best—the elderly women, the spinsters and the bespectacled maidens, and the very serious women of all ages whom he met on church and library and kindergarten committees, who came meekly to him for contributions and advice. He ruled those women by virtue of his superior mentality, his great wealth, and the high place he occupied in the commercial baronage of Hawaii. And he was not afraid of them in the least. Sex, with them, was not obtrusive. Yes, that was it. There was in them something else, or more, than the assertive grossness of life. He was fastidious; he acknowledged that to himself; and these army women, with their bare shoulders and naked arms, their straight-looking eyes, their vitality and challenging femaleness, jarred upon his sensibilities.

Nor did he get on better with the army men, who took life lightly, drinking and smoking and swearing their way through life and asserting the essential grossness of flesh no less shamelessly than their women. He was always uncomfortable in the company of the army men. They seemed uncomfortable, too. And he felt, always, that they were laughing at him up their sleeves, or pitying him, or tolerating him. Then, too, they seemed, by mere contiguity, to emphasize a lack in him, to call attention to that in them which he did not possess and which he thanked God he did not possess. Faugh! They were like their women!

In fact, Percival Ford was no more a woman's man than he was a man's man. A glance at him told the reason. He had a good constitution, never was on intimate terms with sickness, nor even mild disorders; but he lacked vitality. His was a negative organism. No blood with a ferment in it could have nourished and shaped that long and narrow face, those thin lips, lean cheeks, and the small, sharp eyes. The thatch of hair, dust-colored, straight and sparse, advertised the niggard soil, as did the nose, thin, delicately modeled, and just hinting the suggestion of a beak. His meager blood had denied him much of life, and permitted him to be an extremist in one thing only, which thing was righteousness. Over right conduct he pondered and agonized, and that he should do right was as necessary to his nature as loving and being loved were necessary to commoner clay.

He was sitting under the algaroba trees between the *lanai* and the beach. His eyes wandered over the dancers and he turned his head away and gazed seaward across the mellow-sounding surf to the Southern Cross burning low on the horizon. He was irritated by the bare shoulders and arms of the women. If he had a daughter he would never permit it, never. But his hypothesis was the sheerest abstraction. The thought process had been accompanied by no inner vision of that daughter. He did not see a daughter with arms and shoulders. Instead, he smiled at the remote contingency of marriage. He was thirty-five, and, having had no personal experience of love, he looked upon it, not as mythical, but as bestial. Anybody could marry. The Japanese and Chinese coolies, toiling on the sugar plantations and in the rice fields, married. They invariably married at the first opportunity. It was because they were so low in the scale of life. There was nothing else for them to do. They were like the army men and women. But for him there were other and higher things. He was different from them—from all of them. He was proud of how he happened to be. He had come of no petty love-match. He had come of lofty conception of duty and of devotion to a cause. His father had not married for love. Love was a madness that had never perturbed Isaac Ford. When he answered the call to go to the heathen with the message of life, he had had no thought and no desire for marriage. In this they were alike, his father and he. But the Board of Missions was economical. With New England thrift it weighed and measured and decided that married missionaries were less expensive per capita and more efficacious. So the Board commanded Isaac Ford to marry. Furthermore, it furnished him with a wife, another zealous soul with no thought of marriage, intent only on doing the Lord's work among the heathen. They saw each other for the first time in Boston. The Board brought them together, arranged everything, and by the end of the week they were married and started on the long voyage around the Horn.

Percival Ford was proud that he had come of such a union. He had been born high, and he thought of himself as a spiritual aristocrat. And he was proud of his father. It was a passion with him. The erect, austere figure of Isaac Ford had burned itself upon his pride. On his desk was a miniature of that soldier of the Lord. In his bedroom hung the portrait of Isaac Ford, painted at the time when he had served under the Monarchy as prime minister. Not that Isaac Ford had coveted place and worldly wealth, but that, as prime minister, and, later, as banker, he had been of greater service to the missionary cause. The German crowd, and the English crowd, and all the rest of the trading crowd, had sneered at Isaac Ford as a commercial soul-saver; but he, his son, knew different. When the natives, emerging abruptly from their

feudal system, with no conception of the nature and signifi-
cance of property in land, were letting their broad acres slip
through their fingers, it was Isaac Ford who had stepped in
between the trading crowd and its prey and taken possession
of fat, vast holdings. Small wonder the trading crowd did
not like his memory. But he had never looked upon his enormous wealth as his own. He had considered himself God's
steward. Out of the revenues he had built schools, and hos-
pitals, and churches. Nor was it his fault that sugar, after the
slump, had paid forty per cent; that the bank he founded had
prospered into a railroad; and that, among other things,
fifty thousand acres of Oahu pasture land, which he had
bought for a dollar an acre, grew eight tons of sugar to the
acre every eighteen months. No, in all truth Isaac Ford was
a heroic figure, fit, so Percival Ford thought privately, to
stand beside the statue of Kamehameha I in front of the
Judiciary Building. Isaac Ford was gone, but he, his son,
carried on the good work, at least as inflexibly if not as
masterfully.

He turned his eyes back to the lanai. What was the difference, he asked himself, between the shameless, grass-girdled
hula dances and the décolleté dances of the women of his
own race? Was there an essential difference? or was it a matter
of degree?

As he pondered the problem a hand rested on his shoulder.

"Hello, Ford, what are you doing here? Isn't this a bit
festive?"

"I try to be lenient, Dr. Kennedy, even as I look on,"
Percival Ford answered gravely. "Won't you sit down?"

Dr. Kennedy sat down, clapping his palms sharply. A white-
clad Japanese servant answered swiftly.

Scotch and soda was Kennedy's order; then, turning to
the other, he said, "Of course, I don't ask you."

"But I will take something," Ford said firmly. The doctor's
eyes showed surprise, and the servant waited. "Boy, a lemonade, please."

The doctor laughed at it heartily, as a joke on himself, and glanced at the musicians under the hau tree.

"Why, it's the Aloha Orchestra," he said, "I thought they were with the Hawaiian Hotel on Tuesday nights. Some rumpus, I guess."

His eyes paused for a moment and dwelt upon the one who was playing a guitar and singing a Hawaiian song to the accompaniment of all the instruments. His face became grave as he looked at the singer, and it was still grave as he turned it to his companion.

"Look here, Ford, isn't it time you let up on Joe Garland? I understand you are in opposition to the Promotion Committee's sending him to the States on this surfboard proposition, and I've been wanting to speak to you about it. I should have thought you'd be glad to get him out of the country. It would be a good way to end your persecution of him."

"Persecution?" Percival Ford's eyebrows lifted interrogatively.

"Call it by any name you please," Kennedy went on. "You've hounded that poor devil for years. It's not his fault. Even you will admit that."

"Not his fault?" Percival Ford's thin lips drew tightly together for the moment. "Joe Garland is dissolute and idle. He has always been a wastrel, a profligate."

"But that's no reason you should keep on after him the way you do. I've watched you from the beginning. The first thing you did when you returned from college and found him working on the plantation as outside *luna* was to fire him—you with your millions, and he with his sixty dollars a month."

"Not the first thing," Percival Ford said judicially, in the tone he was accustomed to use in committee meetings. "I gave him his warning. The superintendent said he was a capable luna. I had no objection to him on that ground. It was what he did outside working hours. He undid my work faster than I could build it up. Of what use were the Sunday schools, the night schools, and the sewing classes when in the evenings there was Joe Garland with his infernal and eternal tum-tumming of guitar and ukulele, his strong drink, and his hula dancing? After I warned him, I came upon him—I shall never forget it—came upon him, down at the cabins. It was evening. I could hear the hula songs before I saw the scene. And when I did see it, there were the girls, shameless in the moonlight and dancing—the girls upon whom I had worked to teach clean living and right conduct. And there were three girls there, I remember, just graduated from the mission school. Of course I discharged Joe Garland. I know it was the same at Hilo. People said I went out of my way when I persuaded Mason and Fitch to discharge him. But it was the missionaries who requested me to do so. He was undoing their work by his reprehensible example."

"Afterwards, when he got on the railroad, your railroad, he was discharged without cause," Kennedy challenged.

"Not so," was the quick answer. "I had him into my private office and talked with him for half an hour."

"You discharged him for inefficiency?"

"For immoral living, if you please."

Dr. Kennedy laughed with a grating sound. "Who the devil gave it to you to be judge and jury? Does landlordism give you control of the immortal souls of those that toil for you? I have been your physician. Am I to expect tomorrow your ukase that I give up Scotch and soda or your patronage? Bah! Ford, you take life too seriously. Besides, when Joe got into that smuggling scrape (he wasn't in your employ, either), and he sent word to you, asked you to pay his fine, you left him to do his six months hard labor on the reef. Don't forget, you left Joe Garland in the lurch that time. You threw him down, hard; and yet I remember the first day you came to school—we boarded, you were only a day scholar—you had to be initiated. Three times under in the swimming tank—you remember, it was the regular dose every new boy got. And you held back. You denied that you could swim. You were frightened, hysterical—"

"Yes, I know," Percival Ford said slowly. "I was frightened. And it was a lie, for I could swim. . . . And I was frightened."

"And you remember who fought for you? who lied for you harder than you could lie and swore he knew you couldn't swim? Who jumped into the tank and pulled you out after the first under and was nearly drowned for it by the other boys, who had discovered by that time that you *could* swim?"

'Of course I know," the other rejoined coldly. "But a generous act as a boy does not excuse a lifetime of wrong living."

"He has never done wrong to you?—personally and directly, I mean?"

"No," was Percival Ford's answer. "That is what makes my position impregnable. I have no personal spite against him. He is bad, that is all. His life is bad—"

"Which is another way of saying that he does not agree with you in the way life should be lived," the doctor interrupted.

"Have it that way. It is immaterial. He is an idler—"

"With reason," was the interruption, "considering the jobs out of which you have knocked him."

"He is immoral—"

"Oh, hold on now, Ford. Don't go harping on that. You are pure New England stock. Joe Garland is half Kanaka. Your blood is thin. His is warm. Life is one thing to you, another thing to him. He laughs and sings and dances through life, genial, unselfish, childlike, everybody's friend. You go through life like a perambulating prayer wheel, a friend of nobody but the righteous, and the righteous are those who agree with you as to what is right. And after all, who shall say? You live like an anchorite. Joe Garland lives like a good fellow. Who has extracted the most from life? We are paid to live, you know. When the wages are too meager we throw up the job, which is the cause, believe me, of all rational suicide. Joe Garland would starve to death on the wages

you get from life. You see, he is made differently. So would
you starve on his wages, which are singing, and love—"

"Lust, if you will pardon me," was the interruption.

Dr. Kennedy smiled.

"Love, to you, is a word of four letters and a definition
which you have extracted from the dictionary. But love, real
love, dewy and palpitant and tender, you do not know. If
God made you and me, and men and women, believe me
he made love, too. But to come back. It's about time you
quit hounding Joe Garland. It is not worthy of you, and
it is cowardly. The thing for you to do is to reach out and
lend him a hand."

"Why I, any more than you?" the other demanded. "Why
don't you reach him a hand?"

"I have. I'm reaching him a hand now. I'm trying to get
you not to down the Promotion Committee's proposition
of sending him away. I got him the job at Hilo with Mason
and Fitch. I've got him half a dozen jobs, out of every one
of which you drove him. But never mind that. Don't forget
one thing—and a little frankness won't hurt you—it is not
fair play to saddle another's fault on Joe Garland; and you
know that you, least of all, are the man to do it. Why, man,
it's not good taste. It's positively indecent."

"Now I don't follow you," Percival Ford answered. "You're
up in the air with some obscure scientific theory of heredity
and personal irresponsibility. But how any theory can hold
Joe Garland irresponsible for his wrongdoings and at the
same time hold me personally responsible for them—more
responsible than anyone else, including Joe Garland—is beyond me."

"It's a matter of delicacy, I suppose, or of taste, that pre-
vents you from following me," Dr. Kennedy snapped out.
"It's all very well, for the sake of society, tacitly to ignore
some things, but you do more than tacitly ignore."

"What is it, pray, that I tacitly ignore?"

Dr. Kennedy was angry. A deeper red than that of con-
stitutional Scotch and soda suffused his face, as he answered:

"Your father's son."

"Now just what do you mean?"

"Damn it, man, you can't ask me to be plainer spoken than that. But if you will, all right—Isaac's Ford's son—Joe Garland—your brother."

Percival Ford sat quietly, an annoyed and shocked expression on his face. Kennedy looked at him curiously, then, as the slow minutes dragged by, became embarrassed and frightened.

"My God!" he cried finally, "you don't mean to tell me that you didn't know!"

As in answer, Percival Ford's cheeks turned slowly gray.

"It's a ghastly joke," he said; "a ghastly joke."

The doctor had got himself in hand.

"Everybody knows it," he said. "I thought you knew it. And since you don't know it, it's time you did, and I'm glad of the chance of setting you straight. Joe Garland and you are brothers—half brothers."

"It's a lie," Ford cried. "You don't mean it. Joe Garland's mother was Eliza Kunilio." (Dr. Kennedy nodded.) "I remember her well, with her duck pond and *taro* patch. His father was Joseph Garland, the beachcomber." (Dr. Kennedy shook his head.) "He died only two or three years ago. He used to get drunk. There's where Joe got his dissoluteness. There's the heredity for you."

"And nobody told you," Kennedy said wonderingly, after a pause.

"Dr. Kennedy, you have said something terrible, which I cannot allow to pass. You must either prove or, or . . ."

"Prove it yourself. Turn around and look at him. You've got him in profile. Look at his nose. That's Isaac Ford's. Yours is a thin edition of it. That's right. Look. The lines are fuller, but they are all there."

Percival Ford looked at the Kanaka half-breed who played under the *hau* tree, and it seemed, as by some illumination, that he was gazing on a wraith of himself. Feature after feature flashed up an unmistakable resemblance. Or, rather, it was he who was the wraith of that other full-muscled and generously molded man. And his features, and that other man's features, were all reminiscent of Isaac Ford. And nobody had told him. Every line of Isaac Ford's face he knew. Miniatures, portraits, and photographs of his father were passing in review through his mind, and here and there, over and again, in the face before him, he caught resemblances and vague hints of likeness. It was devil's work that could reproduce the austere features of Isaac Ford in the loose and sensuous features before him. Once, the man turned, and for one flashing instant it seemed to Percival Ford that he saw his father, dead and gone, peering at him out of the face of Joe Garland.

"It's nothing at all," he could faintly hear Dr. Kennedy saying. "They were all mixed up in the old days. You know that. You've seen it all your life. Sailors married queens and begat princesses and all the rest of it. It was the usual thing in the Islands."

"But not with my father," Percival Ford interrupted.

"There you are." Kennedy shrugged his shoulders. "Cosmic sap and smoke of life. Old Isaac Ford was strait-laced and all the rest, and I know there's no explaining it, least of all to himself. He understood it no more than you do. Smoke of life, that's all. And don't forget one thing, Ford. There was a dab of unruly blood in old Isaac Ford, and Joe Garland inherited it—all of it, smoke of life and cosmic sap; while you inherited all of old Isaac's ascetic blood. And just because your blood is cold, well-ordered, and well-disciplined, is no reason that you should frown upon Joe Garland. When Joe Garland undoes the work you do, remember that it is only old Isaac Ford on both sides, undoing with one hand what he does with the other. You are Isaac Ford's right hand, let us say; Joe Garland is his left hand."

Percival Ford made no answer, and in the silence Dr. Kennedy finished his forgotten Scotch and soda. From across the grounds an automobile hooted imperatively.

"There's the machine," Dr. Kennedy said, rising. "I've

got to run. I'm sorry I've shaken you up, and at the same
time I'm glad. And know one thing, Isaac Ford's dab of
unruly blood was remarkably small, and Joe Garland got it
all. And one other thing. If your father's left hand offend
you, don't smite it off. Besides, Joe is all right. Frankly, if
I could choose between you and him to live with me on a
desert isle, I'd choose Joe."

Little bare-legged children ran about him, playing, on the
grass; but Percival Ford did not see them. He was gazing
steadily at the singer under the hau tree. He even changed
his position once, to get closer. The clerk of the Seaside went
by, limping with age and dragging his reluctant feet. He
had lived forty years on the Islands. Percival Ford beckoned
to him, and the clerk came respectfully, and wondering that
he should be noticed by Percival Ford.

"John," Ford said, "I want you to give me some information. Won't you sit down?"

The clerk sat down awkwardly, stunned by the unexpected
honor. He blinked at the other and mumbled, "Yes, sir,
thank you."

"John, who is Joe Garland?"

The clerk stared at him, blinked, cleared his throat, and
said nothing.

"Go on," Percival Ford commanded. "Who is he?"

"You're joking me, sir," the other managed to articulate.

"I spoke to you seriously."

The clerk recoiled from him.

"You don't mean to say you don't know?" he questioned,
his question in itself the answer.

"I want to know."

"Why, he's—" John broke off and looked about him helplessly. "Hadn't you better ask somebody else? Everybody
thought you knew. We always thought . . ."

"Yes, go ahead."

"We always thought that that was why you had it in for
him."

Photographs and miniatures of Isaac Ford were trooping

through his son's brain, and ghosts of Isaac Ford seemed in the air about him. "I wish you good night, sir," he could hear the clerk saying, and he saw him beginning to limp away.

"John," he called abruptly.

John came back and stood near him, blinking and nervously moistening his lips.

"You haven't told me yet, you know."

"Oh, about Joe Garland?"

"Yes, about Joe Garland. Who is he?"

"He's your brother, sir, if I say it who shouldn't."

"Thank you, John. Good night."

"And you didn't know?" the old man queried, content to linger, now that the crucial point was past.

"Thank you, John. Good night," was the response.

"Yes, sir, thank you, sir. I think it's going to rain. Good night, sir."

Out of a clear sky, filled only with stars and moonlight, fell a rain so fine and attenuated as to resemble a vapor spray. Nobody minded it; the children played on, running barelegged over the grass and leaping into the sand; and in a few minutes it was gone. In the southeast, Diamond Head, a black blot, sharply defined, silhouetted its crater-form against the stars. At sleepy intervals the surf flung its foam across the sand to the grass, and far out could be seen the black specks of swimmers under the moon. The voices of the singers, singing a waltz, died away; and in the silence, from somewhere under the trees, arose the laugh of a woman that was a love-cry. It startled Percival Ford, and it reminded him of Dr. Kennedy's phrase. Down by the outrigger canoes, where they lay hauled out on the sand, he saw men and women, Kanakas, reclining languorously, like lotus-eaters, the women in white *holokus;* and against one such holoku he saw the dark head of the steersman of the canoe resting upon the woman's shoulder. Farther down, where the strip of sand widened at the entrance to the lagoon, he saw a man and woman walking side by side. As they drew near the light lanai, he saw the woman's hand go down to her waist and disengage a girdling arm. And as they passed him, Percival Ford nodded to a captain he knew, and to a major's daughter. Smoke of life, that was it, an ample phrase. And again, from under the dark algaroba trees arose the laugh of a woman that was a love-cry; and past his chair, on the way to bed, a bare-legged youngster was led by a chiding Japanese nursemaid. The voices of the singers broke softly and meltingly into a Hawaiian love song, and officers and women, with encircling arms, were gliding and whirling on the lanai; and once again the woman laughed under the algaroba trees.

And Percival Ford knew only disapproval of it all. He was irritated by the love-laugh of the woman, by the steersman with pillowed head on the white holoku, by the couples that walked on the beach, by the officers and women that danced, and by the voices of the singers singing of love, and his brother singing there with them under the hau tree. The woman that laughed especially irritated him. A curious train of thought was aroused. He was Isaac Ford's son, and what had happened with Isaac Ford might happen with him. He felt in his cheeks the faint heat of a blush at the thought, and experienced a poignant sense of shame. He was appalled by what was in his blood. It was like learning suddenly that his father had been a leper and that his own blood might bear the taint of that dread disease. Isaac Ford, the austere soldier of the Lord—the old hypocrite! What difference between him and any beachcomber? The house of pride that Percival Ford had builded was tumbling about his ears.

The hours passed, the army people laughed and danced, the native orchestra played on, and Percival Ford wrestled with the abrupt and overwhelming problem that had been thrust upon him. He prayed quietly, his elbow on the table, his head bowed upon his hand, with all the appearance of any tired onlooker. Between the dances the army men and women and the civilians fluttered up to him and buzzed conventionally, and when they went back to the lanai he took up his wrestling where he had left it off.

He began to patch together his shattered ideal of Isaac Ford, and for cement he used a cunning and subtle logic. It was of the sort that is compounded in the brain laboratories of egotists, and it worked. It was incontrovertible that his father had been made of finer clay than those about him; but still, old Isaac had been only in the process of becoming, while he, Percival Ford, had become. As proof of it, he rehabilitated his father and at the same time exalted himself. His lean little ego waxed to colossal proportions. He was great enough to forgive. He glowed at the thought of it. Isaac Ford had been great, but he was greater, for he could forgive Isaac Ford and even restore him to the holy place in his memory, though the place was not quite so holy as it had been. Also, he applauded Isaac Ford for having ignored the outcome of his one step aside. Very well, he, too, would ignore it.

The dance was breaking up. The orchestra had finished "Aloha Oe" and was preparing to go home. Percival Ford clapped his hands for the Japanese servant.

"You tell that man I want to see him," he said, pointing out Joe Garland. "Tell him come here, now."

Joe Garland approached and halted respectfully several paces away, nervously fingering the guitar which he still carried. The other did not ask him to sit down.

"You are my brother," he said.

"Why, everybody knows that," was the reply, in tones of wonderment.

"Yes, so I understand," Percival Ford said dryly. "But I did not know it till this evening."

The half brother waited uncomfortably in the silence that followed, during which Percival Ford coolly considered his next utterance.

"You remember that first time I came to school and the boys ducked me?" he asked. "Why did you take my part?"

The half brother smiled bashfully.

"Because you knew?"

"Yes, that was why."

"But I didn't know," Percival Ford said in the same dry fashion.

"Yes," the other said.

Another silence fell. Servants were beginning to put out the lights on the lanai.

"You know . . . now," the half brother said simply.

Percival Ford frowned. Then he looked the other over with a considering eye.

"How much will you take to leave the Islands and never come back?" he demanded.

"And never come back?" Joe Garland faltered. "It is the only land I know. Other lands are cold. I do not know other lands. I have many friends here. In other lands there would not be one voice to say, 'Aloha, Joe, my boy.' "

"I said never to come back," Percival Ford reiterated. "The Alameda sails tomorrow for San Francisco."

Joe Garland was bewildered.

"But why?" he asked. "You know now that we are brothers."

"That is why," was the retort. "As you said yourself, everybody knows. I will make it worth your while."

All awkwardness and embarrassment disappeared from Joe Garland. Birth and station were bridged and reversed.

"You want me to go?" he demanded.

"I want you to go and never to come back," Percival Ford answered.

And in that moment, flashing and fleeting, it was given him to see his brother tower above him like a mountain, and to feel himself dwindle and dwarf to microscopic insignificance. But it is not well for one to see himself truly, nor can one so see himself for long and live; and only for that flashing moment did Percival Ford see himself and his brother in true perspective. The next moment he was mastered by his meager and insatiable ego.

"As I said, I will make it worth your while. You will not suffer. I will pay you well."

"All right," Joe Garland said. "I'll go."

He started to turn away.

"Joe," the other called. "You see my lawyer tomorrow morning. Five hundred down and two hundred a month as long as you stay away."

"You are very kind," Joe Garland answered softly. "You are too kind. And anyway, I guess I don't want your money. I go tomorrow on the *Alameda*."

He walked away, but did not say good-by.

Percival Ford clapped his hands.

"Boy," he said to the Japanese, "a lemonade."

And over the lemonade he smiled long and contentedly to himself.

KOOLAU THE LEPER

"BECAUSE WE ARE SICK THEY TAKE AWAY OUR LIBERTY. WE have obeyed the law. We have done no wrong. And yet they would put us in prison. Molokai is a prison. That you know. Niuli, there, his sister was sent to Molokai seven years ago. He has not seen her since. Nor will he ever see her. She must stay there until she dies. This is not her will. It is not Niuli's will. It is the will of the white men who rule the land. And who are these white men?

"We know. We have it from our fathers and our fathers' fathers. They came like lambs, speaking softly. Well might they speak softly, for we were many and strong, and all the islands were ours. As I say, they spoke softly. They were of two kinds. The one kind asked our permission, our gracious permission, to preach to us the word of God. The other kind asked our permission, our gracious permission, to trade with us. That was the beginning. Today all the islands are theirs, all the land, all the cattle—everything is theirs. They that preached the word of God and they that preached the word of Rum have foregathered and become great chiefs. They live like kings in houses of many rooms, with multitudes of servants to care for them. They who had nothing have everything, and if you, or I, or any Kanaka be hungry, they sneer and say, 'Well, why don't you work? There are the plantations.' "

Koolau paused. He raised one hand, and with gnarled and twisted fingers lifted up the blazing wreath of hibiscus that crowned his black hair. The moonlight bathed the scene in

39

silver. It was a night of peace, though those who sat about him and listened had all the seeming of battle-wrecks. Their faces were leonine. Here a space yawned in a face where should have been a nose, and there an arm-stump showed where a hand had rotted off. They were men and women beyond the pale, the thirty of them, for upon them had been placed the mark of the beast.

They sat, flower-garlanded, in the perfumed, luminous night, and their lips made uncouth noises and their throats rasped approval of Koolau's speech. They were creatures who once had been men and women. But they were men and women no longer. They were monsters—in face and form grotesque caricatures of everything human. They were hideously maimed and distorted, and had the seeming of creatures that had been racked in millenniums of hell. Their hands, when they possessed them, were like harpy-claws. Their faces were the misfits and slips, crushed and bruised by some mad god at play in the machinery of life. Here and there were features which the mad god had smeared half away, and one woman wept scalding tears from twin pits of horror, where her eyes once had been. Some were in pain and groaned from their chests. Others coughed, making sounds like the tearing of tissue. Two were idiots, more like huge apes marred in the making, until even an ape were an angel. They mowed and gibbered in the moonlight, under crowns of drooping, golden blossoms. One, whose bloated ear-lobe flapped like a fan upon his shoulder, caught up a gorgeous flower of orange and scarlet and with it decorated the monstrous ear that flip-flapped with his every movement.

And over these things Koolau was king. And this was his kingdom,—a flower-throttled gorge, with beetling cliffs and crags, from which floated the blattings of wild goats. On three sides the grim walls rose; festooned in fantastic draperies of tropic vegetation and pierced by cave-entrances—the rocky lairs of Koolau's subjects. On the fourth side the earth fell away into a tremendous abyss, and, far below, could be seen the summits of lesser peaks and crags, at whose bases foamed and rumbled the Pacific surge. In fine weather a boat could land on the rocky beach that marked the entrance of Kalalau Valley, but the weather must be very fine. And a cool-headed mountaineer might climb from the beach to the head of Kalalau Valley, to this pocket among the peaks where Koolau ruled; but such a mountaineer must be very cool of head, and he must know the wild-goat trails as well. The marvel was that the mass of human wreckage that constituted Koolau's people should have been able to drag its helpless misery over the giddy goat-trails to this inaccessible spot.

"Brothers," Koolau began.

But one of the mowing, apelike travesties emitted a wild shriek of madness, and Koolau waited while the shrill ca-chinnation was tossed back and forth among the rocky walls and echoed distantly through the pulseless night.

"Brothers, is it not strange? Ours was the land, and behold, the land is not ours. What did these preachers of the word of God and the word of Rum give us for the land? Have you received one dollar, as much as one dollar, any one of you, for the land? Yet it is theirs, and in return they tell us we can go to work on the land, their land, and that what we produce by our toil shall be theirs. Yet in the old days we did not have to work. Also, when we are sick, they take away our freedom."

"Who brought the sickness, Koolau?" demanded Kiloliana, a lean and wiry man with a face so like a laughing faun's that one might expect to see the cloven hoofs under him. They were cloven, it was true, but the cleavages were great ulcers and livid putrefactions. Yet this was Kiloliana, the most daring climber of them all, the man who knew every goat trail and who had led Koolau and his wretched followers into the recesses of Kalalau.

"Ay, well questioned," Koolau answered. "Because we would not work the miles of sugar cane where once our horses pastured, they brought the Chinese slaves from over-seas. And with them came the Chinese sickness—that which we suffer from and because of which they would imprison us on Molokai. We were born on Kauai. We have been to the other islands, some here and some there, to Oahu, to Maui, to Hawaii, to Honolulu. Yet always did we come back to Kauai. Why did we come back? There must be a reason. Because we love Kauai. We were born here. Here we have lived. And here shall we die—unless—unless—there be weak hearts amongst us. Such we do not want. They are fit for Molokai. And if there be such, let them not remain. Tomorrow the soldiers land on the shore. Let the weak hearts go down to them. They will be sent swiftly to Molokai. As for us, we shall stay and fight. But know that we will not die. We have rifles. You know the narrow trails where men must creep, one by one. I, alone, Koolau, who was once a cowboy on Niihau, can hold the trail against a thousand men. Here is Kapalei, who was once a judge over men and a man with honor, but who is now a hunted rat, like you and me. Hear him. He is wise."

Kapalei arose. Once he had been a judge. He had gone to college at Punahou. He had sat at meat with lords and chiefs and the high representatives of alien powers who protected the interests of traders and missionaries. Such had been Kapalei. But now, as Koolau had said, he was a hunted rat, a creature outside the law, sunk so deep in the mire of human horror that he was above the law as well as beneath it. His face was featureless, save for gaping orifices and for the lidless eyes that burned under hairless brows.

"Let us not make trouble," he began. "We ask to be left alone. But if they do not leave us alone, then is the trouble theirs, and the penalty. My fingers are gone, as you see." He held up his stumps of hands that all might see. "Yet have I the joint of one thumb left, and it can pull a trigger as firmly as did its lost neighbor in the old days. We love Kauai. Let us live here, or die here, but do not let us go to the prison of Molokai. The sickness is not ours. We have not sinned. The men who preached the word of God and the word of Rum brought the sickness with the coolie slaves who work the stolen land. I have been a judge. I know the law and the justice, and I say to you it is unjust to steal a man's land, to make that man sick with the Chinese sickness, and then to put that man in prison for life."

"Life is short, and the days are filled with pain," said Koolau. "Let us drink and dance and be happy as we can."

From one of the rocky lairs calabashes were produced and passed around. The calabashes were filled with the fierce distillation of the root of the *ti* plant; and as the liquid fire coursed through them and mounted to their brains, they forgot that they had once been men and women, for they were men and women once more. The woman who wept scalding tears from open eyepits was indeed a woman apulse with life as she plucked the strings of an ukulele and lifted her voice in a barbaric love-call such as might have come from the dark forest depths of the primeval world. The air tingled with her cry, softly imperious and seductive. Upon a mat, timing his rhythm to the woman's song, Kiloliana danced. It was unmistakable. Love danced in all his movements, and, next, dancing with him on the mat, was a woman whose heavy hips and generous breast gave the lie to her disease-corroded face. It was a dance of the living dead, for in their disintegrating bodies life still loved and longed. Ever the woman whose sightless eyes ran scalding tears chanted her love-cry, ever the dancers danced of love in the warm night, and ever the calabashes went around till in all their brains were maggots crawling of memory and desire. And with the woman on the mat danced a slender maid whose face was beautiful and unmarred, but whose twisted arms that rose and fell marked the disease's ravage. And the two idiots, gibbering and mouthing strange noises, danced apart, grotesque, fantastic, travestying love as they themselves had been travestied by life.

But the woman's love-cry broke midway, the calabashes were lowered, and the dancers ceased, as all gazed into the abyss above the sea, where a rocket flared like a wan phantom through the moonlit air.

"It is the soldiers," said Koolau. "Tomorrow there will be fighting. It is well to sleep and be prepared."

The lepers obeyed, crawling away to their lairs in the cliff, until only Koolau remained, sitting motionless in the moonlight, his rifle across his knees, as he gazed far down to the boats landing on the beach.

The far head of Kalalau Valley had been well chosen as a refuge. Except Kiloliana, who knew back trails up the precipitous walls, no man could win to the gorge save by advancing across a knife-edged ridge. This passage was a hundred yards in length. At best, it was a scant twelve inches wide. On either side yawned the abyss. A slip, and to right or left the man would fall to his death. But once across he would find himself in an earthly paradise. A sea of vegetation laved the landscape, pouring its green billows from wall to wall, dripping from the cliff-lips in great vine masses, and flinging a spray of ferns and air-plants into the multitudinous crevices. During the many months of Koolau's rule, he and his followers had fought with this vegetable sea. The choking jungle, with its riot of blossoms, had been driven back from the bananas, oranges, and mangoes that grew wild. In little clearings grew the wild arrowroot; on stone terraces, filled with soil scrapings, were the taro patches and the melons; and in every open space where the sunshine penetrated were papaya trees burdened with their golden fruit.

Koolau had been driven to this refuge from the lower valley by the beach. And if he were driven from it in turn, he knew of gorges among the jumbled peaks of the inner fastnesses where he could lead his subjects and live. And now he lay with his rifle beside him, peering down through a tangled screen of foliage at the soldiers on the beach. He noted that they had large guns with them, from which the sunshine flashed as from mirrors. The knife-edged passage lay directly before him. Crawling upward along the trail that led to it he could see tiny specks of men. He knew they were not the soldiers, but the police. When they failed, then the soldiers would enter the game.

He affectionately rubbed a twisted hand along his rifle

barrel and made sure that the sights were clean. He had learned to shoot as a wild-cattle hunter on Niihau, and on that island his skill as a marksman was unforgotten. As the toiling specks of men grew nearer and larger, he estimated the range, judged the deflection of the wind that swept at right angles across the line of fire, and calculated the chances of overshooting marks that were so far below his level. But he did not shoot. Not until they reached the beginning of the passage did he make his presence known. He did not disclose himself, but spoke from the thicket.

"What do you want?" he demanded.

"We want Koolau, the leper," answered the man who led the native police, himself a blue-eyed American.

"You must go back," Koolau said.

He knew the man, a deputy sheriff, for it was by him that he had been harried out of Niihau, across Kauai, to Kalalau Valley, and out of the valley to the gorge.

"Who are you?" the sheriff asked.

"I am Koolau, the leper," was the reply.

"Then come out. We want you. Dead or alive, there is a thousand dollars on your head. You cannot escape."

Koolau laughed aloud in the thicket.

"Come out!" the sheriff commanded, and was answered by silence.

He conferred with the police, and Koolau saw that they were preparing to rush him.

"Koolau," the sheriff called. "Koolau, I am coming across to get you."

"Then look first and well about you at the sun and sea and sky, for it will be the last time you behold them."

"That's all right, Koolau," the sheriff said soothingly. "I know you're a dead shot. But you won't shoot me. I have never done you any wrong."

Koolau grunted in the thicket.

"I say, you know, I've never done you any wrong, have I?" the sheriff persisted.

"You do me wrong when you try to put me in prison," was

the reply. "And you do me wrong when you try for the thousand dollars on my head. If you will live, stay where you are."

"I've got to come across and get you. I'm sorry. But it is my duty."

"You will die before you get across."

The sheriff was no coward. Yet was he undecided. He gazed into the gulf on either side, and ran his eyes along the knife-edge he must travel. Then he made up his mind.

"Koolau," he called.

But the thicket remained silent.

"Koolau, don't shoot. I am coming."

The sheriff turned, gave some orders to the police, then started on his perilous way. He advanced slowly. It was like walking a tightrope. He had nothing to lean upon but the air. The lava rock crumbled under his feet, and on either side the dislodged fragments pitched downward through the depths. The sun blazed upon him, and his face was wet with sweat. Still he advanced, until the halfway point was reached.

"Stop!" Koolau commanded from the thicket. "One more step and I shoot."

The sheriff halted, swaying for balance as he stood poised above the void. His face was pale, but his eyes were determined. He licked his dry lips before he spoke.

"Koolau, you won't shoot me. I know you won't."

He started once more. The bullet whirled him half about. On his face was an expression of querulous surprise as he reeled to the fall. He tried to save himself by throwing his body across the knife-edge; but at that moment he knew death. The next moment the knife-edge was vacant. Then came the rush, five policemen, in single file, with superb steadiness, running along the knife-edge. At the same instant the rest of the posse opened fire on the thicket. It was madness. Five times Koolau pulled the trigger, so rapidly that his shots constituted a rattle. Changing his position and crouching low under the bullets that were biting and singing through the bushes, he peered out. Four of the police had followed the sheriff. The fifth lay across the knife-edge, still alive. On the farther side, no longer firing, were the surviving police. On the naked rock there was no hope for them. Before they could clamber down Koolau could have picked off the last man. But he did not fire, and, after a conference, one of them took off a white undershirt and waved it as a flag. Followed by another, he advanced along the knife-edge to their wounded comrade. Koolau gave no sign, but watched them slowly withdraw and become specks as they descended into the lower valley.

Two hours later, from another thicket, Koolau watched a body of police trying to make the ascent from the opposite side of the valley. He saw the wild goats flee before them as they climbed higher and higher, until he doubted his judgment and sent for Kiloliana who crawled in beside him.

"No, there is no way," said Kiloliana.

"The goats?" Koolau questioned.

"They come over from the next valley, but they cannot pass to this. There is no way. Those men are not wiser than goats. They may fall to their deaths. Let us watch."

"They are brave men," said Koolau. "Let us watch."

Side by side they lay among the morning-glories, with the yellow blossoms of the *hau* dropping upon them from overhead, watching the motes of men toil upward, till the thing happened, and three of them, slipping, rolling, sliding, dashed over a cliff-lip and fell sheer half a thousand feet.

Kiloliana chuckled.

"We will be bothered no more," he said.

"They have war guns," Koolau made answer. "The soldiers have not yet spoken."

In the drowsy afternoon, most of the lepers lay in their rock dens asleep. Koolau, his rifle on his knees, fresh-cleaned and ready, dozed in the entrance to his own den. The maid with the twisted arm lay below in the thicket and kept watch on the knife-edge passage. Suddenly Koolau was startled wide awake by the sound of an explosion on the beach. The next instant the atmosphere was incredibly rent asunder. The terrible sound frightened him. It was as if all the gods had caught the envelope of the sky in their hands and were ripping it apart as a woman rips apart a sheet of cotton cloth. But it was such an immense ripping, growing swiftly nearer. Koolau glanced up apprehensively, as if expecting to see the thing. Then high up on the cliff overhead the shell burst in a fountain of black smoke. The rock was shattered, the fragments falling to the foot of the cliff.

Koolau passed his hand across his sweaty brow. He was terribly shaken. He had no experience with shellfire, and this was more dreadful than anything he had imagined.

"One," said Kapahei, suddenly bethinking himself to keep count.

A second and a third shell flew screaming over the top of the wall, bursting beyond view. Kapahei methodically kept the count. The lepers crowded into the open space before the caves. At first they were frightened, but as the shells continued their flight overhead the leper folk became reassured and began to admire the spectacle. The two idiots shrieked with delight, prancing wild antics as each air-tormenting shell went by. Koolau began to recover his confidence. No damage was being done. Evidently they could not aim such large missiles at such long range with the precision of a rifle.

But a change came over the situation. The shells began to fall short. One burst below in the thicket by the knife-edge. Koolau remembered the maid who lay there on watch, and ran down to see. The smoke was still rising from the bushes when he crawled in. He was astounded. The branches were splintered and broken. Where the girl had lain was a hole in the ground. The girl herself was in shattered fragments. The shell had burst right on her.

First peering out to make sure no soldiers were attempting the passage, Koolau started back on the run for the caves. All the time the shells were moaning, whining, screaming by, and the valley was rumbling and reverberating wth the explosions. As he came in sight of the caves, he saw the two idiots cavorting about, clutching each other's hands with their stumps of fingers. Even as he ran, Koolau saw a spout of black smoke rise from the ground, near to the idiots. They were flung apart bodily by the explosion. One lay motionless, but the other was dragging himself by his hands toward the cave. His legs trailed out helplessly behind him, while the blood was pouring from his body. He seemed bathed in blood, and as he crawled he cried like a little dog. The rest of the lepers, with the exception of Kapahei, had fled into the caves.

"Seventeen," said Kapahei. "Eighteen," he added.

This last shell had fairly entered into one of the caves. The explosion caused all the caves to empty. But from the particular cave no one emerged. Koolau crept in through the pungent, acrid smoke. Four bodies, frightfully mangled, lay about. One of them was the sightless woman whose tears till now had never ceased.

Outside, Koolau found his people in a panic and already beginning to climb the goat trail that led out of the gorge and on among the jumbled heights and chasms. The wounded idiot, whining feebly and dragging himself along on the ground by his hands, was trying to follow. But at the first pitch of the wall his helplessness overcame him and he fell back.

"It would be better to kill him," said Koolau to Kapahei, who still sat in the same place.

"Twenty-two," Kapahei answered. "Yes, it would be a wise thing to kill him. Twenty-three—twenty-four."

The idiot whined sharply when he saw the rifle leveled at him. Koolau hesitated, then lowered the gun.

"It is a hard thing to do," he said.

"You are a fool, twenty-six, twenty-seven," said Kapahei. "Let me show you."

He arose and, with a heavy fragment of rock in his hand, approached the wounded thing. As he lifted his arm to strike, a shell burst full upon him, relieving him of the necessity of the act and at the same time putting an end to his count.

Koolau was alone in the gorge. He watched the last of his

people drag their crippled bodies over the brow of the height and disappear. Then he turned and went down to the thicket where the maid had been killed. The shellfire still continued, but he remained; for far below he could see the soldiers climbing up. A shell burst twenty feet away. Flattening himself into the earth, he heard the rush of the fragments above his body. A shower of hau blossoms rained upon him. He lifted his head to peer down the trail, and sighed. He was very much afraid. Bullets from rifles would not have worried him, but this shellfire was abominable. Each time a shell shrieked by he shivered and crouched; but each time he lifted his head again to watch the trail.

At last the shells ceased. This, he reasoned, was because the soldiers were drawing near. They crept along the trail in single file, and he tried to count them until he lost track. At any rate, there were a hundred or so of them—all come after Koolau the leper. He felt a fleeting prod of pride. With war guns and rifles, police and soldiers, they came for him, and he was only one man, a crippled wreck of a man at that. They offered a thousand dollars for him, dead or alive. In all his life he had never possessed that much money. The thought was a bitter one. Kapahei had been right. He, Koolau, had done no wrong. Because the haoles wanted labor with which to work the stolen land, they had brought in the Chinese coolies, and with them had come the sickness. And now, because he had caught the sickness, he was worth a thousand dollars—but not to himself. It was his worthless carcass, rotten with disease or dead from a bursting shell, that was worth all that money.

When the soldiers reached the knife-edged passage, he was prompted to warn them. But his gaze fell upon the body of the murdered maid, and he kept silent. When six had ventured on the knife-edge, he opened fire. Nor did he cease when the knife-edge was bare. He emptied his magazine, reloaded, and emptied it again. He kept on shooting. All his wrongs were blazing in his brain, and he was in a fury of vengeance. All down the goat trail the soldiers were firing, and though they lay flat and sought to shelter themselves in the shallow inequalities of the surface, they were exposed marks to him. Bullets whistled and thudded about him, and an occasional ricochet sang sharply through the air. One bullet ploughed a crease through his scalp, and a second burned across his shoulder blade without breaking the skin.

It was a massacre, in which one man did the killing. The soldiers began to retreat, helping along their wounded. As Koolau picked them off he became aware of the smell of burnt meat. He glanced about him at first, and then discovered that it was his own hands. The heat of the rifle was doing it. The leprosy had destroyed most of the nerves in his hands. Though his flesh burned and he smelled it, there was no sensation.

He lay in the thicket, smiling, until he remembered the war guns. Without doubt they would open up on him again, and this time upon the very thicket from which he had inflicted the damage. Scarcely had he changed his position to a nook behind a small shoulder of the wall where he had noted that no shells fell, than the bombardment recommenced. He counted the shells. Sixty more were thrown into the gorge before the war guns ceased. The tiny area was pitted with their explosions, until it seemed impossible that any creature could have survived. So the soldiers thought, for, under the burning afternoon sun, they climbed the goat trail again. And again the knife-edged passage was disputed, and again they fell back to the beach.

For two days longer Koolau held the passage, though the soldiers contented themselves with flinging shells into his retreat. Then Pahau, a leper boy, came to the top of the wall at the back of the gorge and shouted down to him that Kiloliana, hunting goats that they might eat, had been killed by a fall, and that the women were frightened and knew not what to do. Koolau called the boy down and left him with a spare gun with which to guard the passage. Koolau found his people disheartened. The majority of them were too helpless to forage food for themselves under such forbidding circumstances, and all were starving. He selected two women and a man who were not too far gone with the disease, and sent them back to the gorge to bring up food and mats. The rest he cheered and consoled until even the weakest took a hand in building rough shelters for themselves.

But those he had dispatched for food did not return, and he started back for the gorge. As he came out on the brow of the wall, half a dozen rifles cracked. A bullet tore through the fleshy part of his shoulder, and his cheek was cut by a sliver of rock where a second bullet smashed against the cliff. In the moment that this happened, and he leaped back, he saw that the gorge was alive with soldiers. His own people had betrayed him. The shellfire had been too terrible, and they had preferred the prison of Molokai.

Koolau dropped back and unslung one of his heavy cartridge belts. Lying among the rocks, he allowed the head and shoulders of the first soldier to rise clearly into view before pulling trigger. Twice this happened, and then, after some delay, in place of a head and shoulder a white flag was thrust above the edge of the wall.

"What do you want?" he demanded.

"I want you, if you are Koolau the leper," came the answer.

Koolau forgot where he was, forgot everything, as he lay and marveled at the strange persistence of these haoles who would have their will though the sky fell in. Aye, they would have their will over all men and all things, even though they died in getting it. He could not but admire them, too, what of that will in them that was stronger than life and that bent all things to their bidding. He was convinced of the hopelessness of his struggle. There was no gainsaying that terrible will of the haoles. Though he killed a thousand, yet would they rise like the sands of the sea and come upon him, ever more and more. They never knew when they were beaten. That was their fault and their virtue. It was where his own kind lacked. He could see, now, how the handful of the preachers of God and the preachers of Rum had conquered the land. It was because—

"Well, what have you got to say? Will you come with me?"

It was the voice of the invisible man under the white flag. There he was, like any haole, driving straight toward the end determined.

"Let us talk," said Koolau.

The man's head and shoulders arose, then his whole body. He was a smooth-faced, blue-eyed youngster of twenty-five, slender and natty in his captain's uniform. He advanced until halted, then seated himself a dozen feet away. "You are a brave man," said Koolau wonderingly. "I could kill you like a fly."

"No, you couldn't," was the answer.

"Why not?"

"Because you are a man, Koolau, though a bad one. I know your story. You kill fairly."

Koolau grunted, but was secretly pleased.

"What have you done with my people?" he demanded. "The boy, the two women, and the man?"

"They gave themselves up, as I have now come for you to do."

Koolau laughed incredulously.

"I am a free man," he announced. "I have done no wrong. All I ask is to be left alone. I have lived free, and I shall die free. I will never give myself up."

"Then your people are wiser than you," answered the young captain. "Look—they are coming now."

Koolau turned and watched the remnant of his band approach. Groaning and sighing, a ghastly procession, it dragged its wretchedness past. It was given to Koolau to taste a deeper bitterness, for they hurled imprecations and insults at him as they went by; and the panting hag who brought up the rear halted, and with skinny harpy-claws extended, shaking her snarling death's head from side to side, she laid a curse upon him. One by one they dropped over the lip-edge and surrendered to the hiding soldiers.

"You can go now," said Koolau to the captain. "I will never give myself up. That is my last word. Good-by."

The captain slipped over the cliff to his soldiers. The next moment, and without a flag of truce, he hoisted his hat on his scabbard, and Koolau's bullet tore through it. That afternoon they shelled him out from the beach, and as he retreated into the high inaccessible pockets beyond, the soldiers followed him.

For six weeks they hunted him from pocket to pocket, over the volcanic peaks and along the goat trails. When he hid in the lantana jungle, they formed lines of beaters, and through lantana jungle and guava scrub they drove him like a rabbit. But ever he turned and doubled and eluded. There was no cornering him. When pressed too closely, his sure rifle held them back and they carried their wounded down the goat trails to the beach. There were times when they did the shooting as his brown body showed for a moment through the underbrush. Once, five of them caught him on an exposed goat trail between pockets. They emptied their rifles at him as he limped and climbed along his dizzy way. Afterward they found bloodstains and knew that he was wounded. At the end of six weeks they gave up. The soldiers and police returned to Honolulu, and Kalalau Valley was left to him for his own, though head-hunters ventured after him from time to time and to their own undoing.

Two years later, and for the last time, Koolau crawled unto a thicket and lay down among the ti leaves and wild ginger blossoms. Free he had lived, and free he was dying. A slight drizzle of rain began to fall, and he drew a ragged blanket about the distorted wreck of his limbs. His body was covered with an oilskin coat. Across his chest he laid his Mauser rifle, lingering affectionately for a moment to wipe the dampness from the barrel. The hand with which he wiped had no fingers left upon it with which to pull the trigger.

He closed his eyes, for, from the weakness in his body and the fuzzy turmoil in his brain, he knew that his end was near. Like a wild animal he had crept into hiding to die. Half-conscious, aimless and wandering, he lived back in his life to his early manhood on Niihau. As life faded and the drip of the rain grew dim in his ears, it seemed to him that he was once more in the thick of the horse-breaking, with raw colts rearing and bucking under him, his stirrups tied together beneath, or charging madly about the breaking corral and driving the helping cowboys over the rails. The next instant, and with seeming naturalness, he found himself pursuing the wild bulls of the upland pastures, roping them and leading them down to the valleys. Again the sweat and dust of the branding pen stung his eyes and bit his nostrils.

All his lusty, whole-bodied youth was his, until the sharp pangs of impending dissolution brought him back. He lifted his monstrous hands and gazed at them in wonder. But how? Why? Why should the wholeness of that wild youth of his change to this? Then he remembered, and once again, and for a moment, he was Koolau, the leper. His eyelids fluttered wearily down and the drip of the rain ceased in his ears. A prolonged trembling set up in his body. This, too, ceased. He half lifted his head, but it fell back. Then his eyes opened, and did not close. His last thought was of his Mauser, and he pressed it against his chest with his folded, fingerless hands.

GOOD-BY, JACK

HAWAII IS A QUEER PLACE. EVERYTHING SOCIALLY IS WHAT I MAY call topsy-turvy. Not but what things are correct. They are almost too much so. But still things are sort of upside down. The most ultra-exclusive set there is the "Missionary Crowd." It comes with rather a shock to learn that in Hawaii the obscure, martydom-seeking missionary sits at the head of the table of the moneyed aristocracy. But it is true. The humble New Englanders who came out in the third decade of the nineteenth century came for the lofty purpose of teaching the Kanakas the true religion, the worship of the one only genuine and undeniable God. So well did they succeed in this, and also in civilizing the Kanaka, that by the second or third generation he was practically extinct. This being the fruit of the seed of the Gospel, the fruit of the seed of the missionaries (the sons and the grandsons) was the possession of the islands themselves—of the land, the ports, the town sites, and the sugar plantations. The missionary who came to give the bread of life remained to gobble up the whole heathen feast.

But that is not the Hawaiian queerness I started out to tell. Only one cannot speak of things Hawaiian without mentioning the missionaries. There is Jack Kersdale, the man I wanted to tell about; he came of missionary stock. That is, on his grandmother's side. His grandfather was old Benjamin Kersdale, a Yankee trader, who got his start for a million in the old days by selling cheap whisky and square-face gin. There's another queer thing. The old missionaries and old traders were mortal enemies. You see, their interests conflicted. But their children made it up by intermarrying and dividing the islands between them.

Life in Hawaii is a song. That's the way Stoddard put it in his "Hawaii Nei":

"Thy life is music—Fate the notes prolong!
Each isle a stanza, and the whole a song."

And he was right. Flesh is golden there. The native women are sun-ripe Junos, the native men bronzed Apollos. They sing, and dance, and all are flower-bejeweled and flower-crowned. And, outside the rigid "Missionary Crowd," the white men yield to the climate and the sun, and no matter how busy they may be, are prone to dance and sing and wear flowers behind their ears and in their hair. Jack Kersdale was one of these fellows. He was one of the busiest men I ever met. He was a several-times millionaire. He was a sugar king, a coffee planter, a rubber pioneer, a cattle rancher, and a promoter of three out of every four new enterprises launched in the islands. He was a society man, a club man, a yachtsman, a bachelor, and withal as handsome a man as was ever doted upon by mamas with marriageable daughters. Incidentally, he had finished his education at Yale, and his head was crammed fuller with vital statistics and scholarly information concerning Hawaii Nei than any other islander I ever encountered. He turned off an immense amount of work, and he sang and danced and put flowers in his hair as immensely as any of the idlers.

He had grit, and had fought two duels—both political—when he was no more than a raw youth essaying his first adventures in politics. In fact, he played a most creditable and courageous part in the last revolution, when the native dynasty was overthrown; and he could not have been over sixteen at the time. I am pointing out that he was no coward, in order that you may appreciate what happens later on. I've seen him in the breaking yard at the Haleakala Ranch, conquering a four-year-old brute that for two years had defied the pick of Von Tempsky's cowboys. And I must tell of one other thing. It was down in Kona—or up, rather, for the Kona people scorn to live at less than a thousand feet elevation. We were all on the *lanai* of Doctor Goodhue's bungalow. I was talking with Dottie Fairchild when it happened. A big centipede—it was seven inches, for we measured it afterward—fell from the rafters overhead squarely into her coiffure. I confess, the hideousness of it paralyzed me. I couldn't move. My mind refused to work. There, within two feet of me, the ugly venomous devil was writhing in her hair. It threatened at any moment to fall down upon her exposed shoulders—we had just come out from dinner.

"What is it?" she asked, starting to raise her hand to her head.

"Don't!" I cried. "Don't!"

"But what is it?" she insisted, growing frightened by the fright she read in my eyes and on my stammering lips.

My exclamation attracted Kersdale's attention. He glanced our way carelessly, but in that glance took in everything. He came over to us, but without haste.

"Please don't move, Dottie," he said quietly.

He never hesitated, nor did he hurry and make a bungle of it.

"Allow me," he said.

And with one hand he caught her scarf and drew it tightly around her shoulders so that the centipede could not fall inside her bodice. With the other hand—the right—he reached into her hair, caught the repulsive abomination as near as he was able by the nape of the neck, and held it tightly between thumb and forefinger as he withdrew it from her hair. It was as horrible and heroic a sight as man could wish to see. It made my flesh crawl. The centipede, seven inches of squirming legs, writhed and twisted and dashed itself about his hand, the body twining around the fingers and the legs digging into the skin and scratching as the beast endeavored to free itself. It bit him twice—I saw it—though he assured the ladies that he was not harmed as he dropped it upon the walk and stamped it into the gravel. But I saw him in the surgery five minutes afterward, with Doctor Goodhue scarifying the wounds and injecting permanganate of potash. The next morning Kersdale's arm was as big as a barrel, and it was three weeks before the swelling went down.

All of which has nothing to do with my story, but which I could not avoid giving in order to show that Jack Kersdale was anything but a coward. It was the cleanest exhibition of grit I have ever seen. He never turned a hair. The smile never left his lips. And he dived with thumb and forefinger into Dottie Fairchild's hair was gaily as if it had been a box of salted almonds. Yet that was the man I was destined to see stricken with fear a thousand times more hideous even than the fear that was mine when I saw that writhing abomination in Dottie Fairchild's hair, dangling over her eyes and the trap of her bodice.

I was interested in leprosy, and upon that, as upon every other island subject, Kersdale had encyclopedic knowledge. In fact, leprosy was one of his hobbies. He was an ardent defender of the settlement at Molokai, where all the island lepers were segregated. There was much talk and feeling among the natives, fanned by the demagogues, concerning the cruelties of Molokai, where men and women, not alone banished from friends and family, were compelled to live in perpetual imprisonment until they died. There were no reprieves, no commutations of sentences. "Abandon hope" was written over the portal of Molokai.

"I tell you they are happy there," Kersdale insisted. "And they are infinitely better off than their friends and relatives outside who have nothing the matter with them. The horrors of Molokai are all poppycock. I can take you through any hospital or any slum in any of the great cities of the world and show you a thousands times worse horrors. The living death! The creatures that once were men! Bosh! You ought to see those living deaths racing horses on the Fourth of July. Some of them own boats. One has a gasoline launch. They have nothing to do but have a good time. Food, shelter, clothes, medical attendance, everything, is theirs. They are the wards of the Territory. They have a much finer climate than Honolulu, and the scenery is magnificent. I shouldn't mind going down there myself for the rest of my days. It is a lovely spot."

So Kersdale on the joyous leper. He was not afraid of leprosy. He said so himself, and that there wasn't one chance in a million for him or any other white man to catch it, though he confessed afterward that one of his school chums, Alfred Starter, had contracted it, gone to Molokai, and there died.

"You know, in the old days," Kersdale explained, "there was no certain test for leprosy. Anything unusual or abnormal was sufficient to send a fellow to Molokai. The result was that dozens were sent there who were no more lepers than you or I. But they don't make that mistake now. The Board of Health tests are infallible. The funny thing is that when the test was discovered they immediately went down to Molokai and applied it, and they found a number who were not lepers. These were immediately deported. Happy to get away? They wailed harder at leaving the settlement than when they left Honolulu to go to it. Some refused to leave, and really had to be forced out. One of them even married a leper woman in the last stages and then wrote pathetic letters to the Board of Health, protesting against his expulsion on the ground that no one was so well able as he to take care of his poor old wife."

"What is this infallible test?" I demanded.

"The bacteriological test. There is no getting away from it. Doctor Hervey—he's our expert, you know—was the first man to apply it here. He is a wizard. He knows more about leprosy than any living man, and if a cure is ever discovered, he'll be that discoverer. As for the test, it is very simple. They have succeeded in isolating the *bacillus leprae* and studying it. They know it now when they see it. All they do is to snip a bit of skin from the suspect and subject it to the bacteriological test. A man without any visible symptoms may be chock-full of the leprosy bacilli."

"Then you or I, for all we know," I suggested, "may be full of it now."

Kersdale shrugged his shoulders and laughed.

"Who can say? It takes seven years for it to incubate. If you have any doubts go and see Doctor Hervey. He'll just snip out a piece of your skin and let you know in a jiffy."

Later on he introduced me to Dr. Hervey, who loaded me down with Board of Health reports and pamphlets on the subject, and took me out to Kalihi, the Honolulu receiving station, where suspects were examined and confirmed lepers were held for deportation to Molokai. These deportations occurred about once a month, when, the last good-bys said, the lepers were marched on board the little steamer, the *Noeau,* and carried down to the settlement.

One afternoon, writing letters at the club, Jack Kersdale dropped in on me.

"Just the man I want to see," was his greeting. "I'll show you the saddest aspect of the whole situation—the lepers wailing as they depart for Molokai. The *Noeau* will be taking them on board in a few minutes. But let me warn you not to let your feelings be harrowed. Real as their grief is, they'd wail a whole sight harder a year hence if the Board of Health tried to take them away from Molokai. We've just time for a whisky and soda. I've a carriage outside. It won't take us five minutes to get down to the wharf."

To the wharf we drove. Some forty sad wretches, amid their mats, blankets, and luggage of various sorts, were squatting on the stringer piece. The *Noeau* had just arrived and was making fast to a lighter that lay between her and the wharf. A Mr. McVeigh, the superintendent of the settlement, was overseeing the embarkation, and to him I was introduced, also to Dr. Georges, one of the Board of Health physicians whom I had already met at Kalihi. The lepers were a woebegone lot. The faces of the majority were hideous—too horrible for me to describe. But here and there I noticed fairly good-looking persons, with no apparent signs of the fell disease upon them. One, I noticed, a little white girl, not more than twelve, with blue eyes and golden hair. One cheek, however, showed the leprous bloat. On my remarking upon the sadness of her alien situation among the brown-skinned afflicted ones, Doctor Georges replied: "Oh, I don't know. It's a happy day in her life. She comes from Kauai. Her father is a brute. And now that she has developed the disease she is going to join her mother at the settlement. Her mother was sent down three years ago—a very bad case."

"You can't always tell from appearances," Mr. McVeigh explained. "That man there, that big chap, who looks the pink of condition, with nothing the matter with him, I happen to know has a perforating ulcer in his foot and another in his shoulder blade. Then there are others—there, see that girl's hand, the one who is smoking the cigarette. See her twisted fingers. That's the anesthetic form. It attacks the nerves. You could cut her fingers off with a dull knife, or rub them off on a nutmeg-grater, and she would not experience the slightest sensation."

"Yes, but that fine-looking woman, there," I persisted; "surely, surely, there can't be anything the matter with her. She is too glorious and gorgeous altogether."

"A sad case," Mr. McVeigh answered over his shoulder, already turning away to walk down the wharf with Kersdale.

She was a beautiful woman, and she was pure Polynesian. From my meager knowledge of the race and its types I could not but conclude that she had descended from old chief stock. She could not have been more than twenty-three or four. Her lines and proportions were magnificent, and she was just beginning to show the amplitude of the women of her race.

"It was a blow to all of us," Dr. Georges volunteered. "She gave herself up voluntarily, too. No one suspected. But somehow she had contracted the disease. It broke us all up, I assure you. We've kept it out of the papers, though. Nobody but us and her family knows what has become of her. In fact, if you were to ask any man in Honolulu, he'd tell you it was his impression that she was somewhere in Europe. It was at her request that we've been so quiet about it. Poor girl, she has a lot of pride."

"But who is she?" I asked. "Certainly, from the way you talk about her, she must be somebody."

"Did you ever hear of Lucy Mokunui?" he asked.

"Lucy Mokunui?" I repeated, haunted by some familiar association. I shook my head. "It seems to me I've heard the name, but I've forgotten it."

"Never heard of Lucy Mokunui! The Hawaiian nightingale! I beg your pardon. Of course you are a *malihini*, and could not be expected to know. Well, Lucy Mokunui was the best beloved of Honolulu—of all Hawaii, for that matter."

"You say was," I interrupted.

"And I mean it. She is finished." He shrugged his shoulders pityingly. "A dozen haoles—I beg your pardon, white men— have lost their hearts to her at one time or another. And I'm not counting in the ruck. The dozen I refer to were haoles of position and prominence.

"She could have married the son of the Chief Justice if she'd wanted to. You think she's beautiful, eh? But you should hear her sing. Finest native woman singer in Hawaii Nei. Her throat is pure silver and melted sunshine. We adored her. She toured America first with the Royal Hawaiian Band. After that she made two more trips on her own—concert work."

"Oh!" I cried. "I remember now. I heard her two years ago at the Boston Symphony. So that is she. I recognize her now."

I was oppressed by a heavy sadness. Life was a futile thing at best. A short two years and this magnificent creature, at the summit of her magnificent success, was one of the leper squad awaiting deportation to Molokai. Henley's lines came into my mind:

"The poor old tramp explains his poor old ulcers;
Life is, I think, a blunder and a shame."

I recoiled from my own future. If this awful fate fell to Lucy Mokunui, what might not my lot be?—or anybody's lot? I was thoroughly aware that in life we are in the midst of death—but to be in the midst of living death, to die and not be dead, to be one of that draft of creatures that once were men, aye, and women, like Lucy Mokunui, the epitome of all Polynesian charms, an artist as well, and well beloved of men—I am afraid I must have betrayed my perturbation, for Doctor Georges hastened to assure me that they were very happy down in the settlement.

It was all too inconceivably monstrous. I could not bear to look at her. A short distance away, behind a stretched rope guarded by a policeman, were the lepers' relatives and friends. They were not allowed to come near. There were no last embraces, no kisses of farewell. They called back and forth to one another—last messages, last words of love, last reiterated instructions. And those behind the rope looked with terrible intensity. It was the last time they would behold the faces of their loved ones, for they were the living dead, being carted away in the funeral ship to the graveyard of Molokai.

Doctor Georges gave the command, and the unhappy wretches dragged themselves to their feet and under their burdens of luggage began to stagger across the lighter and aboard the steamer. It was the funeral procession. At once the wailing started from those behind the rope. It was blood-curdling; it was heart-rending. I never heard such woe, and I hope never to again. Kersdale and McVeigh were still at the other end of the wharf, talking earnestly—politics, of course, for both were head-over-heels in the particular game. When Lucy Mokunui passed me, I stole a look at her. She *was* beautiful. She was beautiful by our standards, as well—one of those rare blossoms that occur but once in generations. And she, of all women, was doomed to Molokai. She walked like a queen, across the lighter, straight on board, and aft on the open deck where the lepers huddled by the rail, wailing, now, to their dear ones on shore.

The lines were cast off, and the *Noeau* began to move away from the wharf. The wailing increased. Such grief and despair! I was just resolving that never again would I be a witness to the sailing of the *Noeau,* when McVeigh and Kersdale returned. The latter's eyes were sparkling, and his lips could not quite hide the smile of delight that was his. Evidently the politics they had talked had been satisfactory. The rope had been flung aside, and the lamenting relatives now crowded the stringer piece on either side of us.

"That's her mother," Doctor Georges whispered, indicating an old woman next to me, who was rocking back and forth and gazing at the steamer rail out of tear-blinded eyes. I noticed that Lucy Mokunui was also wailing. She stopped abruptly and gazed at Kersdale. Then she stretched forth her arms in that adorable, sensuous way that Olga Nethersole has of embracing an audience. And with arms outspread, she cried:

"Good-by, Jack! Good-by!"

He heard the cry, and looked. Never was a man overtaken by more crushing fear. He reeled on the stringer piece, his face went white to the roots of his hair, and he seemed to shrink and wither away inside his clothes. He threw up his hands and groaned, "My God! My God!" Then he controlled himself by a great effort.

"Good-by, Lucy! Good-by!" he called.

And he stood there on the wharf, waving his hands to her till the *Noeau* was clear away and the faces lining her afterrail were vague and indistinct.

"I thought you knew," said McVeigh, who had been regarding him curiously. "You, of all men, should have known. I thought that was why you were here."

"I know now," Kersdale answered with immense gravity. "Where's the carriage?"

He walked rapidly—half ran—to it. I had to half run myself to keep up with him.

"Drive to Doctor Hervey's," he told the driver. "Drive as fast as you can."

He sank down in the seat, panting and gasping. The pallor of his face had increased. His lips were compressed and the sweat was standing out on his forehead and upper lip. He seemed in some horrible agony.

"For God's sake, Martin, make those horses go!" he broke out suddenly. "Lay the whip into them!—do you hear?—lay the whip into them!"

"They'll break, sir," the driver remonstrated.

"Let them break," Kersdale answered. "I'll pay your fine and square you with the police. Put it to them. That's right. Faster! Faster!

"And I never knew, I never knew," he muttered, sinking back in the seat and with trembling hands wiping the sweat away.

The carriage was bouncing, swaying and lurching around corners at such a wild pace as to make conversation impossible. Besides, there was nothing to say. But I could hear him muttering over and over, "And I never knew. I never knew."

ALOHA OE

NEVER ARE THERE SUCH DEPARTURES AS FROM THE DOCK AT Honolulu.

The great transport lay with steam up, ready to pull out. A thousand persons were on her decks; five thousand stood on the wharf. Up and down the long gangway passed native princes and princesses, sugar kings and the high officials of the Territory. Beyond, in long lines, kept in order by the native police, were the carriages and motor cars of the Honolulu aristocracy. On the wharf the Royal Hawaiian Band played "Aloha Oe," and when it finished, a stringed orchestra of native musicians on board the transport took up the same sobbing strains, the native woman singer's voice rising bird-like above the instruments and the hubbub of departure. It was silver reed, sounding its clear, unmistakable note in the great diapason of farewell.

Forward, on the lower deck, the rail was lined six deep with khaki-clad young boys, whose bronzed faces told of three years' campaigning under the sun. But the farewell was not for them. Nor was it for the white-clad captain on the lofty bridge, remote as the stars, gazing down upon the tumult beneath him. Nor was the farewell for the young officers farther aft, returning from the Philippines, nor for the white-faced, climate-ravaged women by their sides. Just aft the gangway, on the promenade deck, stood a score of United States senators with their wives and daughters—the senatorial junketing party that for a month had been dined

and wined, surfeited with statistics, and dragged up volcanic
hill and down lava dale to behold the glories and resources
of Hawaii. It was for the junketing party that the transport
had called in at Honolulu, and it was to the junketing party
that Honolulu was saying good-by.

The senators were garlanded and bedecked with flowers.
Senator Jeremy Sambrooke's stout neck and portly bosom
were burdened with a dozen wreaths. Out of this mass of
bloom and blossom projected his head and the greater portion of his freshly sunburned and perspiring face. He thought
the flowers an abomination, and as he looked out over the
multitude on the wharf it was with a statistical eye that saw
none of the beauty, but that peered into the labor power, the
factories, the railroads, and the plantations that lay back of
the multitude and which the multitude expressed. He saw
resources and thought development, and he was too busy
with dreams of material achievement and empire to notice
his daughter at his side, talking with a young fellow in a
natty summer suit and straw hat, whose eager eyes seemed
only for her and never left her face. Had Senator Jeremy had
eyes for his daughter, he would have seen that, in place
of the young girl of fifteen he had brought to Hawaii a
short month before, he was now taking away with him a
woman.

Hawaii has a ripening climate, and Dorothy Sambrooke
had been exposed to it under exceptionally ripening circumstances. Slender, pale, with blue eyes a trifle tired from por-
ing over the pages of books and trying to muddle into an
understanding of life—such she had been the month before.
But now the eyes were warm instead of tired, the cheeks
were touched with the sun, and the body gave the first hint
and promise of swelling lines. During that month she had left
books alone, for she had found greater joy in reading from
the book of life. She had ridden horses, climbed volcanoes,
and learned surf swimming. The tropics had entered into
her blood, and she was aglow with the warmth and color and

sunshine. And for a month she had been in the company of a man—Stephen Knight, athlete, surfboard rider, a bronzed god of the sea who bitted the crashing breakers, leaped upon their backs, and rode them in to shore.

Dorothy Sambrooke was unaware of the change. Her consciousness was still that of a young girl, and she was surprised and troubled by Steve's conduct in this hour of saying good-by. She had looked upon him as her playfellow, and for the month he had been her playfellow; but now he was not parting like a playfellow. He talked excitedly and disconnectedly, or was silent, by fits and starts. Sometimes he did not hear what she was saying, or if he did, failed to respond in his wonted manner. She was perturbed by the way he looked at her. She had not known before that he had such blazing eyes. There was something in his eyes that was terrifying. She could not face it, and her own eyes continually drooped before it. Yet there was something alluring about it, as well, and she continually returned to catch a glimpse of that blazing, imperious, yearning something that she had never seen in human eyes before. And she was herself strangely bewildered and excited.

The transport's huge whistle blew a deafening blast, and the flower-crowned multitude surged closer to the side of the dock. Dorothy Sambrooke's fingers were pressed to her ears; and as she made a *moue* of distaste at the outrage of sound, she noticed again the imperious, yearning blaze in Steve's eyes. He was not looking at her, but at her ears, delicately pink and transparent in the slanting rays of the afternoon sun. Curious and fascinated, she gazed at that strange something in his eyes until he saw that he had been caught. She saw his cheeks flush darkly and heard him utter inarticulately. He was embarrassed, and she was aware of embarrassment herself. Stewards were going about nervously begging shore-going persons to be gone. Steve put out his hand. When she felt the grip of the fingers that had gripped hers a thousand times on surfboards and laval slopes, she heard the words

of the song with a new understanding as they sobbed in the
Hawaiian woman's silver throat:

> *"Ka halia ko aloha kai hiki mai,*
> *Ke hone ae nei i ku'u manawa,*
> *O oe no ka'u aloha*
> *A loko e hana nei."*

Steve had taught her air and words and meaning—so she
had thought, till this instant; and in this instant of the last
finger clasp and warm contact of palms she divined for the
first time the real meaning of the song. She scarcely saw him
go, nor could she note him on the crowded gangway, for she
was deep in a memory maze, living over the four weeks just
past, rereading events in the light of revelation.

When the senatorial party had landed, Steve had been
one of the committee of entertainment. It was he who had
given them their first exhibition of surf riding, out at Waikiki
Beach, paddling his narrow board seaward until he became
a disappearing speck, and then, suddenly reappearing, rising
like a sea-god from out of the welter of spume and churning
white—rising swiftly higher and higher, shoulders and chest
and loins and limbs, until he stood poised on the smoking
crest of a mighty, mile-long billow, his feet buried in the
flying foam, hurling beachward with the speed of an express
train and stepping calmly ashore at their astounded feet.
That had been her first glimpse of Steve. He had been the
youngest man on the committee, a youth, himself, of twenty.
He had not entertained by speechmaking, nor had he shone
decoratively at receptions. It was in the breakers at Waikiki,
in the wild cattle drive on Mauna Kea, and in the breaking
yard of the Haleakala Ranch that he had performed his share
of the entertaining.

She had not cared for the interminable statistics and eternal speechmaking of the other members of the committee.
Neither had Steve. And it was with Steve that she had stolen
away from the open-air feast at Hamakua, and from Abe

Louisson, the coffee planter, who had talked coffee, coffee, nothing but coffee, for two mortal hours. It was then, as they rode among the tree ferns, that Steve had taught her the words of "Aloha Oe," the song that had been sung to the visiting senators at every village, ranch, and plantation departure.

Steve and she had been much together from the first. He had been her playfellow. She had taken possession of him while her father had been occupied in taking possession of the statistics of the island territory. She was too gentle to tyrannize over her playfellow, yet she had ruled him abjectly, except when in canoe, or on horse or surfboard, at which times he had taken charge and she had rendered obedience. And now, with this last singing of the song, as the lines were cast off and the big transport began backing slowly out from the dock, she knew that Steve was something more to her than playfellow.

Five thousand voices were singing "Aloha Oe"—*My love be with you till we meet again*—and in that first moment of known love she realized that she and Steve were being torn apart. When would they ever meet again? He had taught her those words himself. She remembered listening as he sang them over and over under the hau tree at Waikiki. Had it been prophesy? And she had admired his singing, had told him that he sang with such expression. She laughed aloud, hysterically, at the recollection. With such expression!—when he had been pouring his heart out in his voice. She knew now, and it was too late. Why had he not spoken? Then she realized that girls of her age did not marry. But girls of her age did marry—in Hawaii—was her instant thought. Hawaii had ripened her—Hawaii, where flesh is golden and where all women are ripe and sun-kissed.

Vainly she scanned the packed multitude on the dock. What had become of him? She felt that she could pay any price for one more glimpse of him, and she almost hoped that some mortal sickness would strike the lonely captain on the bridge and delay departure. For the first time in her life she looked at her father with a calculating eye, and as she did she noted with newborn fear the lines of will and determination. It would be terrible to oppose him. And what chance would she have in such a struggle? But why had Steve not spoken? Now it was too late. Why had he not spoken under the hau tree at Waikiki?

And then, with a great sinking of the heart, it came to her that she knew why. What was it she had heard one day? Oh, yes, it was at Mrs. Stanton's tea, that afternoon when the ladies of the "Missionary Crowd" had entertained the ladies of the senatorial party. It was Mrs. Hodgkins, the tall blond woman, who had asked the question. The scene came back to her vividly—the broad *lanai,* the tropic flowers, the noiseless Asiatic attendants, the hum of the voices of the many women, and the question Mrs. Hodgkins had asked in the group next to her. Mrs. Hodgkins had been away on the mainland for years, and was evidently inquiring after old island friends of her maiden days. "What has become of Susie Maydwell?" was the question she had asked. "Oh, we never see her any more; she married Willie Kupele," another island woman answered. And Senator Behrend's wife laughed and wanted to know why matrimony had affected Susie Maydwell's friendships. *"Hapa-haole,"* was the answer; "he was a half-caste, you know, and we of the Islands have to think about our children."

Dorothy turned to her father, resolved to put it to the test.

"Papa, if Steve ever comes to the United States, mayn't he come and see us some time?"

"Who? Steve?"

"Yes, Stephen Knight—you know him. You said good-by to him not five minutes ago. Mayn't he, if he happens to be in the United States some time, come and see us?"

"Certainly not," Jeremy Sambrooke answered shortly. "Stephen Knight is a hapa-haole and you know what that means."

"Oh," Dorothy said faintly, while she felt a numb despair creep into her heart.

Steve was not a hapa-haole—she knew that; but she did know that a quarter-strain of tropic sunshine streamed in his veins, and she knew that that was sufficient to put him outside the marriage pale. It was a strange world. There was the Honorable A. S. Cleghorn, who had married a dusky princess of the Kamehameha blood, yet men considered it an honor to know him, and the most exclusive women of the ultra-exclusive "Missionary Crowd" were to be seen at his afternoon teas. And there was Steve. No one had disapproved of his teaching her to ride a surfboard, nor of his leading her by the hand through the perilous places of the crater of Kilauea. He could have dinner with her and her father, dance with her, and be a member of the entertainment committee; but because there was tropic sunshine in his veins he could not marry her.

And he didn't show it. One had to be told to know. And he was so good looking. The picture of him limned itself on her inner vision, and before she was aware she was pleasuring in the memory of the grace of his magnificent body, of his splendid shoulders, of the power in him that tossed her lightly on a horse, bore her safely through the thundering breakers, or towed her at the end of an alpenstock up the stern lava crest of the House of the Sun. There was something subtler and mysterious that she remembered, and that she was even then just beginning to understand—the aura of the male creature that is man, all man, masculine man. She came to herself with a shock of shame at the thoughts she had been thinking. Her cheeks were dyed with the hot blood which quickly receded and left them pale at the thought that she would never see him again. The stem of the transport was already out in the stream, and the promenade deck was passing abreast of the end of the dock.

"There's Steve now," her father said. "Wave good-by to him, Dorothy."

Steve was looking up at her with eager eyes, and he saw in her face what he had not seen before. By the rush of glad-

ness into his own face she knew that he knew. The air was
throbbing with the song—

> My love to you.
> My love be with you till we meet again.

There was no need for speech to tell their story. About her,
passengers were flinging their garlands to their friends on
the dock. Steve held up his hands and his eyes pleaded. She
slipped her own garland over her head, but it had become
entangled in the string of Oriental pearls that Mervin, an
elderly sugar king, had placed around her neck when he
drove her and her father down to the steamer.

She fought with the pearls that clung to the flowers. The
transport was moving steadily on. Steve was already beneath
her. This was the moment. The next moment and he would
be past. She sobbed, and Jeremy Sambrooke glanced at her
inquiringly.

"Dorothy!" he cried sharply.

She deliberately snapped the string, and, amid a shower
of pearls, the flowers fell to the waiting lover. She gazed at
him until the tears blinded her and she buried her face on
the shoulder of Jeremy Sambrooke, who forgot his beloved
statistics in wonderment at girl babies that insisted on growing up. The crowd sang on, the song growing fainter in the
distance, but still melting with the sensuous love-languor of
Hawaii, the words biting into her heart like acid because of
their untruth.

> *Aloha oe, Aloha oe, e ke onaona no ho ika lipo,*
> *A fond embrace, ahoi ae au, until we meet again.*

CHUN AH CHUN

THERE WAS NOTHING STRIKING IN THE APPEARANCE OF CHUN Ah Chun. He was rather undersized, as Chinese go, and the Chinese narrow shoulders and spareness of flesh were his. The average tourist, casually glimpsing him on the streets of Honolulu, would have concluded that he was a good-natured little Chinese, probably the proprietor of a prosperous laundry or tailor shop. In so far as good nature and prosperity went, the judgment would be correct, though beneath the mark; for Ah Chun was as good-natured as he was prosperous, and of the latter no man knew a tithe the tale. It was well known that he was enormously wealthy, but in his case "enormous" was merely the symbol for the unknown.

Ah Chun had shrewd little eyes, black and beady and so very little that they were like gimlet holes. But they were wide apart, and they sheltered under a forehead that was patently the forehead of a thinker. For Ah Chun had his problems, and had had them all his life. Not that he ever worried over them. He was essentially a philosopher, and whether as coolie, or multimillionaire and master of many men, his poise of soul was the same. He lived always in the high equanimity of spiritual repose, undeterred by good fortune, unruffled by ill fortune. All things went well with him, whether they were blows from the overseer in the cane field or a slump in the price of sugar when he owned those cane fields himself. Thus, from the steadfast rock of his sure content he mastered problems such as are given to few men to consider, much less to a Chinese peasant.

He was precisely that—a Chinese peasant, born to labor in the fields all his days like a beast, but fated to escape from the fields like the prince in a fairy tale. Ah Chun did not remember his father, a small farmer in a district not far from Canton; nor did he remember much of his mother, who had died when he was six. But he did remember his respected uncle, Ah Kow, for him had he served as a slave from his sixth year to his twenty-fourth. It was then that he escaped by contracting himelf as a coolie to labor for three years on the sugar plantations of Hawaii for fifty cents a day.

Ah Chun was observant. He perceived little details that not one man in a thousand ever noticed. Three years he worked in the field, at the end of which time he knew more about cane-growing than the overseers or even the superintendent, while the superintendent would have been astounded at the knowledge the wizened little coolie possessed of the reduction processes in the mill. But Ah Chun did not study only sugar processes. He studied to find out how men came to be owners of sugar mills and plantations. One judgment he achieved early, namely, that men did not become rich from the labor of their own hands. He knew, for he had labored for a score of years himself. The men who grew rich did so from the labor of the hands of others. That man was richest who had the greatest number of his fellow creatures toiling for him.

So, when his term of contract was up, Ah Chun invested his savings in a small importing store, going into partnership with one Ah Yung. The firm ultimately became the great one of "Ah Chun & Ah Yung," which handled anything from India silks and ginseng to guano islands and blackbird brigs. In the meantime, Ah Chun hired out as cook. He was a good cook, and in three years he was the highest-paid chef in Honolulu. His career was assured, and he was a fool to abandon it, as Dantin, his employer, told him; but Ah Chun knew his own mind best, and for knowing it was called a triple-fool and given a present of fifty dollars over and above the wages due him.

The firm of Ah Chun & Ah Yung was prospering. There was no need for Ah Chun longer to be a cook. There were boom times in Hawaii. Sugar was being extensively planted, and labor was needed. Ah Chun saw the chance, and went into the labor-importing business. He brought thousands of Cantonese coolies into Hawaii, and his wealth began to grow. He made investments. His beady black eyes saw bargains where other men saw bankruptcy. He bought a fishpond for a song, which later paid five hundred per cent and was the opening wedge by which he monopolized the fish market of Honolulu. He did not talk for publication, nor figure in politics, nor play at revolutions, but he forecast events more clearly and farther ahead than did the men who engineered them. In his mind's eye he saw Honolulu a modern, electric-lighted city at a time when it straggled, unkempt and sand-tormented, over a barren reef of uplifted coral rock. So he bought land. He bought land from merchants who needed ready cash, from impecunious natives, from riotous traders' sons, from widows and orphans and the lepers deported to Molokai; and, somehow, as the years went by, the pieces of land he had bought proved to be needed for warehouses, or office buildings, or hotels. He leased, and rented, sold and bought, and resold again.

But there were other things as well. He put his confidence and his money into Parkinson, the renegade captain whom nobody would trust. And Parkinson sailed away on mysterious voyages in the little *Vega*. Parkinson was taken care of until he died, and years afterward Honolulu was astonished when the news leaked out that the Drake and Acorn guano islands had been sold to the British Phosphate Trust for three-quarters of a million. Then there were the fat, lush days of King Kalakaua, when Ah Chun paid three hundred thousand dollars for the opium license. If he paid a third of a million for the drug monopoly, the investment was nevertheless a good one, for the dividends bought him the Kalalau Plantation, which, in turn, paid him thirty per cent for seventeen years and was ultimately sold by him for a million and a half.

It was under the Kamehamehas, long before, that he had served his own country as Chinese consul—a position that was not altogether unlucrative; and it was under Kamehameha IV that he changed his citizenship, becoming a Hawaiian subject in order to marry Stella Allendale, herself a subject of the brown-skinned king, though more of Anglo-Saxon blood ran in her veins than of Polynesian. In fact, the random breeds in her were so attenuated that they were valued at eighths and sixteenths. In the latter proportion was the blood of her great-grandmother, Paahao—the Princess Paahao, for she came of the royal line. Stella Allendale's great-grandfather had been a Captain Blunt, an English adventurer who took service under Kamehameha I and was made a tabu chief himself. Her grandfather had been a New Bedford whaling captain, while through her own father had been introduced a remote blend of Italian and Portuguese which had been grafted upon his own English stock. Legally a Hawaiian, Ah Chun's spouse was more of any one of three other nationalities.

And into this conglomerate of the races, Ah Chun introduced the Mongolian mixture. Thus, his children by Mrs. Ah Chun were one thirty-second Polynesian, one-sixteenth Italian, one-sixteenth Portuguese, one-half Chinese, and eleven thirty-seconds English and American. It might well be that Ah Chun would have refrained from matrimony could he have foreseen the wonderful family that was to spring from this union. It was wonderful in many ways. First, there was its size. There were fifteen sons and daughters, mostly daughters. The sons had come first, three of them, and then had followed, in unswerving sequence, a round dozen of girls. The blend of the races was excellent. Not alone fruitful did it prove, for the progeny, without exception, was healthy and without blemish. But the most amazing thing about the family was its beauty. All the girls were beautiful—delicately, ethereally beautiful. Mama Ah Chun's

rotund lines seemed to modify papa Ah Chun's lean angles,
so that the daughters were willowy without being lathy,
round-muscled without being chubby. In every feature of
every face were haunting reminiscences of Asia, all manip-
ulated over and disguised by old England, New England,
and South of Europe. No observer, without information,
would have guessed the heavy Chinese strain in their veins;
nor could any observer, after being informed, fail to note
immediately the Chinese traces.

As beauties, the Ah Chun girls were something new. Nothing like them had been seen before. They resembled nothing
so much as they resembled one another, and yet each girl
was sharply individual. There was no mistaking one for another. On the other hand, Maud, who was blue-eyed and
yellow-haired, would remind one instantly of Henrietta, an
olive brunette with large, languishing dark eyes and hair
that was blue-black. The hint of resemblance that ran through
them all, reconciling every differentiation, was Ah Chun's
contribution. He had furnished the groundwork upon which
had been traced the blended patterns of the races. He had
furnished the slim-boned Chinese frame, upon which had
been builded the delicacies and subtleties of Saxon, Latin,
and Polynesian flesh.

Mrs. Ah Chun had ideas of her own to which Ah Chun
gave credence, though never permitting them expression
when they conflicted with his own philosophic calm. She had
been used all her life to living in European fashion. Very
well. Ah Chun gave her a European mansion. Later, as his
sons and daughters grew able to advise, he built the bungalow, a spacious, rambling affair, as unpretentious as it was
magnificent. Also, as time went by, there arose a mountain
house on Tantalus, to which the family could flee when the
"sick wind" blew from the south. And at Waikiki he built
a beach residence on an extensive site so well chosen that
later on, when the United States government condemned it
for fortification purposes, an immense sum accompanied the
condemnation. In all his houses were billiard and smoking

rooms and guest rooms galore, for Ah Chun's wonderful progeny was given to lavish entertainment. The furnishing was extravagantly simple. Kings' ransoms were expended without display—thanks to the educated tastes of the progeny.

Ah Chun had been liberal in the matter of education. "Never mind expense," he had argued in the old days with Parkinson when that slack mariner could see no reason for making the *Vega* seaworthy; "you sail the schooner, I pay the bills." And so with his sons and daughters. It had been for them to get the education and never mind the expense. Harold, the eldest-born, had gone to Harvard and Oxford; Albert and Charles had gone through Yale in the same classes. And the daughters, from the eldest down, had undergone their preparation at Mills Seminary in California and passed on to Vassar, Wellesley, or Bryn Mawr. Several, having so desired, had had the finishing touches put on in Europe. And from all the world Ah Chun's sons and daughters returned to him to suggest and advise in the garnishment of the chaste magnificence of his residences. Ah Chun himself preferred the voluptuous glitter of Oriental display; but he was a philosopher, and he clearly saw that his children's tastes were correct according to Western standards.

Of course, his children were not known as the Ah Chun children. As he had evolved from a coolie laborer to a multi-millionaire, so had his name evolved. Mama Ah Chun had spelled it A'Chun, but her wiser offspring had elided the apostrophe and spelled it Achun. Ah Chun did not object. The spelling of his name interfered no whit with his comfort nor his philosophic calm. Besides, he was not proud. But when his children arose to the height of a starched shirt, a stiff collar, and a frock coat, they did interfere with his comfort and calm. Ah Chun would have none of it. He preferred the loose-flowing robes of China, and neither could they cajole nor bully him into making the change. They tried both courses, and in the latter one failed especially disastrously. They had not been to America for nothing. They had learned the virtues of the boycott as employed by organized labor, and he, their father, Chun Ah Chun, they boycotted in his own house, Mama Achun aiding and abetting. But Ah Chun himself, while unversed in Western culture, was thoroughly conversant with Western labor conditions. An extensive employer of labor himself, he knew how to cope with its tactics. Promptly he imposed a lockout on his rebellious progeny and erring spouse. He discharged his scores of servants, locked up his stables, closed his houses, and went to live in the Royal Hawaiian Hotel, in which enterprise he happened to be the heaviest stockholder. The family fluttered distractedly on visits about with friends, while Ah Chun calmly managed his many affairs, smoked his long pipe with the tiny silver bowl, and pondered the problem of his wonderful progeny.

This problem did not disturb his calm. He knew in his philosopher's soul that when it was ripe he would solve it. In the meantime he enforced the lesson that, complacent as he might be, he was nevertheless the absolute dictator of the Achun destinies. The family held out for a week, then returned, along with Ah Chun and the many servants, to occupy the bungalow once more. And thereafter no question was raised when Ah Chun elected to enter his brilliant drawing room in blue silk robe, wadded slippers, and black silk skullcap with red button peak, or when he chose to draw at his slender-stemmed silver-bowled pipe among the cigarette- and cigar-smoking officers and civilians on the broad verandas or in the smoking room.

Ah Chun occupied a unique position in Honolulu. Though he did not appear in society, he was eligible anywhere. Except among the Chinese merchants of the city, he never went out; but he received, and he was always the center of his household and the head of his table. Himself peasant-born Chinese, he presided over an atmosphere of culture and refinement second to none in all the islands. Nor were there any in all the islands too proud to cross his threshold and enjoy his hospitality. First of all, the Achun bungalow was of irreproachable tone. Next, Ah Chun was a power. And, finally, Ah Chun was a moral paragon and an honest businessman. Despite the fact that business morality was higher than on the mainland, Ah Chun outshone the businessmen of Honolulu in the scrupulous rigidity of his honesty. It was a saying that his word was as good as his bond. His signature was never needed to bind him. He never broke his word. Twenty years after Hotchkiss, of Hotchkiss, Morterson Company, died, they found among mislaid papers a memorandum of a loan of thirty thousand dollars to Ah Chun. It had been incurred when Ah Chun was privy counselor to Kamehameha II. In the bustle and confusion of those heyday, money-making times, the affair had slipped Ah Chun's mind. There was no note, no legal claim against him, but he settled in full with the Hotchkiss' Estate, voluntarily paying a compound interest that dwarfed the principal. Likewise, when he verbally guaranteed the disastrous Kakiku Ditch Scheme, at a time when the least sanguine did not dream a guarantee necessary—"Signed his check for two hundred thousand without a quiver, gentlemen, without a quiver," was the report of the secretary of the defunct enterprise, who had been sent on the forlorn hope of finding out Ah Chun's intentions. And on top of the many similar actions that were true of his word, there was scarcely a man of repute in the islands that at one time or another had not experienced the helping financial hand of Ah Chun.

So it was that Honolulu watched his wonderful family grow up into a perplexing problem and secretly sympathized with him, for it was beyond any of them to imagine what he was going to do with it. But Ah Chun saw the problem more clearly than they. No one knew as he knew the extent to which he was an alien in his family. His own family did not guess it. He saw that there was no place for him amongst this marvelous seed of his loins, and he looked forward to his declining years and knew that he would grow more and more alien. He did not understand his children. Their conversation was of things that did not interest him and about which he knew nothing. The culture of the West had passed

him by. He was Asiatic to the last fiber, which meant that
he was heathen. Their Christianity was to him so much nonsense. But all this he would have ignored as extraneous and
irrelevant, could he have but understood the young people
themselves. When Maud, for instance, told him that the
housekeeping bills for the month were thirty thousand—that
he understood, as he understood Albert's request for five
thousand with which to buy the schooner yacht *Muriel* and
become a member of the Hawaiian Yacht Club. But it was
their remoter, complicated desires and mental processes that
obfuscated him. He was not slow in learning that the mind
of each son and daughter was a secret labyrinth which he
could never hope to tread. Always he came upon the wall
that divides East from West. Their souls were inaccessible
to him, and by the same token he knew that his soul was
inaccessible to them.

Besides, as the years came upon him, he found himself
harking back more and more to his own kind. The reeking
smells of the Chinese quarter were spicy to him. He sniffed
them with satisfaction as he passed along the street, for in
his mind they carried him back to the narrow tortuous alleys
of Canton swarming with life and movement. He regretted
that he had cut off his queue to please Stella Allendale in
the prenuptial days, and he seriously considered the advis-
ability of shaving his crown and growing a new one. The
dishes his highly paid chef concocted for him failed to tickle
his reminiscent palate in the way that the weird messes did
in the stuffy restaurant down in the Chinese quarter. He enjoyed vastly more a half-hour's smoke and chat with two or
three Chinese chums than to preside at the lavish and elegant
dinners for which his bungalow was famed, where the pick
of the Americans and Europeans sat at the long table, men
and women on equality, the women with jewels that blazed
in the subdued light against white necks and arms, the men
in evening dress, and all chattering and laughing over topics
and witticisms that, while they were not exactly Greek to
him, did not interest him nor entertain.

But it was not merely his alienness and his growing desire to return to his Chinese fleshpots that constituted the problem. There was also his wealth. He had looked forward to a placid old age. He had worked hard. His reward should have been peace and repose. But he knew that with his immense fortune peace and repose could not possibly be his. Already there were signs and omens. He had seen similar troubles before. There was his old employer, Dantin, whose children had wrested from him, by due process of law, the management of his property, having the court appoint guardians to administer it for him. Ah Chun knew, and knew thoroughly well, that had Dantin been a poor man, it would have been found that he could quite rationally manage his own affairs. And old Dantin had had only three children and half a million, while he, Chun Ah Chun, had fifteen children and no one but himself knew how many millions.

"Our daughters are beautiful women," he said to his wife, one evening. "There are many young men. The house is always full of young men. My cigar bills are very heavy. Why are there no marriages?"

Mama Achun shrugged her shoulders and waited.

"Women are women and men are men—it is strange there are no marriages. Perhaps the young men do not like our daughters."

"Ah, they like them well enough," Mama Achun answered; "but you see, they cannot forget that you are your daughters' father."

"Yet you forgot who my father was," Ah Chun said gravely. "All you asked was for me to cut off my queue."

"The young men are more particular than I was, I fancy."

"What is the greatest thing in the world?" Ah Chun demanded with abrupt irrelevance.

Mama Achun pondered for a moment, then replied: "God."

He nodded. "There are gods and gods. Some are paper, some are wood, some are bronze. I use a small one in the

office for a paperweight. In the Bishop Museum are many
gods of coral rock and lava stone."

"But there is only one God," she announced decisively,
stiffening her ample frame argumentatively.

Ah Chun noted the danger signal and sheered off.

"What is greater than God, then?" he asked. "I will tell
you. It is money. In my time I have had dealings with Jews
and Christians, Mohammedans and Buddhists, and with little
black men from the Solomons and New Guinea who carried
their god about them, wrapped in oiled paper. They possessed various gods, these men, but they all worshiped money.
There is that Captain Higginson. He seems to like Henrietta."

"He will never marry her," retorted Mama Achun. "He
will be an admiral before he dies—"

"A rear admiral," Ah Chun interpolated. "Yes, I know.
That is the way they retire."

"His family in the United States is a high one. They would
not like it if he married . . . if he did not marry an American
girl."

Ah Chun knocked the ashes out of his pipe and thought-
fully refilled the silver bowl with a tiny pledget of tobacco.
He lighted it and smoked it out before he spoke.

"Henrietta is the oldest girl. The day she marries I will
give her three hundred thousand dollars. That will fetch
that Captain Higginson and his high family along with him.
Let the word go out to him. I leave it to you."

And Ah Chun sat and smoked on, and in the curling
smoke-wreaths he saw take shape the face and figure of Toy
Shuey—Toy Shuey, the maid of all work in his uncle's house
in the Cantonese village, whose work was never done and
who received for a whole year's work one dollar. And he
saw his youthful self arise in the curling smoke, his youthful
self who had toiled eighteen years in his uncle's field for little
more. And now he, Ah Chun, the peasant, dowered his
daughter with three hundred thousand years of such toil.

And she was but one daughter of a dozen. He was not elated at the thought. It struck him that it was a funny, whimsical world, and he chuckled aloud and startled Mama Achun from a reverie which he knew lay deep in the hidden crypts of her being where he had never penetrated.

But Ah Chun's word went forth, as a whisper, and Captain Higginson forgot his rear-admiralship and his high family and took to wife three hundred thousand dollars and a refined and cultured girl who was one thirty-second Polynesian, one-sixteenth Italian, one sixteenth Portuguese, eleven thirty-seconds English and Yankee, and one-half Chinese.

Ah Chun's munificence had its effect. His daughers became suddenly eligible and desirable. Clara was the next, but when the Secretary of the Territory formally proposed for her, Ah Chun informed him that he must await his turn, that Maud was the oldest and that she must be married first. It was shrewd policy. The whole family was made vitally interested in marrying off Maud, which it did in three months, to Ned Humphreys, the United States immigration commissioner. Both he and Maud complained, for the dowry was only two hundred thousand. Ah Chun explained that his initial generosity had been to break the ice, and that after that his daughters could not expect otherwise than to go more cheaply.

Clara followed Maud, and thereafter, for a space of two years, there was a continuous round of weddings in the bungalow. In the meantime Ah Chun had not been idle. Investment after investment was called in. He sold out his interests in a score of enterprises, and step by step, so as not to cause a slump in the market, he disposed of his large holdings in real estate. Toward the last he did precipitate a slump and sold at sacrifice. What caused this haste were the squalls he saw already rising above the horizon. By the time Lucille was married, echoes of bickerings and jealousies were already rumbling in his ears. The air was thick with schemes and counterschemes to gain his favor and to prejudice him against one or another or all but one of his sons-in-law. All of which was not conducive to the peace and repose he had planned for his old age.

He hastened his efforts. For a long time he had been in correspondence with the chief banks in Shanghai and Macao. Every steamer for several years had carried away drafts drawn in favor of one Chun Ah Chun, for deposit in those Far Eastern banks. The drafts now became heavier. His two youngest daughters were not yet married. He did not wait, but dowered them with a hundred thousand each, which sums lay in the Bank of Hawaii, drawing interest and awaiting their wedding day. Albert took over the business of the firm of Ah Chun & Ah Yung, Harold, the eldest, having elected to take a quarter of a million and go to England to live. Charles, the youngest, took a hundred thousand, a legal guardian, and a course in a Keeley institute. To Mama Achun was given the bungalow, the mountain house on Tantalus, and a new seaside residence in place of the one Ah Chun sold to the government. Also, to Mama Achun was given half a million in money well invested.

Ah Chun was now ready to crack the nut of the problem. One fine morning when the family was at breakfast—he had seen to it that all his sons-in-law and their wives were present—he announced that he was returning to his ancestral soil. In a neat little homily he explained that he had made ample provision for his family, and he laid down various maxims that he was sure, he said, would enable them to dwell together in peace and harmony. Also, he gave business advice to his sons-in-law, preached the virtues of temperate living and safe investments, and gave them the benefit of his encyclopedic knowledge of industrial and business conditions in Hawaii. Then he called for his carriage, and, in the company of the weeping Mama Achun, was driven down to the Pacific Mail steamer, leaving behind him a panic in the bungalow. Captain Higginson clamored wildly for an injunction. The daughters shed copious tears. One of their husbands, an ex-federal judge, questioned Ah Chun's sanity, and hastened to the proper authorities to inquire into it. He returned with the information that Ah Chun had appeared before the commission the day before, demanded an examination, and passed with flying colors. There was nothing to be done, so they went down and said good-by to the little old man, who waved farewell from the promenade deck as the big steamer poked her nose seaward through the coral reef.

But the little old man was not bound for Canton. He knew his own country too well, and the squeeze of the Mandarins, to venture into it with the tidy bulk of wealth that remained to him. He went to Macao. Now Ah Chun had long exercised the power of a king and he was imperious as a king. When he landed at Macao and went into the office of the biggest European hotel to register, the clerk closed the book on him. Chinese were not permitted. Ah Chun called for the manager and was treated with contumely. He drove away, but in two hours he was back again. He called the clerk and manager in, gave them a month's salary, and discharged them. He had made himself the owner of the hotel; and in the finest suite he settled down during the many months the gorgeous palace in the suburbs was building for him. In the meantime, with the inevitable ability that was his, he increased the earnings of his big hotel from three per cent to thirty.

The troubles Ah Chun had flown began early. There were sons-in-law that made bad investments, others that played ducks and drakes with the Achun dowries. Ah Chun being out of it, they looked at Mama Achun and her half million, and looking, engendered not the best of feeling toward one another. Lawyers waxed fat in the striving to ascertain the construction of trust deeds. Suits, cross-suits, and counter-suits cluttered the Hawaiian courts. Nor did the police courts escape. There were angry encounters in which harsh words and harsher blows were struck. There were such things as flowerpots being thrown to add emphasis to winged words. And suits for libel arose that dragged their way through the courts and kept Honolulu agog with excitement over the revelations of the witnesses.

In his palace, surrounded by all dear delights of the Orient, Ah Chun smokes his placid pipe and listens to the turmoil overseas. Each mail steamer, in faultless English, typewritten on an American machine, a letter goes from Macao to Honolulu, in which, by admirable texts and precepts, Ah Chun advises his family to live in unity and harmony. As for himself, he is out of it all and well content. He has won to peace and repose. At times he chuckles and rubs his hands, and his slant little black eyes twinkle merrily at the thought of the funny world. For out of all his living and philosophizing that remains to him—the conviction that it is a very funny world.

THE SHERIFF OF KONA

"YOU CANNOT ESCAPE LIKING THE CLIMATE," CUDWORTH SAID, in reply to my panegyric on the Kona coast. "I was a young fellow, just out of college, when I came here eighteen years ago. I never went back, except, of course, to visit. And I warn you, if you have some spot dear to you on earth, not to linger here too long, else you will find this dearer."

We had finished dinner, which had been served on the big *lanai,* the one with a northerly exposure, though "exposure" is indeed a misnomer in so delectable a climate.

The candles had been put out, and a slim, white-clad Japanese slipped like a ghost through the silvery moonlight, presented us with cigars, and faded away into the darkness of the bungalow. I looked through a screen of banana and lehua trees, and down across the guava scrub to the quiet sea a thousand feet beneath. For a week, ever since I had landed from the tiny coasting-steamer, I had been stopping with Cudworth, and during that time no wind had ruffled that unvexed sea. True, there had been breezes, but they were the gentlest zephyrs that ever blew through summer isles. They were not winds; they were sighs—long, balmy sighs of a world at rest.

"A lotus land," I said.

"Where each day is like every day, and every day is a paradise of days," he answered. "Nothing ever happens. It is not too hot. It is not too cold. It is always just right. Have you noticed how the land and the sea breathe turn and turn about?"

Indeed I had noticed that delicious, rhythmic, breathing. Each morning I had watched the sea breeze begin at the shore and slowly extend seaward as it blew the mildest, softest whiff of ozone to the land. It played over the sea, just faintly darkening its surface, with here and there and everywhere long lanes of calm, shifting, changing, drifting, according to the capricious kisses of the breeze. And each evening I had watched the sea breath die away to heavenly calm, and heard the land breath softly make its way through the coffee trees and monkeypods.

"It is a land of perpetual calm," I said. "Does it ever blow here?—ever really blow? You know what I mean."

Cudworth shook his head and pointed eastward.

"How can it blow, with a barrier like that to stop it?"

Far above towered the huge bulks of Mauna Kea and Mauna Loa, seeming to blot out half the starry sky. Two miles and a half above our heads they reared their own heads, white with snow that the tropic sun had failed to melt.

"Thirty miles away, right now, I'll wager, it is blowing forty miles an hour."

I smiled incredulously.

Cudworth stepped to the lanai telephone. He called up, in succession, Waimea, Kohala, and Hamakua. Snatches of his conversation told me that the wind was blowing: "Ripsnorting and back-jumping, eh?... How long?... Only a week?... Hello, Abe, is that you?... Yes, yes.... You *will* plant coffee on the Hamakua coast.... Hang your windbreaks! You should see *my* trees.

"Blowing a gale," he said to me, turning from hanging up the receiver. "I always have to joke Abe on his coffee. He has five hundred acres, and he's done marvels in windbreaking, but how he keeps the roots in the ground is beyond me. Blow? It always blows on the Hamakua side. Kohala reports a schooner under double reefs beating up the channel between Hawaii and Maui, and making heavy weather of it."

"It is hard to realize," I said lamely. "Doesn't a little whiff of it ever eddy around somehow, and get down here?"

"Not a whiff. Our land breeze is absolutely of no kin, for it begins this side of Mauna Kea and the Mauna Loa. You see, the land radiates its heat quicker than the sea, and so, at night, the land breathes over the sea. In the day the land becomes warmer than the sea, and the sea breathes over the land. . . . Listen! Here comes the land breath now, the mountain wind."

I could hear it coming, rustling softly through the coffee trees, stirring the monkeypods, and sighing through the sugar cane. On the lanai the hush still reigned. Then it came, the first feel of the mountain wind, faintly balmy, fragrant and spicy, and cool, deliciously cool, a silken coolness, a wine-like coolness—cool as only the mountain wind of Kona can be cool.

"Do you wonder that I lost my heart to Kona eighteen years ago?" he demanded. "I could never leave it now. I think I should die. It would be terrible. There was another man who loved it, even as I. I think he loved it more, for he was born here on the Kona coast. He was a great man, my best friend, my more than brother. But he left it, and he did not die."

"Love?" I queried. "A woman?"

Cudworth shook his head.

"Nor will he ever come back, though his heart will be here until he dies."

He paused and gazed down upon the beach lights of Kailua. I smoked silently and waited.

"He was already in love . . . with his wife. Also, he had three children, and he loved them. They are in Honolulu now. The boy is going to college."

"Some rash act?" I questioned, after a time, impatiently.

He shook his head. "Neither guilty of anything criminal, nor charged with anything criminal. He was the sheriff of Kona."

"You choose to be paradoxical," I said.

"I suppose it does sound that way," he admitted, "and that is the perfect hell of it."

He looked at me searchingly for a moment, and then abruptly took up the tale.

"He was a leper. No, he was not born with it—no one is born with it; it came upon him. This man—what does it matter? Lyte Gregory was his name. Every *kamaaina* knows the story. He was straight American stock, but he was built like the chieftains of old Hawaii. He stood six feet three. His stripped weight was two hundred and twenty pounds, not an ounce of which was not clean muscle or bone. He was the strongest man I have ever seen. He was an athlete and a giant. He was a god. He was my friend. And his heart and his soul were as big and as fine as his body.

"I wonder what you would do if you saw your friend, your brother, on the slippery lip of a precipice, slipping, slipping, and you were able to do nothing. That was just it. I could do nothing. I saw it coming, and I could do nothing. My God, man! what could I do? There it was, malignant and incontestable, the mark of the thing on his brow. No one else saw it. It was because I loved him so, I do believe, that I alone saw it. I could not credit the testimony of my senses. It was too incredibly horrible. Yet there it was, on his brow, on his ears. I had seen it, the slight puff of the earlobes—oh, so imperceptibly slight. I watched it for months. Then, next, hoping against hope, the darkening of the skin above both eyebrows—oh, so faint, just like the dimmest touch of sunburn. I should have thought it sunburn but that there was a shine to it, such an invisible shine, like a little highlight seen for a moment and gone the next. I tried to believe it was sunburn, only I could not. I knew better. No one noticed it but me. No one ever noticed it except Stephen Kaluna, and I did not know that till afterward. But I saw it coming, the whole damnable, unnamable awfulness of it; but I refused to think about the future. I was afraid. I could not. And of nights I cried over it.

"He was my friend. We fished sharks on Niihau together. We hunted wild cattle on Mauna Kea and Mauna Loa. We broke horses and branded steers on the Carter Ranch. We hunted goats through Haleakala. He taught me diving and surfing until I was nearly as clever as he, and he was cleverer than the average Kanaka. I have seen him dive in fifteen fathoms, and he could stay down two minutes. He was an amphibian and a mountaineer. He could climb wherever a goat dared climb. He was afraid of nothing. He was on the wrecked *Luga,* and he swam thirty miles in thirty-six hours in a heavy sea. He could fight his way out through breaking combers that would batter you and me to a jelly. He was a great, glorious man-god. We went through the Revolution together. We were both romantic loyalists. He was shot twice and sentenced to death. But he was too great a man for the republicans to kill. He laughed at them. Later, they gave him honor and made him sheriff of Kona. He was a simple man, a boy that never grew up. His was no intricate brain pattern. He had no twists nor quirks in his mental processes. He went straight to the point, and his points were always simple.

"And he was sanguine. Never have I known so confident a man, nor a man so satisfied and happy. He did not ask anything from life. There was nothing left to be desired. For him life had no arrears. He had been paid in full, cash down, and in advance. What more could he possibly desire than that magnificent body, that iron constitution, that immunity from all ordinary ills, and that lowly wholesomeness of soul? Physically he was perfect. He had never been sick in his life. He did not know what a headache was. When I was so afflicted he used to look at me in wonder, and make me laugh with his clumsy attempts at sympathy. He did not understand such a thing as a headache. He could not understand. Sanguine? No wonder. How could he be otherwise with that tremendous vitality and incredible health?

"Just to show you what faith he had in his glorious star, and, also, what sanction he had for that faith. He was a youngster at the time—I had just met him—when he went into a poker game at Wailuku. There was a big German in it, Schultz his name was, and he played a brutal, domineering game. He had had a run of luck as well, and he was quite insufferable, when Lyte Gregory dropped in and took a hand. The very first hand it was Schultz's blind. Lyte came in, as well as the others, and Schultz raised them out—all except Lyte. He did not like the German's tone, and he raised him back. Schultz raised in turn, and in turn Lyte raised Schultz. So they went, back and forth. The stakes were big. And do you know what Lyte held? A pair of kings and three little clubs. It wasn't poker. Lyte wasn't playing poker. He was playing his optimism. He didn't know what Schultz held, but he raised and raised until he made Schultz squeal, and Schultz held three aces all the time. Think of it! A man with a pair of kings compelling three aces to see before the draw!

"Well, Schultz called for two cards. Another German was dealing, Schultz's friend at that. Lyte knew then that he was up against three of a kind. Now what did he do? What would you have done? Drawn three cards and held up the kings, of course. Not Lyte, he was playing optimism. He threw the kings away, held up the three little clubs, and drew two cards. He never looked at them. He looked across at Schultz to bet, and Schultz did bet, big. Since he himself held three aces he knew he had Lyte, because he played Lyte for threes, and, necessarily, they would have to be smaller threes. Poor Schultz! He was perfectly correct under the premises. His mistake was that he thought Lyte was playing poker. They bet back and forth for five minutes, until Schultz's certainty began to ooze out. And all the time Lyte had never looked at his two cards, and Schultz knew it. I could see Schultz think, and revive, and splurge with his bets again. But the strain was too much for him.

" 'Hold on, Gregory,' he said at last. 'I've got you beaten from the start. I don't want any of your money. I've got—'

" 'Never mind what you've got,' Lyte interrupted. 'You don't know what I've got. I guess I'll take a look.'

"He looked, and raised the German a hundred dollars. Then they went at it again, back and forth and back and forth, until Schultz weakened and called, and laid down his three aces. Lyte faced his five cards. They were all black. He had drawn two more clubs. Do you know, he just about broke Schultz's nerve as a poker player. He never played in the same form again. He lacked confidence after that, and was a bit wobbly.

" 'But how could you do it?' I asked Lyte afterward. 'You knew he had you beaten when he drew two cards. Besides, you never looked at your own draw.'

" 'I didn't have to look,' was Lyte's answer. 'I knew they were two clubs all the time. They just had to be two clubs. Do you think I was going to let that big Dutchman beat me? It was impossible that he should beat me. It is not my way to be beaten. I just have to win. Why, I'd have been the most surprised man in this world if they hadn't been all clubs.'

"That was Lyte's way, and maybe it will help you to appreciate his colossal optimism. As he put it, he just had to succeed, to fare well, to prosper. And in that same incident, as in ten thousand others, he found his sanction. The thing was that he did succeed, did prosper. That was why he was afraid of nothing. Nothing could ever happen to him. He knew it, because nothing had ever happened to him. That time the *Luga* was lost and he swam thirty miles, he was in the water two whole nights and a day. And during all that terrible stretch of time he never lost hope once, never once doubted the outcome. He just knew he was going to make the land. He told me so himself, and I know it was the truth.

"Well, that is the kind of a man Lyte Gregory was. He was of a different race from ordinary, ailing mortals. He was a lordly being, untouched by common ills and misfortunes. Whatever he wanted he got. He won his wife—one of the Caruthers, a little beauty—from a dozen rivals. And she settled down and made him the finest wife in the world. He wanted a boy. He got it. He wanted a girl and another boy. He got them. And they were just right, without spot or blemish, with chests like little barrels, and with all the inheritance of his own health and strength.

"And then it happened. The mark of the beast was laid

upon him. I watched it for a year. It broke my heart. But he did not know it, nor did anybody else guess it except that cursed *hapa-haole*, Stephen Kaluna. He knew it, but I did not know that he did. And—yes—Doc Strowbridge knew it. He was the federal physician, and he had developed the leper eye. You see, part of his business was to examine suspects and order them to the receiving station at Honolulu. And Stephen Kaluna had developed the leper eye. The disease ran strong in his family, and four or five of his relatives were already on Molokai.

"The trouble arose over Stephen Kaluna's sister. When she became suspect, and before Doc Strowbridge could get hold of her, her brother spirited her away to some hiding place. Lyte was sheriff of Kona, and it was his business to find her.

"We were all over at Hilo that night, in Ned Austin's. Stephen Kaluna was there when we came in, by himself, in his cups, and quarrelsome. Lyte was laughing over some joke —that huge, happy laugh of a giant boy. Kaluna spat contemptuously on the floor. Lyte noticed, so did everybody; but he ignored the fellow. Kaluna was looking for trouble. He took it as a personal grudge that Lyte was trying to apprehend his sister. In half a dozen ways he advertised his displeasure at Lyte's presence, but Lyte ignored him. I imagined Lyte was a bit sorry for him, for the hardest duty of his office was the apprehension of lepers. It is not a nice thing to go into a man's house and tear away a father, mother, or child, who has done no wrong, and to send such a one to perpetual banishment on Molokai. Of course, it is necessary as a protection to society, and Lyte, I do believe, would have been the first to apprehend his own father did he become suspect.

"Finally, Kaluna blurted out: 'Look here, Gregory, you think you're going to find Kalaniweo, but you're not.'

"Kalaniweo was his sister. Lyte glanced at him when his name was called, but he made no answer. Kaluna was furious. He was working himself up all the time.

" 'I'll tell you one thing,' he shouted. 'You'll be on Molo-kai yourself before ever you get Kalaniweo there. I'll tell you what you are. You've no right to be in the company of honest men. You've made a terrible fuss talking about your duty, haven't you? You've sent many lepers to Molokai, and knowing all the time you belonged there yourself.'

"I'd seen Lyte angry more than once, but never quite so angry as at that moment. Leprosy with us, you know, is not a thing to jest about. He made one leap across the floor, dragging Kaluna out of his chair with a clutch on his neck. He shook him back and forth savagely, till you could hear the half-caste's teeth rattling.

" 'What do you mean?' Lyte was demanding. 'Spit it out, man, or I'll choke it out of you!'

"You know, in the West there is a certain phrase that a man must smile while uttering. So with us of the islands, only our phrase is related to leprosy. No matter what Kaluna was, he was no coward. As soon as Lyte eased the grip on his throat he answered:—

" 'I'll tell you what I mean. You are a leper yourself.'

"Lyte suddenly flung the half-caste sidewise into a chair, letting him down easily enough. Then Lyte broke out into honest, hearty laughter. But he laughed alone, and when he discovered it he looked around at our faces. I had reached his side and was trying to get him to come away, but he took no notice of me. He was gazing, fascinated, at Kaluna, who was brushing at his own throat in a flurried, nervous way, as if to brush off the contamination of the fingers that had clutched him. The action was unreasoned, genuine.

"Lyte looked around at us, slowly passing from face to face.

" 'My God, fellows! My God!' he said.

"He did not speak it. It was more a hoarse whisper of fright and horror. It was fear that fluttered in his throat, and I don't think that ever in his life before he had known fear.

"Then his colossal optimism asserted itself, and he laughed again.

" 'A good joke—whoever put it up,' he said. 'The drinks are on me. I had a scare for a moment. But, fellows, don't do it again, to anybody. It's too serious. I tell you I died a thousand deaths in that moment. I thought of my wife and kids, and . . .'

"His voice broke, and the half-caste, still throat-brushing, drew his eyes. He was puzzled and worried.

" 'John,' he said, turning toward me.

"His jovial, rotund voice rang in my ears. But I could not answer. I was swallowing hard at that moment, and besides, I knew my face didn't look just right.

" 'John,' he called again, taking a step nearer.

"He called timidly, and of all nightmares of horrors the most frightful was to hear timidity in Lyte Gregory's voice.

" 'John, John, what does it mean?' he went on, still more timidly. 'It's a joke, isn't it? John, here's my hand. If I were a leper would I offer you my hand? Am I a leper, John?'

"He held out his hand, and what in high heaven or hell did I care? He was my friend. I took his hand, though it cut me to the heart to see the way his face brightened.

" 'It was only a joke, Lyte,' I said. 'We fixed it up on you. But you're right. It's too serious. We won't do it again.'

"He did not laugh this time. He smiled, as a man awakened from a bad dream and still oppressed by the substance of the dream.

" 'All right, then,' he said. 'Don't do it again, and I'll stand for the drinks. But I may as well confess that you fellows had me going south for a moment. Look at the way I've been sweating.'

"He sighed and wiped the sweat from his forehead as he started to step toward the bar.

" 'It is no joke,' Kaluna said abruptly.

"I looked murder at him, and I felt murder, too. But I dared not speak or strike. That would have precipitated the catastrophe which I somehow had a mad hope of still averting.

" 'It is no joke,' Kaluna repeated. 'You are a leper, Lyte

Gregory, and you've no right putting your hands on honest men's flesh—on the clean flesh of honest men.'

"Then Gregory flared up.

"'The joke has gone far enough! Quit it! Quit it, I say, Kaluna, or I'll give you a beating!'

"'You undergo a bacteriological examination,' Kaluna answered, 'and then you can beat me—to death, if you want to. Why, man, look at yourself there in the glass. You can see it. Anybody can see it. You're developing the lion face. See where the skin is darkened there over your eyes.'

"Lyte peered and peered, and I saw his hands trembling.

"'I can see nothing,' he said finally, then turned on the hapa-haole. 'You have a black heart, Kaluna. And I am not ashamed to say that you have given me a scare that no man has a right to give another. I take you at your word. I am going to settle this thing now. I am going straight to Doc Strowbridge. And when I come back, watch out.'

"He never looked at us, but started for the door.

"'You wait here, John,' he said, waving me back from accompanying him.

"We stood around like a group of ghosts.

"'It is the truth,' Kaluna said. 'You could see it for yourselves.'

"They looked at me, and I nodded. Harry Burnley lifted his glass to his lips, but lowered it untasted. He spilled half of it over the bar. His lips were trembling like a child that is about to cry. Ned Austin made a clatter in the ice chest. He wasn't looking for anything. I don't think he knew what he was doing. Nobody spoke. Harry Burnley's lips were trembling harder than ever. Suddenly, with a most horrible, malignant expression he drove his fist into Kaluna's face. He followed it up. We made no attempt to separate them. We didn't care if he killed the half-caste. It was a terrible beating. We weren't interested. I don't even remember when Burnley ceased and let the poor devil crawl away. We were all too dazed.

"Doc Strowbridge told me about it afterward. He was

working late over a report when Lyte came into his office. Lyte had already recovered his optimism, and came swinging in, a trifle angry with Kaluna to be sure, but very certain of himself. 'What could I do?' Doc asked me. 'I knew he had it. I had seen it coming on for months. I couldn't answer him. I couldn't say yes. I don't mind telling you I broke down and cried. He pleaded for the bacteriological test. "Snip out a piece, Doc," he said, over and over. "Snip out a piece of skin and make the test." '

"The way Doc Strowbridge cried must have convinced Lyte. The *Claudine* was leaving next morning for Honolulu. We caught him when he was going aboard. You see, he was headed for Honolulu to give himself up to the Board of Health. We could do nothing with him. He had sent too many to Molokai to hang back himself. We argued for Japan. But he wouldn't hear of it. 'I've got to take my medicine, fellows,' was all he would say, and he said it over and over. He was obsessed with the idea.

"He wound up all his affairs from the Receiving Station at Honolulu, and went down to Molokai. He didn't get on well there. The resident physician wrote us that he was a shadow of his old self. You see he was grieving about his wife and the kids. He knew we were taking care of them, but it hurt him just the same. After six months or so I went down to Molokai. I sat on one side of a plate-glass window, and he on the other. We looked at each other through the glass, and talked through what might be called a speaking tube. But it was hopeless. He had made up his mind to remain. Four mortal hours I argued. I was exhausted at the end. My steamer was whistling for me, too.

"But we couldn't stand for it. Three months later we chartered the schooner *Halcyon*. She was an opium smuggler, and she sailed like a witch. Her master was a squarehead who would do anything for money, and we made a charter to China worth his while. He sailed from San Francisco, and a few days later we took out Landhouse's sloop for a cruise. She was only a five-ton yacht, but we slammed her fifty miles to windward into the northeast trade. Seasick? I never suffered so in my life. Out of sight of land we picked up the *Halcyon,* and Burnley and I went aboard.

"We ran down to Molokai, arriving about eleven at night. The schooner hove to and we landed through the surf in a whaleboat at Kalawao—the place, you know, where Father Damien died. That squarehead was game. With a couple of revolvers strapped on him he came right along. The three of us crossed the peninsula to Kalaupapa, something like two miles. Just imagine hunting in the dead of night for a man in a settlement of over a thousand lepers. You see, if the alarm was given, it was all off with us. It was strange ground, and pitch dark. The lepers' dogs came out and bayed at us, and we stumbled around till we got lost.

"The squarehead solved it. He led the way into the first detached house. We shut the door after us and struck a light. There were six lepers. We routed them up, and I talked in native. What I wanted was a *kokua*. A kokua is, literally, a helper, a native who is clean that lives in the settlement and is paid by the Board of Health to nurse the lepers, dress their sores, and such things. We stayed in the house to keep track of the inmates, while the squarehead led one of them off to find a kokua. He got him, and he brought him along at the point of his revolver. But the kokua was all right. While the squarehead guarded the house, Burnley and I were guided by the kokua to Lyte's house. He was all alone.

' "I thought you fellows would come,' Lyte said. 'Don't touch me, John. How's Ned, and Charley, and all the crowd? Never mind, tell me afterward. I am ready to go now. I've had nine months of it. Where's the boat?'

"We started back for the other house to pick up the squarehead. But the alarm had got out. Lights were showing in the houses, and doors were slamming. We had agreed that there was to be no shooting unless absolutely necessary, and when we were halted we went at it with our fists and the butts of our revolvers. I found myself tangled up with a big man. I couldn't keep him off of me, though twice I smashed him fairly in the face with my fist. He grappled with me, and we went down, rolling and scrambling and struggling for grips. He was getting away with me, when someone came running up with a lantern. Then I saw his face. How shall I describe the horror of it! It was not a face—only wasted or wasting features—a living ravage, noseless, lipless, with one ear swollen and distorted, hanging down to the shoulder. I was frantic. In a clinch he hugged me close to him until that ear flapped in my face. Then I guess I went insane. It was too terrible. I began striking him with my revolver. How it happened I don't know, but just as I was getting clear he fastened upon me with his teeth. The whole side of my hand was in that lipless mouth. Then I struck him with the revolver butt squarely between the eyes, and his teeth relaxed."

Cudworth held his hand to me in the moonlight, and I could see the scars. It looked as if it had been mangled by a dog.

"Weren't you afraid?" I asked.

"I was. Seven years I waited. You know, it takes that long for the disease to incubate. Here in Kona I waited, and it did not come. But there was never a day of those seven years, and never a night, that I did not look out on . . . on all this. . . ." His voice broke as he swept his eyes from the moon-bathed sea beneath to the snowy summits above. "I could not bear to think of losing it, of never again beholding Kona. Seven years! I stayed clean. But that is why I am single. I was engaged. I could not dare to marry while I was in doubt. She did not understand. She went away to the States, and married. I have never seen her since.

"Just at the moment I got free of the leper policeman there was a rush and clatter of hoofs like a cavalry charge. It was the squarehead. He had been afraid of a rumpus and he had improved his time by making those blessed lepers he was guarding saddle up four horses. We were ready for him. Lyte had accounted for three kokuas, and between us we untangled Burnley from a couple more. The whole settlement was in an uproar by that time, and as we dashed away somebody opened up on us with a Winchester. It must have been Jack McVeigh, the superintendent of Molokai.

"That was a ride! Leper horses, leper saddles, leper bridles, pitch-black darkness, whistling bullets, and a road none of the best. And the squarehead's horse was a mule, and he didn't know how to ride, either. But we made the whale-boat, and as we shoved off through the surf we could hear the horses coming down the hill from Kalaupapa.

"You're going to Shanghai. You look Lyte Gregory up. He is employed in a German firm there. Take him out to dinner. Open up wine. Give him everything of the best, but don't let him pay for anything. Send the bill to me. His wife and the kids are in Honolulu, and he needs the money for them. I know. He sends most of his salary, and lives like an anchorite. And tell him about Kona. There's where his heart is. Tell him all you can about Kona."

On the Makaloa Mat

ON THE MAKALOA MAT

UNLIKE THE WOMEN OF MOST WARM RACES, THOSE OF HAWAII age well and nobly. With no pretense of make-up or cunning concealment of time's inroads, the woman who sat under the hau tree might have been permitted as much as fifty years by a judge competent anywhere over the world save in Hawaii. Yet her children and her grandchildren, and Roscoe Scandwell, who had been her husband for forty years, knew that she was sixty-four and would be sixty-five come the next twenty-second day of June. But she did not look it, despite the fact that she thrust reading glasses on her nose as she read her magazine and took them off when her gaze desired to wander in the direction of the half-dozen children playing on the lawn.

It was a noble situation—noble as the ancient hau tree, the size of a house, where she sat as if in a house, so spaciously and comfortably houselike was its shade furnished; noble as the lawn that stretched away landward, its plush of green at an appraisement of two hundred dollars a front foot, to a bungalow equally dignified, noble, and costly. Seaward, glimpsed through a fringe of hundred-foot coconut palms, was the ocean, beyond the reef a dark blue that grew indigo blue to the horizon, within the reef all the silken gamut of jade and emerald and tourmaline.

And this was but one of the half-dozen houses belonging to Martha Scandwell. Her town house, a few miles away in Honolulu, on Nuuanu Drive, between the first and second showers, was a palace. Hosts of guests had known the comfort

and joy of her mountain house on Tantalus, and of her volcano house, her *mauka* (mountainward) house, and her
makai (seaward) house on the big island of Hawaii. Yet this
Waikiki house stressed no less than the rest in beauty, in dig-
nity and in expensiveness of upkeep. Two Japanese yard boys
were trimming hibiscus, a third was engaged expertly with
the long hedge of night-blooming cereus that was shortly
expectant of unfolding in its mysterious night bloom. In im-
maculate ducks, a house Japanese brought out the tea things,
followed by a Japanese maid, pretty as a butterfly in the dis-
tinctive garb of her race and fluttery as a butterfly to attend
on her mistress. Another Japanese maid, an array of Turkish
towels on her arm, crossed the lawn well to the right in the
direction of the bathhouses, from which the children, in
swimming suits, were beginning to emerge. Beyond, under
the palms at the edge of the sea, two Chinese nursemaids, in
their pretty native costume of white *yeeshon* and straight-
lined trousers, their black braids of hair down their backs,
attended each on a baby in a perambulator.

And all these—servants, and nurses, and grandchildren—
were Martha Scandwell's. So likewise was the color of the
skin of the grandchildren—the unmistakable Hawaiian color,
tinted beyond shadow of mistake by exposure to the Hawaiian sun. One eighth and one sixteenth Hawaiian were
they, which meant that seven eighths and fifteen sixteenths
white blood informed that skin, yet failed to obliterate the
modicum of golden tawny brown of Polynesia. But in this
again, only a trained observer would have known that the
frolicking children were aught but pure-blooded white. Roscoe Scandwell, grandfather, was pure white; Martha, three-
quarters white; the many sons and daughters of them seven-
eighths white; the grandchildren graded up to fifteen-six-
teenths white, or, in the cases when their seven-eighths fathers
and mothers had married seven-eighths, themselves fourteen-
sixteenths or seven-eighths white. On both sides the stock was
good, Roscoe straight descended from the New England
Puritans, Martha no less straight descended from the royal

chief stocks of Hawaii whose genealogies were chanted in *meles* a thousand years before written speech was acquired.

In the distance a machine stopped and deposited a woman whose utmost years might have been guessed as sixty, who walked across the lawn as lightly as a well-cared-for woman of forty, and whose actual calendar age was sixty-eight. Martha rose to greet her in the hearty Hawaiian way, arms about, lips on lips, faces eloquent and bodies no less eloquent with sincereness and frank excessiveness of emotion. And it was "Sister Bella," and "Sister Martha," back and forth, intermingled with almost incoherent inquiries about each other, and about Uncle This and Brother That and Aunt Some One Else, until, the first tremulousness of meeting over, eyes moist with tenderness of love, they sat gazing at each other across their teacups. Apparently, they had not seen nor embraced for years. In truth, two months marked the interval of their separation. And one was sixty-four, the other sixty-eight. But the thorough comprehension resided in the fact that in each of them one fourth of them was the sun-warm, love-warm heart of Hawaii.

The children flooded about Aunt Bella like a rising tide and were capaciously hugged and kissed ere they departed with their nurses to the swimming beach.

"I thought I'd run out to the beach for several days—the trades had stopped blowing," Martha explained.

"You've been here two weeks already," Bella smiled fondly at her younger sister. "Brother Edward told me. He met me at the steamer and insisted on running me out first of all to see Louise and Dorothy and that first grandchild of his. He's as mad as a silly hatter about it."

"Mercy!" Martha exclaimed. "Two weeks! I had not thought it that long."

"Where's Annie?—and Margaret?" Bella asked.

Martha shrugged her voluminous shoulders with voluminous and forgiving affection for her wayward, matronly daughters who left their children in her care for the afternoon.

"Margaret's at a meeting of the Outdoor Circle—they're planning the planting of trees and hibiscus all along both sides of Kalakaua Avenue," she said. "And Annie's wearing out eighty dollars' worth of tires to collect seventy-five dollars for the British Red Cross—this is their tag day, you know."

"Roscoe must be very proud," Bella said, and observed the bright glow of pride that appeared in her sister's eyes. "I got the news in San Francisco of Ho-o-la-a's first dividend. Remember when I put a thousand in it at seventy-five cents for poor Abbie's children, and said I'd sell when it went to ten dollars?"

"And everybody laughed at you, and at anybody who bought a share," Martha nodded. "But Rosco knew. It's selling today at twenty-four."

"I sold mine from the steamer by wireless—at twenty even," Bella continued. "And now Abbie's wildly dressmaking. She's going with May and Tootsie to Paris."

"And Carl?" Martha queried.

"Oh, he'll finish Yale all right—"

"Which he would have done anyway, and you *know* it," Martha charged, lapsing charmingly into twentieth-century slang.

Bella affirmed her guilt of intention of paying the way of her school friend's son through college, and added complacently:

"Just the same it was nicer to have Ho-o-la-a pay for it. In a way, you see, Roscoe is doing it, because it was his judgment I trusted to when I made the investment." She gazed slowly about her, her eyes taking in, not merely the beauty and comfort and repose of all they rested on, but the immensity of beauty and comfort and repose represented by them, scattered in similar oases all over the islands. She sighed pleasantly and observed: "All our husbands have done well by us with what we brought them."

"And happily . . ." Martha agreed, then suspended her utterance with suspicious abruptness.

"And happily, all of us, except Sister Bella," Bella forgivingly completed the thought for her.

"It was too bad, that marriage," Martha murmured, all softness of sympathy. "You were so young. Uncle Robert should never have made you."

"I was only nineteen," Bella nodded. "But it was not George Castner's fault. And look what he, out of the grave, has done for me. Uncle Robert was wise. He knew George had the faraway vision of far ahead, the energy, and the steadiness. He saw, even then, and that's fifty years ago, the value of the Nahala water rights which nobody else valued then. They thought he was struggling to buy cattle range. He struggled to buy the future of the water—and how well he succeeded, you know. I'm almost ashamed to think of my income sometimes. No; whatever else, the unhappiness of our marriage was not due to George. I could have lived happily with him, I know, even to this day, had he lived." She shook her head slowly. "No; it was not his fault. Nor anybody's. Nor even mine. If it was anybody's fault—" The wistful fondness of her smile took the sting out of what she was about to say. "If it was anybody's fault, it was Uncle John's."

"Uncle John's!" Martha cried with sharp surprise. "If it had to be one or the other, I should have said Uncle Robert. But Uncle John!"

Bella smiled with slow positiveness.

"But it was Uncle Robert who made you marry George Castner," her sister urged.

"That is true," Bella nodded corroboration. "But it was not the matter of a husband, but of a horse. I wanted to borrow a horse from Uncle John, and Uncle John said yes. That is how it all happened."

A silence fell, pregnant and cryptic, and, while the voices of the children and the soft mandatory protests of the Asiatic maids drew nearer from the beach, Martha Scandwell felt herself vibrant and tremulous with sudden resolve of daring. She waved the children away.

"Run along, dears, run along. Grandma and Aunt Bella want to talk."

And as the shrill, sweet treble of child voices ebbed away across the lawn, Martha, with scrutiny of the heart, observed the sadness of the lines graven by secret woe for half a century in her sister's face. For nearly fifty years had she watched those lines. She steeled all the melting softness of the Hawaiian of her to break the half century of silence.

"Bella," she said. "We never knew. You never spoke. But we wondered, oh, often and often—"

"And never asked," Bella murmured gratefully.

"But I am asking now, at the last. This is our twilight. Listen to them! Sometimes it almost frightens me to think that they are grandchildren, *my* grandchildren—*I*, who only the other day, it would seem, was as heart-free, leg-free, care-free a girl as ever bestrode a horse, or swam in the big surf, or gathered *opihis* at low tide, or laughed at a dozen lovers. And here in our twilight let us forget everything save that I am your dear sister as you are mine."

The eyes of both were dewy moist. Bella palpably trembled to utterance.

"We thought it was George Castner," Martha went on; "and we could guess the details. He was a cold man. You were warm Hawaiian. He must have been cruel. Brother Walcott always insisted he must have beaten you—"

"No! No!" Bella broke in. "George Castner was never a brute, a beast. Almost have I wished, often, that he had been. He never laid hand on me. He never raised hand to me. He never raised his voice to me. Never—oh, can you believe it?— do, please, sister, believe it—did we have a high word nor a cross word. But that house of his, of ours, at Nahala, was gray. All the color of it was gray and cool and chill while I was bright with all colors of sun and earth and blood and birth. It was very cold, gray cold, with that cold gray husband of mine at Nahala.—You know he was gray, Martha. Gray like those portraits of Emerson we used to see at school. His skin was gray. Sun and weather and all hours in the saddle could never tan it. And he was as gray inside as out.

"And I was only nineteen, when Uncle Robert decided on the marriage. How was I to know? Uncle Robert talked to me. He pointed out how the wealth and property of Hawaii was already beginning to pass into the hands of the haoles (whites). The Hawaiian chiefs let their possessions slip away from them. The Hawaiian chiefesses who married haoles had their possessions, under the management of their haole husbands, increase prodigiously. He pointed back to the original Grandfather Roger Wilton, who had taken Grandmother Wilton's poor mauka lands and added to them and built up about them the Kilohana Ranch—"

"Even then it was second only to the Parker Ranch," Martha interrupted proudly.

"—And he told me that had our father, before he died, been as farseeing as grandfather, half the then Parker holdings would have been added to Kilohana, making Kilohana first. And he said that never, forever and ever, would beef be cheaper. And he said that the big future of Hawaii would be in sugar. That was fifty years ago, and he has been more than proved right. And he said that the young haole, George Castner, saw far and would go far, and that there were many girls of us, and that the Kilohana lands ought by rights to go to the boys, and that if I married George my future was assured in the biggest way.

"I was only nineteen. Just back from the Royal Chief School—that was before our girls went to the States for their educations. You were among the first, Sister Martha, who got their education on the mainland. And what did I know of love and lovers, much less of marriage? All women married. It was their business in life. Mother and grandmother, all the way back they had married. It was my business in life to marry George Castner. Uncle Robert said so in his wisdom, and I knew he was very wise. And I went to live with my husband in the gray house at Nahala.

"You remember it. No trees, only the rolling grass lands,

the high mountains behind, the sea beneath, and the wind!—
the Waimea and Nahala winds, we got them both, and the
kona wind as well. Yet little would I have minded them, any
more than we minded them at Kilohana, or than they minded
them at Mana, had not Nahala itself been so gray, and Husband George so gray. We were alone. He was managing
Nahala for the Glenns, who had gone back to Scotland.
Eighteen hundred a year, plus beef, horses, cowboy service,
and the ranch house, was what he received—"

"It was a high salary in those days," Martha said.

"And for George Castner, and the service he gave, it was
very cheap," Bella defended. "I lived with him for three
years. There was never a morning that he was out of his bed
later than half-past four. He was the soul of devotion to his
employers. Honest to a penny in his accounts, he gave them
full measure and more of his time and energy. Perhaps that
was what helped make our life so gray. But listen, Martha.
Out of his eighteen hundred, he laid aside sixteen hundred
each year. Think of it! The two of us lived on two hundred
a year. Luckily he did not drink or smoke. Also, we dressed
out of it as well. I made my own dresses. You can imagine
them. Outside of the cowboys who chored the firewood, I did
the work. I cooked and baked and scrubbed—"

"You who had never known anything but servants from
the time you were born!" Martha pitied. "Never less than a
regiment of them at Kilohana."

"Oh, but it was the bare, naked, pinching meagerness of
it!" Bella cried out. "How far I was compelled to make a
pound of coffee go! A broom worn down to nothing before a
new one was bought! And beef! French beef and jerky, morning, noon, and night! And porridge! Never since have I eaten
porridge or any breakfast food."

She arose suddenly and walked a dozen steps away to gaze
a moment with unseeing eyes at the color-lavish reef while
she composed herself. And she returned to her seat with the
splendid, sure, gracious, high-breasted, noble-headed port of
which no outbreeding can ever rob the Hawaiian woman.

Very haole was Bella Castner, fair-skinned, fine-textured. Yet, as she returned, the high pose of head, the level-lidded gaze of her long brown eyes under royal arches of eyebrows, the softly set lines of her small mouth that fairly sang sweetness of kisses after sixty-eight years—all made her the very picture of a chiefess of old Hawaii full-bursting through her ampleness of haole blood. Taller she was than her sister Martha, if anything more queenly.

"You know we were notorious as poor feeders," Bella laughed lightly enough. "It was many a mile on either side from Nahala to the next roof. Belated travelers, or storm-bound ones, would, on occasion, stop with us overnight. And you know the lavishness of the big ranches, then and now. How we were the laughingstock! 'What do we care?' George would say. 'They live today and now. Twenty years from now will be our turn, Bella. They will be where they are now, and they will eat out of our hand. We will be compelled to feed them, they will need to be fed, and we will feed them well; for we will be rich, Bella, so rich that I am afraid to tell you. But I know what I know, and you must have faith in me.'

"George was right. Twenty years afterward, though he did not live to see it, my income was a thousand a month. Goodness! I do not know what it is today. But I was only nineteen, and I would say to George: 'Now! now! We live now. We may not be alive twenty years from now. I do want a new broom. And there is a third-rate coffee that is only two cents a pound more than the awful stuff we are using. Why couldn't I fry eggs in butter—now? I should dearly love at least one new tablecloth. Our linen! I'm ashamed to put a guest between the sheets, though heaven knows they dare come seldon enough.'

" 'Be patient,' he would reply. 'In a little while, in only a few years, those that scorn to sit at our table now or sleep between our sheets will be proud of an invitation—those of them who will not be dead. You remember how Stevens passed out last year—free living and easy, everybody's friend but his own. The Kohala crowd had to bury him, for he left

nothing but debts. Watch the others going the same pace.
There's your brother Hal. He can't keep it up and live five
years, and he's breaking his uncles' hearts. And there's Prince
Lilolilo. Dashes by me with half a hundred mounted, able-
bodied, roistering Kanakas in his train who would be better
at hard work and looking after their futures, for he will
never be King of Hawaii. He will not live to be King of
Hawaii.'

"George was right. Brother Hal died. So did Prince Lilolilo. But George was not *all* right. He, who neither drank
nor smoked, who never wasted the weight of his arms in an
embrace, nor the touch of his lips a second longer than the
most perfunctory kisses, who was invariably up before cock-
crow and asleep ere the kerosene lamp had a tenth emptied
itself, and who never thought to die, was dead even more
quickly than Brother Hal and Prince Lilolilo.

" 'Be patient, Bella,' Uncle Robert would say to me.
'George Castner is a coming man. I have chosen well for you.
Your hardships now are the hardships on the way to the
promised land. Not always will the Hawaiians rule in Hawaii. Just as they let their wealth slip out of their hands, so
will their rule slip out of their hands. Political power and the
land always go together. There will be great changes, revolutions no one knows how many nor of what sort, save that in
the end the haole will possess the land and the rule. And in
that day you may well be first lady of Hawaii, just as surely
as George Castner will be ruler of Hawaii. It is written in
the books. It is ever so where the haole conflicts with the
easier races. I, your Uncle Robert, who am half Hawaiian
and half haole, know whereof I speak. Be patient, Bella, be
patient.'

" 'Dear Bella,' Uncle John would say; and I knew his
heart was tender for me. Thank God, he never told me to be
patient. He knew. He was very wise. He was warm, human,
and, therefore, wiser than Uncle Robert and George Castner,
who sought the thing, not the spirit, who kept records in
ledgers rather than numbered heartbeats breast to breast,

who added columns of figures rather than remembered embraces and endearments of look and speech and touch. 'Dear Bella,' Uncle John would say. He knew. You have heard always how he was the lover of the Princess Naomi. He was a true lover. He loved but the once. After her death they said he was eccentric. He was. He was the one lover, once and always. Remember that tabu inner room of his at Kilohana that we entered only after his death and found it his shrine to her. 'Dear Bella,' it was all he ever said to me, but I knew he knew.

"And I was nineteen, and sun-warm Hawaiian in spite of my three quarters haole blood, and I knew nothing save my girlhood splendors at Kilohana and my Honolulu education at the Royal Chief School, and my gray husband at Nahala with his gray preachments and practices of sobriety and thrift, and those two childless uncles of mine, the one with far cold vision, the other the brokenhearted, forever-dreaming lover of a dead princess.

"Think of that gray house! I, who had known the ease and the delights and the ever-laughing joys of Kilohana, and of the Parkers at old Mana, and of Puuwaawaa! You remember. We did live in feudal spaciousness in those days. Would you, can you believe it, Martha?—at Nahala the only sewing machine I had was one of those the early missionaries brought, a tiny, crazy thing that one cranked around by hand!

"Robert and John had each given Husband George five thousand dollars at my marriage. But he had asked for it to be kept secret. Only the four of us knew. And while I sewed my cheap *holokus* on that crazy machine, he bought land with the money—the upper Nahala lands, you know— a bit at a time, each purchase a hard-driven bargain, his face the very face of poverty. Today the Nahala Ditch alone pays me forty thousand a year.

"But was it worth it? I starved. If only once, madly, he had crushed me in his arms! If only once, he could have lingered with me five minutes from his own business or from his fidelity to his employers! Sometimes I could have screamed, or showered the eternal bowl of hot porridge into his face, or smashed the sewing machine upon the floor and danced a hula on it, just to make him burst out and lose his temper and be human, be a brute, be a man of some sort instead of a gray, frozen demigod."

Bella's tragic expression vanished, and she laughed outright in sheer genuineness of mirthful recollection.

"And when I was in such moods he would gravely look me over, gravely feel my pulse, examine my tongue, gravely dose me with castor oil, and gravely put me to bed early with hot stove lids and assure me that I'd feel better in the morning. Early to bed! Our wildest sitting up was nine o'clock. Eight o'clock was our regular bedtime. It saved kerosene. We did not eat dinner at Nahala—remember the great table at Kilohana where we did have dinner? But Husband George and I had supper. And then he would sit close to the lamp on one side the table and read old borrowed magazines for an hour, while I sat on the other side and darned his socks and underclothing. He always wore such cheap, shoddy stuff. And when he went to bed, I went to bed. No wastage of kerosene with only one to benefit by it. And he went to bed always the same way, winding up his watch, entering the day's weather in his diary, and taking off his shoes, right foot first invariably, left foot second, and placing them just so, side by side, on the floor, at the foot of the bed, on his side.

"He was the cleanest man I ever knew. He never wore the same undergarment a second time. I did the washing. He was so clean it hurt. He shaved twice a day. He used more water on his body than any Kanaka. He did more work than any two haoles. And he saw the future of the Nahala water."

"And he made you wealthy, but did not make you happy," Martha observed.

Bella sighed and nodded.

"What is wealth, after all, Sister Martha? My new Pierce-Arrow came down on the steamer with me. My third in two years. But oh, all the Pierce-Arrows and all the incomes in the world compared with a lover!—the one lover, the one mate, to be married to, to toil beside and suffer and joy beside, the one male man lover husband—"

Her voice trailed off, and the sisters sat in soft silence while an ancient crone, staff in hand, twisted, doubled, and shrunken under a hundred years of living, hobbled across the lawn to them. Her eyes, withered to scarcely more than peepholes, were sharp as a mongoose's, and at Bella's feet she first sank down, in pure Hawaiian mumbling and chanting a toothless mele of Bella and Bella's ancestry and adding it to an extemporized welcome back to Hawaii after her absence across the great sea to California. And while she chanted her mele, the old crone's shrewd fingers *lomied* or massaged Bella's silk-stockinged legs from ankle and calf to knee and thigh.

Both Bella's and Martha's eyes were luminous-moist, as the old retainer repeated the lomi and the mele to Martha, and as they talked with her in the ancient tongue and asked the immemorial questions about her health and age and great-great-grandchildren—she, who had lomied them as babies in the great house at Kilohana, as her ancestresses had lomied their ancestresses back through the unnumbered generations. The brief duty visit over, Martha arose and accompanied her back to the bungalow, putting money into her hand, commanding proud and beautiful Japanese housemaids to wait upon the dilapidated aborigine with poi, which is compounded of the roots of the water lily, with *iamaka*, which is raw fish, and with pounded *kukui* nut and *limu*, which latter is seaweed tender to the toothless, digestible and savory. It was the old feudal tie, the faithfulness of the commoner to the chief, the responsibility of the chief to the commoner; and Martha, three quarters haole with the Anglo-Saxon blood of New England, was four quarters Hawaiian in her remembrance and observance of the well-nigh vanished customs of old days.

As she came back across the lawn to the hau tree, Bella's eyes dwelt upon the moving authenticity of her and of the blood of her, and embraced her and loved her. Shorter than Bella was Martha a trifle, but the merest trifle, less queenly of port; but beautifully and generously proportioned, mellowed rather than dismantled by years, her Polynesian chiefess figure eloquent and glorious under the satisfying lines of a half-fitting, grandly sweeping, black silk holoku trimmed with black lace more costly than a Paris gown.

And as both sisters resumed their talk, an observer would have noted the striking resemblance of their pure, straight profiles, of their broad cheekbones, of their wide and lofty foreheads, of their iron-gray abundance of hair, of their sweet-lipped mouths set with the carriage of decades of assured and accomplished pride, and of their lovely, slender eyebrows arched over equally lovely long brown eyes. The hands of both of them, little altered or defaced by age, were wonderful in their slender, tapering finger tips, love-lomied and love-formed while they were babies by old Hawaiian women like to the one even then eating poi and iamaka and limu in the house.

"I had a year of it," Bella resumed, "and, do you know, things were beginning to come right. I was beginning to draw to Husband George. Women are so made. I was such a woman at any rate. For he *was* good. He *was* just. All the old sterling Puritan virtues were his. I was coming to draw to him, to like him, almost, might I say, to love him. And had not Uncle John loaned me that horse, I know that I would have truly loved him and have lived ever happily with him— in a quiet sort of way, of course.

"You see, I knew nothing else, nothing different, nothing better in the way of man. I came gladly to look across the table at him while he read in the brief interval between supper and bed, gladly to listen for and to catch the beat of his horse's hoofs coming home at night from his endless riding over the ranch. And his scant praise was praise indeed, that made me tingle with happiness—yes, Sister Martha, I knew what it was to blush under his precise, just praise for the things I had done right or correctly.

"And all would have been well for the rest of our lives together, except that he had to take the steamer to Honolulu. It was business. He was to be gone two weeks or longer, first, for the Glenns in ranch affairs, and, next, for himself, to arrange the purchase of still more of the upper Nahala lands. Do you know, he bought lots of the wilder and up-and-down lands, worthless for aught save water, and the very heart of the watershed, for as low as five and ten cents an acre. And he suggested I needed a change. I wanted to go with him to Honolulu. But, with an eye to expense, he decided Kilohana for me. Not only would it cost him nothing for me to visit at the old home, but he saved the price of the poor food I should have eaten had I remained alone at Nahala, which meant the purchase price of more Nahala acreage. And at Kilohana Uncle John said yes, and loaned me the horse.

"Oh, it was like heaven, getting back those first several days. It was difficult to believe at first that there was so much food in all the world. The enormous wastage of the kitchen appalled me. I saw waste everywhere, so well trained had I been by Husband George. Why, out in the servants' quarters the aged relatives and most distant hangers-on of the servants fed better than George and I ever fed. You remember our Kilohana way, same as the Parker way, a bullock killed for every meal, fresh fish by runners from the ponds of Waipio and Kiholo, and the best and rarest at all times of everything. . . .

"And love, our family way of loving! You know what Uncle John was. And Brother Walcott was there, and Brother Edward, and all the younger sisters save you and Sally away at school. And Aunt Elizabeth, and Aunt Janet with her husband and all her children on a visit. It was arms around, and perpetual endearings, and all that I had missed for a weary twelvemonth. I was thirsty for it. I was like a survivor from the open boat falling down on the sand and lapping the fresh, bubbling springs at the roots of the palms.

"And *they* came, riding up from Kawaihae, where they had landed from the royal yacht, the whole glorious cavalcade of them, two by two, flower-garlanded, young and happy, gay, on Parker Ranch horses, thirty of them in the party, a hundred Parker Ranch cowboys and as many more of their own retainers—a royal progress. It was Princess Lihue's progress, of course, she flaming and passing as we all knew with the dreadful tuberculosis; but with her were her nephews, Prince Lilolilo, hailed everywhere as the next king, and his brothers, Prince Kahekili and Prince Kamalau. And with the Princess was Ella Higginsworth, who rightly claimed higher chief bloodlines through the Kauai descent than belonged to the reigning family, and Dora Niles, and Emily Lowcroft, and— oh, why enumerate them all! Ella Higginsworth and I had been roommates at the Royal Chief School. And there was a great resting time for an hour—no luau, for the luau waited them at the Parkers'—but beer and stronger drinks for the men, and lemonade, and oranges, and refreshing watermelon for the women.

"And it was arms around with Ella Higginsworth and me, and the Princess, who remembered me, and all the other girls and women, and Ella spoke to the Princess, and the Princess herself invited me to the progress, joining them at Mana whence they would depart two days later. And I was mad, mad with it all—I, from a twelvemonth of imprisonment at gray Nahala. And I was nineteen yet, just turning twenty within the week.

"Oh, I had no thought of what was to happen. So occupied was I with the women that I did not see Lilolilo, except at a distance, bulking large and tall above the other men. But I had never been on a progress. I had seen them entertained at Kilohana and Mana, but I had been too young to be invited along, and after that it had been school and marriage. I knew what it would be like—two weeks of paradise, and little enough for another twelvemonth at Nahala.

"And I asked Uncle John to lend me a horse, which meant three horses, of course—one mounted cowboy and a pack horse to accompany me. No roads then. No automobiles. And the horse for myself! It was Hilo. You don't remember him. You were away at school, then, and before you came home, the following year, he'd broken his back and his rider's neck wild-cattle-roping up Mauna Kea. You heard about it—that young American naval officer."

"Lieutenant Bowsfield," Martha nodded.

"But Hilo! I was the first woman on his back. He was a three-year-old, almost a four-year, and just broken. So black and in such vigor of coat that the highlights on him clad him in shimmering silver. He was the biggest riding animal on the ranch, descended from the King's Sparklingdew with a range mare for dam, and roped wild only weeks before. I never have seen so beautiful a horse. He had the round, deep-chested, big-hearted, well-coupled body of the ideal mountain pony, and his head and neck were true thoroughbred, slender, yet full, with lovely alert ears not too small to be vicious nor too large to be stubborn mulish. And his legs and feet were lovely, too, unblemished, sure and firm, with long springy pasterns that made him a wonder of ease under the saddle."

"I remember hearing Prince Lilolilo tell Uncle John that you were the best woman rider in all Hawaii," Martha interrupted to say. "That was two years afterward when I was back from school and while you were still living at Nahala."

"Lilolilo said that!" Bella cried. Almost as with a blush, her long brown eyes were illumined, as she bridged the years to her lover near half a century dead and dust. With the gentleness of modesty so innate in the women of Hawaii, she covered her spontaneous exposure of her heart with added panegyric of Hilo.

"Oh, when he ran with me up the long-grass slopes, and down the long-grass slopes, it was like hurdling in a dream, for he cleared the grass at every bound, leaping like a deer, a rabbit, or a fox terrier—you know how they do. And cut up, and prance, and high life! He was a mount for a general, for a Napoleon or a Kitchener. And he had, not a wicked eye, but, oh, such a roguish eye, intelligent and looking as if it cherished a joke behind and wanted to laugh or to perpetrate it. And I asked Uncle John for Hilo. And Uncle John looked at me, and I looked at him; and, though he did not say it, I knew he was *feeling* 'Dear Bella,' and I knew, somewhere in his seeing of me, was all his vision of the Princess Naomi. And Uncle John said yes. That is how it happened.

"But he insisted that I should try Hilo out—myself, rather —at private rehearsal. He was a *handful*, a glorious handful. But not vicious, not malicious. He got away from me over and over again, but I never let him know. I was not afraid, and that helped me keep always a *feel* of him that prevented him from thinking that he was even a jump ahead of me.

"I have often wondered if Uncle John dreamed of what possibly might happen. I know I had no thought of it my-self, that day I rode across and joined the Princess at Mana. Never was there such festal time. You know the grand way the old Parkers had of entertaining. The pigsticking and wild-cattle shooting, the horse-breaking and the branding. The servants' quarters overflowing. Parker cowboys in from everywhere. And all the girls from Waimea up, and the girls from Waipio, and Honokaa, and Paauilo—I can see them yet, sitting in long rows on top the stone walls of the breaking pen and making leis (flower garlands) for their cowboy lovers. And the nights, the perfumed nights, the chanting of the meles and the dancing of the hulas, and the big Mana grounds with lovers everywhere strolling two by two under the trees.

"And the Prince . . ." Bella paused, and for a long minute her small fine teeth, still perfect, showed deep in her under-lip as she sought and won control and sent her gaze vacantly out across the far blue horizon. As she relaxed, her eyes came back to her sister.

"He was a prince, Martha. You saw him at Kilohana be-fore . . . after you came home from seminary. He filled the eyes of any woman, yes, and of any man. Twenty-five he was, in all glorious ripeness of man, great and princely in body as he was great and princely in spirit. No matter how wild the fun, how reckless mad the sport, he never seemed to for-get that he was royal and that all his forebears had been high chiefs even to that one first one they sang in the genealogies, who had navigated his double canoes to Tahiti and Raiatea and back again. He was gracious, sweet, kindly, comradely, all friendliness—and severe, and stern, and harsh, if he were crossed too grievously. It is hard to express what I mean. He was all man, man, man, and he was all prince, with a strain of the merry boy in him, and the iron in him that would have made him a good and strong King of Hawaii had he come to the throne.

"I can see him yet, as I saw him that first day and touched his hand and talked with him . . . few words and bashful, and anything but a year-long married woman to a gray haole at gray Nahala. Half century ago it was, that meeting—you remember how our young men then dressed in white shoes and trousers, white silk shirts, with, slashed around the middle, the gorgeously colorful Spanish sashes—and for half a century that picture of him has not faded in my heart. He was the center of a group on the lawn, and I was being brought by Ella Higginsworth to be presented. The Princess Lihue had just called some teasing chaff to her which had made her halt to respond and left me halted a pace in front of her.

"His glance chanced to light on me, alone there, perturbed, embarrassed. Oh, how I see him!—his head thrown back a little, with that high, bright, imperious, and utterly carefree poise that was so usual of him. Our eyes met. His head bent forward, or straightened to me. I don't know what happened. Did he command? Did I obey? I do not know. I know only that I was good to look upon, crowned with fragrant *maile*, clad in Princess Naomi's wonderful holoku loaned me by Uncle John from his tabu room; and I know that I advanced alone to him across the Mana lawn, and that he stepped forth from those about him to meet me halfway. We came to each other across the grass, unattended, as if we were coming to each other across our lives.

"Was I very beautiful, Sister Martha, when I was young? I do not know. I don't know. But in that moment, with all his beauty and truly royal manness crossing to me and penetrating to the heart of me, I felt a sudden sense of beauty in myself—how shall I say?—as if in him and from him perfection were engendered and conjured within myself.

"No word was spoken. But, oh, I know I raised my face in frank answer to the thunder and trumpets of the message unspoken, and that, had it been death for that one look and that one moment, I could not have refrained from the gift of myself that must have been in my face and eyes, in the very body of me that breathed so high.

"Was I beautiful, very beautiful, Martha, when I was nineteen, just turning into twenty?"

And Martha, threescore and four, looked upon Bella, threescore and eight, and nodded genuine affirmation, and to herself added the appreciation of the instant in what she beheld—Bella's neck, still full and shapely, longer than the ordinary Hawaiian woman's neck, a pillar that carried regally her high-cheeked, high-browed, high-chiefess face and head; Bella's hair, high-piled, intact, sparkling the silver of the years, ringleted still and contrasting definitely and sharply with her clean, slim, black brows and deep brown eyes. And Martha's glance, in modest overwhelming of modesty by what she saw, dropped down the splendid breast of her and generously true lines of body to the feet, silken clad, high-heeled-slippered, small, plump, with a almost Spanish arch and faultlessness of instep.

"When one is young, the one young time!" Bella laughed. "Lilolilo was a prince. I came to know his every feature and their every phase ... afterward, in our wonder days and nights by the singing waters, by the slumber-drowsy surfs, and on the mountain ways. I knew his fine, brave eyes, with their straight black brows, the nose of him that was assuredly a Kamehameha nose, and the last, least, lovable curve of his mouth. There is no mouth more beautiful than the Hawaiian, Martha.

"And his body. He was a king of athletes, from his wicked, wayward hair to his ankles of bronzed steel. Just the other day I heard one of the Wilder grandsons referred to as 'The

Prince of Harvard.' Mercy! What would they, what could they, have called my Lilolilo could they have matched him against this Wilder lad and all his team at Harvard!"

Bella ceased and breathed deeply, the while she clasped her fine, small hands in her ample silken lap. But her pink fairness blushed faintly through her skin and warmed her eyes as she relived her prince days.

"Well—you have guessed?" Bella said, with defiant shrug of shoulders and a straight gaze into her sister's eyes. "We rode out from gay Mana and continued the gay progress—down the lava trails to Kiholo to the swimming and the fishing and the feasting and the sleeping in the warm sand under the palms; and up to Puuwaawaa, and more pigsticking, and roping and driving, and wild mutton from the upper pasture lands; and on through Kona, now mauka (mountainward), now down to the King's palace at Kailua, and to the swimming at Keauhou, and to Kealakekua Bay, and Napoopoo and Honaunau. And everywhere the people turning out, in their hands gifts of flowers, and fruit, and fish, and pig, in their hearts love and song, their heads bowed in obeisance to the royal ones while their lips ejaculated exclamations of amazement or chanted meles of old and unforgotten days.

"What would you, Sister Martha? You know what we Hawaiians are. You know what we were half a hundred years ago. Lilolilo was wonderful. I was reckless. Lilolilo of himself could make any woman reckless. I was twice reckless, for I had cold, gray Nahala to spur me on. I knew. I had never a doubt. Never a hope. Divorces in those days were undreamed. The wife of George Castner could never be Queen of Hawaii, even if Uncle Robert's prophesied revolutions were delayed, and if Lilolilo himself became king. But I never thought of the throne. What I wanted would have been the queendom of being Lilolilo's wife and mate. But I made no mistake. What was impossible was impossible, and I dreamed no false dreams.

"It was the very atmosphere of love. And Lilolilo was a lover. I was forever crowned with leis (wreaths) by him, and

he had his runners bring me leis all the way from the rose
gardens of Mana—you remember them; fifty miles across the
lava and the ranges, dewy fresh as the moment they were
plucked, in their jewel cases of banana bark; yard long they
were, the tiny pink buds like threaded beads of Neapolitan
coral. And at the luaus (feasts), the forever never-ending
luaus, I must be seated on Lilolilo's makaloa mat, the Prince's
mat, his alone and tabu to any lesser mortal save by his own
condescension and desire. And I must dip my fingers into his
own *pa wai holoi* (finger bowl) where scented flower petals
floated in the warm water. Yes, and careless that all should
see his extended favor, I must dip into his *pa paakai* for my
pinches of red salt, and limu, and kukui nut and chili pepper;
and into his *ipu kai* (fish sauce dish) of *kou* wood that the
great Kamehameha himself had eaten from on many a similar progress. And it was the same for special delicacies that
were for Lilolilo and the Princess alone—for his *nelu,* and
the *ake,* and the *palu,* and the *alaala.* And his *kahilis* were
waved over me, and his attendants were mine, and he was
mine; and from my flower-crowned hair to my happy feet
I was a woman loved."

Once again Bella's small teeth pressed into her underlip,
as she gazed vacantly seaward and won control of herself and
her memories.

"It was on, and on, through all Kona, and all Kau, from
Hoopuloa and Kapua to Honuapo and Punaluu, a lifetime
of living compressed into two short weeks. A flower blooms
but once. That was my time of bloom—Lilolilo beside me,
myself on my wonderful Hilo, a queen, not of Hawaii but
of Lilolilo and love. He said I was a bubble of color and
beauty on the black back of Leviathan; that I was a fragile
dewdrop on the smoking crest of a lava flow; that I was rain-
bow riding the thunder cloud. . . ."

Bella paused for a moment.

"I shall tell you no more of what he said to me," she
declared gravely; "save that the things he said were fire of
love and essence of beauty, and that he composed hulas to

me, and sang them to me, before all, of nights under the stars as we lay on our mats at the feasting, and I on the makaloa mat of Lilolilo.

"And it was on to Kilauea—the dream so near its ending; and of course we tossed into the pit of sea-surging lava our offerings to Pele (Fire Goddess) of maile leis and of fish and hard poi wrapped moist in the ti leaves. And we continued down through old Puna, and feasted and danced and sang at Kohoualea and Kamaili and Opihikao, and swam in the clear, sweet-water pools of Kalapana. And in the end came to Hilo by the sea.

"It was the end. We had never spoken. It was the end recognized and unmentioned. The yacht waited. We were days late. Honolulu called, and the news was that the King had gone particularly *pupule* (insane), that there were Catholic and Protestant missionary plottings, and that trouble with France was brewing. As they had landed at Kawaihae two weeks before with laughter and flowers and song, so they departed from Hilo. It was a merry parting, full of fun and frolic and a thousand last messages and reminders and jokes. The anchor was broken out to a song of farewell from Lilolilo's singing boys on the quarterdeck, while we, in the big canoes and whaleboats, saw the first breeze fill the vessel's sails and the distance begin to widen.

"Through all the confusion and excitement Lilolilo, at the rail, who must say last farewells and quip last jokes to many, looked squarely down at me. On his head he wore my *ilima* lei, which I had made for him and placed there. And into the canoes, to the favored ones, they on the yacht began tossing their many leis. I had no expectancy of hope ... And yet I hoped, in a small, wistful way that I know did not show in my face, which was as proud and merry as any there. But Lilolilo did what I knew he would do, what I had known from the first he would do. Still looking me squarely and honestly in the eyes, he took my beautiful ilima lei from his head and tore it across. I saw his lips shape, but not utter aloud, the single word *pau* (finish). Still looking at me, he broke both parts of the lei in two again and tossed the deliberate fragments, not to me, but down overside into the widening water. Pau. It was finished. . . ."

For a long space Bella's vacant gaze rested on the sea horizon. Martha ventured no mere voice expression of the sympathy that moistened her own eyes.

"And I rode on that day, up the old bad trail along the Hamakua coast," Bella resumed, with a voice at first singularly dry and harsh. "That first day was not so hard. I was numb. I was too full with the wonder of all I had to forget to know that I had to forget it. I spent the night at Laupahoehoe. Do you know, I had expected a sleepless night. Instead, weary from the saddle, still numb, I slept the night through as if I had been dead.

"But the next day, in driving wind and drenching rain! How it blew and poured! The trail was really impassable. Again and again our horses went down. At first the cowboy Uncle John had loaned me with the horses protested, then he followed stolidly in the rear, shaking his head, and, I know, muttering over and over that I was pupule. The pack horse was abandoned at Kukuihaele. We almost swam up Mud Lane in a river of mud. At Waimea the cowboy had to exchange for a fresh mount. But Hilo lasted through. From daybreak till midnight I was in the saddle, till Uncle John, at Kilohana, took me off my horse, in his arms, and carried me in, and routed the women from their beds to undress me and lomi me, while he plied me with hot toddies and drugged me to sleep and forgetfulness. I know I must have babbled and raved. Uncle John must have guessed. But never to another, nor even to me, did he breathe a whisper. Whatever he guessed he locked away in the tabu room of Naomi.

"I do have fleeting memories of some of that day, all a brokenhearted, mad rage against fate—of my hair down and whipped wet and stinging about me in the driving rain; of endless tears of weeping contributed to the general deluge of passionate outbursts and resentments against a world all twisted and wrong, of beatings of my hands upon my saddle pommel, of asperities to my Kilohana cowboy, of spurs into the ribs of poor magnificent Hilo, with a prayer on my lips, bursting out from my heart, that the spurs would so madden him as to make him rear and fall on me and crush my body forever out of all beauty for man, or topple me off the trail and finish me at the foot of the *palis* (precipices), writing pau at the end of my name as final as the unuttered pau on Lilo-lilo's lips when he tore across my ilima lei and dropped it in the sea. . . .

"Husband George was delayed in Honolulu. When he came back to Nahala I was there waiting for him. And solemnly he embraced me, perfunctorily kissed my lips, gravely examined my tongue, decried my looks and state of health, and sent me to bed with hot stove lids and a dosage of castor oil. Like entering into the machinery of a clock and becoming one of the cogs or wheels, inevitably and remorselessly turning around and around, so I entered back into the gray life of Nahala. Out of bed was Husband George at half after four every morning, and out of the house and astride his horse at five. There was the eternal porridge, and the horrible cheap coffee, and the fresh beef and jerky, the fresh beef and jerky. I cooked, and baked, and scrubbed. I ground around the crazy hand sewing machine and made my cheap holokus. Night after night, through the endless centuries of two years more, I sat across the table from him until eight o'clock, mending his cheap socks and shoddy underwear while he read the years-old borrowed magazines he was too thrifty to subscribe to. And then it was bedtime— kerosene must be economized—and he wound his watch, entered the weather in his diary, and took off his shoes, the right shoe first, and placed them, just so, side by side, at the foot of the bed on his side.

"But there was no more of my drawing to Husband George, as had been the promise ere the Princess Lihue invited me on the progress and Uncle John loaned me the horse. You see, Sister Martha, nothing would have happened had Uncle John refused me the horse. But I had known love, and I had

known Lilolilo; and what chance, after that, had Husband
George to win from me heart of esteem or affection? And for
two years, at Nahala, I was a dead woman, who somehow
walked and talked, and baked and scrubbed, and mended
socks and saved kerosene. . . . The doctors said it was the
shoddy underwear that did for him, pursuing as always the
high-mountain Nahala waters in the drenching storms of
midwinter.

"When he died, I was not sad. I had been sad too long
already. Nor was I glad. Gladness had died at Hilo when
Lilolilo dropped my ilima lei into the sea, and my feet were
never happy again. Lilolilo passed within a month after
Husband George. I had never seen him since the parting at
Hilo. La, la, suitors a-many have I had since; but I was like
Uncle John. Mating for me was but once. Uncle John had
his Naomi room at Kilohana. I have had my Lilolilo room
for fifty years in my heart. You are the first, Sister Martha,
whom I have permitted to enter that room. . . ."

A machine swung the circle of the drive, and from it,
across the lawn, approached the husband of Martha. Erect,
slender, gray-haired, of graceful military bearing, Roscoe
Scandwell was a member of the "Big Five," which, by the
interlocking of interests, determined the destinies of all
Hawaii. Himself pure haole, New England born, he kissed
Bella first, arms around, full-hearty, in the Hawaiian way.
His alert eye told him that there had been a woman talk,
and, despite the signs of all generousness of emotion, that
all was well and placid in the twilight wisdom that was theirs.

"Elsie and the younglings are coming—just got a wireless
from their steamer," he announced, after he had kissed his
wife. "And they'll be spending several days with us before
they go on to Maui."

"I was going to put you in the Rose Room, Sister Bella,"
Martha Scandwell planned aloud. "But it will be better for
her and the children and the nurses and everything there, so
you shall have Queen Emma's Room."

"I had it last time, and I prefer it," Bella said.

Roscoe Scandwell, himself well taught of Hawaiian love and love ways, erect, slender, dignified, between the two nobly proportioned women, an arm around each of their sumptuous waists, proceeded with them toward the house.

THE BONES OF KAHEKILI

FROM OVER THE LOFTY KOOLAU MOUNTAINS, VAGRANT WISPS of the trade wind drifted, faintly swaying the great, unwhipped banana leaves, rustling the palms, and fluttering and setting up a whispering among the lace-leaved algaroba trees. Only intermittently did the atmosphere so breathe, for breathing it was, the suspiring of the languid Hawaiian afternoon. In the intervals between the soft breathings, the air grew heavy and balmy with perfume of flowers and exhalations of fat, living soil.

Of humans about the low bungalowlike house, there were many; but one only of them slept. The rest were on the tense tiptoes of silence. At the rear of the house a tiny babe piped up a thin, blatting wail that the quickly thrust breast could not appease. The mother, a slender hapa-haole (half-white), clad in a loose-flowing holoku of white muslin, hastened away swiftly among the banana and papaya trees to remove the babe's noise by distance. Other women, hapa-haole and full native, watched her anxiously as she fled.

At the front of the house, on the grass, squatted a score of Hawaiians. Well-muscled, broad-shouldered, they were all strapping men. Brown-skinned, with luminous brown eyes and black, their features large and regular, they showed all the signs of being as good-natured, merry-hearted, and soft-tempered as the climate. To all of which a seeming contradiction was given by the ferociousness of their accouterment. Into the tops of their rough leather leggings were thrust long knives, the handles projecting. On their heels were huge-

134

roweled Spanish spurs. They had the appearance of banditti, save for the incongruous wreaths of flowers and fragrant *maile* that encircled the crowns of their flopping cowboy hats. One of them, deliciously and roguishly handsome as a faun, with the eyes of a faun, wore a flaming, double-hibiscus bloom coquettishly tucked over his ear. Above them, casting a shelter of shade from the sun, grew a wide-spreading canopy of poinciana regia, itself a flame of scarlet blossoms, out of each of which sprang pompons of feathery stamens. From far off, muffled by distance, came the faint stamping of their tethered horses. The eyes of all were intently fixed upon the solitary sleeper who lay on his back on a *lauhala* mat a hundred feet away under the monkeypod trees.

Large as were the Hawaiian cowboys, the sleeper was larger. Also, as his snow-white hair and beard attested, he was much older. The thickness of his wrist and the greatness of his fingers made authentic the mighty frame of him hidden under loose dungaree pants and cotton shirt, buttonless, open from midriff to Adam's apple, exposing a chest matted with a thatch of hair as white as that of his head and face. The depth and breadth of that chest, its resilience, and its relaxed and plastic muscles, tokened the knotty strength that still resided in him. Further, no bronze and beat of sun and wind availed to hide the testimony of his skin that he was all haole —a white man.

On his back, his great white beard, thrust skyward, untrimmed of barbers, stiffened and subsided with every breath, while with the outblow of every exhalation the white mustache erected perpendicularly like the quills of a porcupine and subsided with each intake. A young girl of fourteen, clad only in a single shift, or *muumuu*, herself a granddaughter of the sleeper, crouched beside him and with a feathered fly flapper brushed away the flies. In her face were depicted solicitude and nervousness and awe, as if she attended on a god.

And truly, Hardman Pool, the sleeping, whiskered one, was to her, and to many and sundry, a god—a source of life,

a source of food, a fount of wisdom, a giver of law, a smiling
beneficence, a blackness of thunder and punishment; in
short, a man master whose record was fourteen living and
adult sons and daughters, six great-grandchildren, and more
grandchildren than could he in his most lucid moments
enumerate.

Fifty-one years before, he had landed from an open boat
at Laupahoehoe on the windward coast of Hawaii. The boat
was the only surviving one of the whaler *Black Prince* of New
Bedford. Himself New Bedford born, twenty years of age,
by virtue of his driving strength and ability he had served as
second mate on the lost whale ship. Coming to Honolulu and
casting about for himself, he had first married Kalama
Kamaiopili, next acted as pilot of Honolulu Harbor, after
that started a saloon and boarding house, and, finally, on the
death of Kalama's father, engaged in cattle ranching on the
broad pasture lands she had inherited.

For over half a century he had lived with the Hawaiians,
and it was conceded that he knew their language better than
did most of them. By marrying Kalama, he had married not
merely her land but her own chief rank, and the fealty owed
by the commoners to her by virtue of her genealogy was also
accorded him. In addition, he possessed of himself all the
natural attributes of chiefship: the gigantic stature, the fearlessness, the pride, and the high hot temper that could brook
no impudence nor insult, that could be neither bullied nor
awed by any utmost magnificence of power that walked on
two legs, and that could compel service of lesser humans, not
through any ignoble purchase by bargaining but through
an unspoken but expected condescending of largesse. He
knew his Hawaiians from the outside and the in, knew them
better than themselves—their Polynesian circumlocutions,
faiths, customs, and mysteries.

And at seventy-one, after a morning in the saddle over the
ranges that began at four o'clock, he lay under the monkeypods in his customary and sacred siesta that no retainer dared
to break nor would dare permit any equal of the great one

to break. Only to the King was such a right accorded, and, as the King had early learned, to break Hardman Pool's siesta was to gain awake a very irritable and grumpy Hardman Pool who would talk straight from the shoulder and say unpleasant but true things that no King would care to hear.

The sun blazed down. The horses stamped remotely. The fading trade-wind wisps sighed and rustled between longer intervals and quiescence. The perfume grew heavier. The woman brought back babe, quiet again, to the rear of the house. The monkeypods folded their leaves and swooned to a siesta of their own in the soft air above the sleeper. The girl, breathless as ever from the enormous solemnity of her task, still brushed the flies away; and the score of cowboys still intently and silently watched.

Hardman Pool awoke. The next outbreath, expected of the long rhythm, did not take place. Neither did the white, long mustache rise up. Instead, the cheeks, under the whiskers, puffed; the eyelids lifted, exposing blue eyes, choleric and fully and immediately conscious; the right hand went out to the half-smoked pipe beside him, while the left hand reached the matches.

"Get me my gin and milk," he ordered, in Hawaiian, of the little maid, who had been startled into a tremble by his waking.

He lighted the pipe, but gave no sign of awareness of the presence of his waiting retainers until the tumbler of gin and milk had been brought and drunk.

"Well?" he demanded abruptly, and in the pause, while twenty faces wreathed in smiles and twenty pairs of dark eyes glowed luminously with well-wishing pleasure, he wiped the lingering drops of gin and milk from his hairy lips. "What are you hanging around for? What do you want? Come over here."

Twenty giants, most of them young, uprose and with a great clanking and jangling of spurs and spur chains strode over to him. They grouped before him in a semicircle, trying bashfully to wedge their shoulders, one behind another's, their faces a-grin and apologetic and at the same time expressing a casual and unconscious democraticness. In truth, to them Hardman Pool was more than mere chief. He was elder brother, or father, or patriarch; and to all of them he was related, in one way or another, according to Hawaiian custom, through his wife and through the many marriages of his children and grandchildren. His slightest frown might perturb them, his anger terrify them, his command compel them to certain death; yet, on the other hand, not one of them would have dreamed of addressing him otherwise than intimately by his first name, which name, "Hardman," was transmuted by their tongues into Kanaka Oolea.

At a nod from him, the semicircle seated itself on the *manienie* grass, and with further deprecatory smiles waited his pleasure.

"What do you want?" he demanded, in Hawaiian, with a brusqueness and sternness they knew was put on.

They smiled more broadly, and deliciously squirmed their broad shoulders and great torsos with the appeasingness of so many wriggling puppies. Hardman Pool singled out one of them.

"Well, Iliiopoi, what do *you* want?"

"Ten dollars, Kanaka Oolea."

"Ten dollars," Pool cried, in apparent shock at mention of so vast a sum. "Does it mean you are going to take a second wife? Remember the missionary teaching. One wife at a time, Iliiopoi; one wife at a time. For he who entertains a plurality of wives will surely go to hell."

Giggles and flashings of laughing eyes from all greeted the joke.

"No, Kanaka Oolea," came the reply. "The devil knows I am hard put to get *kow-kow* for one wife and her several relations."

"Kow-kow?" Pool repeated the Chinese-introduced word for food which the Hawaiians had come to substitute for their own *paina*. "Didn't you boys get kow-kow here this noon?"

"Yes, Kanaka Oolea," volunteered an old, withered native who had just joined the group from the direction of the house. "All of them had kow-kow in the kitchen, and plenty of it. They ate like lost horses brought down from the lava."

"And what do you want, Kumuhana?" Pool diverted to the old one, at the same time motioning to the little maid to flap flies from the other side of him.

"Twelve dollars," said Kumuhana. "I want to buy a jack-ass and a secondhand saddle and bridle. I am growing too old for my legs to carry me in walking."

"You wait," his haole lord commanded. "I will talk with you about the matter, and about other things of importance, when I am finished with the rest and they are gone."

The withered old one nodded and proceeded to light his pipe.

"The kow-kow in the kitchen was good," Iliipoi resumed, licking his lips. "The poi was one-finger, the pig fat, the salmon belly unstinking, the fish of great freshness and plenty, though the *opihis* (tiny rock-clinging shellfish) had been salted and thereby made tough. Never should the opihis be salted. Often have I told you, Kanaka Oolea, that opihis should never be salted. I am full of good kow-kow. My belly is heavy with it. Yet is my heart not light of it because there is no kow-kow in my own house, where is my wife, who is the aunt of your fourth son's second wife, and where is my baby daughter, and my wife's old mother, and my wife's old mother's feeding child that is a cripple, and my wife's sister who lives likewise with us along with her three children, the father being dead of a wicked dropsy—"

"Will five dollars save all of you from funerals for a day or several?" Pool testily cut the tale short.

"Yes, Kanaka Oolea, and as well it will buy my wife a new comb and some tobacco for myself."

From a gold sack drawn from the hip pocket of his dungarees, Hardman Pool drew the gold piece and tossed it accurately into the waiting hand.

To a bachelor who wanted six dollars for new leggings, tobacco, and spurs, three dollars were given; the same to another who needed a hat; and to a third, who modestly asked for two dollars, four were given with a flowery-worded compliment anent his prowess in roping a recent wild bull from the mountains. They knew, as a rule, that he cut their requisitions in half, wherefore they doubled the size of their requisitions. And Hardman Pool knew they doubled, and smiled to himself. It was his way, and, further, it was a very good way with his multitudinous relatives and did not reduce his stature in their esteem.

"And you, Ahuhu?" he demanded of one whose name meant "poison weed."

"And the price of a pair of dungarees," Ahuhu concluded his list of needs. "I have ridden much and hard after your cattle, Kanaka Oolea, and where my dungarees have pressed against the seat of the saddle there is no seat to my dungarees. It is not well that it be said that a Kanaka Oolea cowboy, who is also a cousin of Kanaka Oolea's wife's half sister, should be shamed to be seen out of the saddle save that he walks backward from all that behold him."

"The price of a dozen pairs of dungarees be thine, Ahuhu," Hardman Pool beamed, tossing to him the necessary sum. "I am proud that my family shares my pride. Afterward, Ahuhu, out of the dozen dungarees you will give me one, else shall I be compelled to walk backward, my own and only dungarees being in like manner well worn and shameful."

And in laughter of love at their haole chief's final sally, all the sweet-child-minded and physically gorgeous company of them departed to their waiting horses, save the old withered one, Kumuhana, who had been bidden to wait.

For a full five minutes they sat in silence. Then Hardman Pool ordered the little maid to fetch a tumbler of gin and milk, which, when she brought it, he nodded her to hand to Kumuhana. The glass did not leave his lips until it was empty, whereupon he gave a great audible outbreath of "A-a-ah," and smacked his lips.

"Much *awa* have I drunk in my time," he said reflectively. "Yet is the awa but a common man's drink while the haole liquor is a drink for chiefs. The awa has not the liquor's hot willingness, its spur in the ribs of feeling, its biting alive of oneself that is very pleasant, since it is pleasant to be alive."

Hardman Pool smiled and nodded agreement, and old Kumuhana continued:

"There is a warmingness to it. It warms the belly and the soul. It warms the heart. Even the soul and the heart grow cold, when one is old."

"You *are* old," Pool conceded. "Almost as old as I."

Kumuhana shook his head and murmured: "Were I no older than you I would be as young as you."

"I am seventy-one," said Pool.

"I do not know ages that way," was the reply. "What happened when you were born?"

"Let me see," Pool calculated. "This is 1880. Subtract 71, and it leaves 9. I was born in 1809, which is the year Kelii-maikai died, which is the year the Scotchman, Archibald Campbell, lived in Honolulu."

"Then am I truly older than you, Kanaka Oolea. I remember the Scotchman well, for I was playing among the grass houses of Honolulu at the time, and already riding a surf-board in the wahine (woman) surf of Waikiki. I can take you now to the spot where was the Scotchman's grass house. The Seaman's Mission stands now on the very ground. Yet do I know when I was born. Often my grandmother and my mother told me of it. I was born when Madame Pele (the Fire Goddess or Volcano Goddess) became angry with the people of Paiea because they sacrificed no fish to her from their fish pond, and she sent down a flow of lava from Hual-alai and filled up their pond. Forever was the fish pond of Paiea filled up. That was when I was born."

"That was in 1801, when James Boyd was building ships

for Kamehameha at Hilo," Pool cast back through the calendar; "which makes you seventy-nine, or eight years older than I. You are very old."

"Yes, Kanaka Oolea," muttered Kumuhana, pathetically attempting to swell his shrunken chest with pride.

"And you are very wise."

"Yes, Kanaka Oolea."

"And you know many of the secret things that are known only to old men."

"Yes, Kanaka Oolea."

"And then you know—" Hardman Pool broke off, the more effectively to impress and hypnotize the other ancient with the set stare of his pale-washed blue eyes. "They say the bones of Kahekili were taken from their hiding place and lie today in the Royal Mausoleum. I have heard it whispered that you alone of all living men truly know."

"I know," was the proud answer. "I alone know."

"Well, do they lie there? Yes or no."

"Kahekili was an *alii* (high chief). It is from his straight line that your wife Kalama came. She is an alii." The old retainer paused and pursed his lean lips in meditation. "I belong to her as all my people before me belonged to her people before her. She only can command the great secrets of me. She is wise, too wise ever to command me to speak this secret. To you, O Kanaka Oolea, I do not answer yes, I do not answer no. This is a secret of the aliis that even the aliis do not know."

"Very good, Kumuhana," Hardman Pool commended. "Yet do you forget that I am an alii, and that what my good Kalama does not dare ask, I command to ask. I can send for her, now, and tell her to command your answer. But such would be foolishness unless you prove yourself doubly foolish. Tell me the secret, and she will never know. A woman's lips must pour out whatever flows in through her ears, being so made. I am a man, and man is differently made. As you well know, my lips suck tight on secrets as a squid sucks to the salty rock. If you will not tell me alone, then will you tell

Kalama and me together, and her lips will talk, her lips will talk, so that the latest *malihini* will shortly know what, otherwise, you and I alone will know."

Long time Kumuhana sat on in silence, debating the argument and finding no way to evade the fact logic of it.

"Great is your haole wisdom," he conceded at last.

"Yes or no?" Hardman Pool drove home the point of steel.

Kumuhana looked about him first, then slowly let his eyes come to rest on the fly-flapping maid.

"Go," Pool commanded her. "And come not back without you hear a clapping of my hands."

Hardman Pool spoke no further, even after the flapper had disappeared into the house; yet his face adamantly looked: "Yes—or no?"

Again Kumuhana looked carefully about him, and up into the monkeypod boughs as if to apprehend a lurking listener. His lips were very dry. With his tongue he moistened them repeatedly. Twice he essayed to speak, but was inarticulately husky. And finally, with bowed head, he whispered, so low and solemn that Hardman Poole bent his own head to hear: "No."

Pool clapped his hands, and the little maid ran out of the house to him in tremulous, fluttery haste.

"Bring a milk and gin for old Kumuhana, here," Pool commanded; and, to Kumuhana: "Now tell me the whole story."

"Wait," was the answer. "Wait till the little wahine has come and gone."

And when the maid was gone, and the gin and milk had traveled the way predestined of gin and milk when mixed together, Hardman Pool waited without further urge for the story. Kumuhana pressed his hand to his chest and coughed hollowly at intervals, bidding for encouragement; but in the end, of himself, spoke out.

"It was a terrible thing in the old days when a great alii died. Kahekili was a great alii. He might have been King had he lived. Who can tell? I was a young man, not yet married.

You know, Kanaka Oolea, when Kahekili died, and you can tell me how old I was. He died when Governor Boki ran the Blonde Hotel here in Honolulu. You have heard?"

"I was still on windward Hawaii," Pool answered. "But I have heard. Boki made a distillery, and leased Manoa lands to grow sugar for it, and Kaahumanu, who was regent, canceled the lease, rooted out the cane, and planted potatoes. And Boki was angry, and prepared to make war, and gathered his fighting men, with a dozen whale-ship deserters and five brass six-pounders, out at Waikiki—"

"That was the very time Kahekili died," Kumuhana broke in eagerly. "You are very wise. You know many things of the old days better than we old Kanakas."

"It was 1829," Pool continued complacently. "You were twenty-eight years old, and I was twenty, just coming ashore in the open boat after the burning of the *Black Prince*."

"I was twenty-eight," Kumuhana resumed. "It sounds right. I remember well Boki's brass guns at Waikiki. Kahekili died, too, at the time, at Waikiki. The people to this day believe his bones were taken to the *Hale o Keawe* (mausoleum) at Honaunau, in Kona—"

"And long afterward were brought to the Royal Mausoleum here in Honolulu," Pool supplemented.

"Also, Kanaka Oolea, there are some who believe to this day that Queen Alice has them stored with the rest of her ancestral bones in the big jars in her tabu room. All are wrong. I know. The sacred bones of Kahekili are gone and forever gone. They rest nowhere. They have ceased to be. And many kona winds have whitened the surf at Waikiki since the last man looked upon the last of Kahekili. I alone remain alive of those men. I am the last man, and I was not glad to be at the finish.

"For, see! I was a young man, and my heart was white-hot lava for Malia, who was in Kahekili's household. So was Anapuni's heart white-hot for her, though the color of his heart was black, as you shall see. We were at a drinking that night—Anapuni and I—the night that Kahekili died. Anapuni

and I were only commoners, as were all of us Kanakas and
wahines who were at the drinking with the common sailors
and whale-ship men from before the mast. We were drinking
on the mats by the·beach at Waikiki, close to the old *heiau*
(temple) that is not far from what is now the Wilders' beach
place. I learned then and forever what quantities of drink
haole sailormen could stand. As for us Kanakas, our heads
were hot and light and rattly as dry gourds with the whisky
and the rum.

"It was past midnight, I remember well, when I saw Malia,
whom never had I seen at a drinking, come across the wet-
hard sand of the beach. My brain burned like red cinders of
hell as I looked upon Anapuni look upon her, he being nearest to her by being across from me in the drinking circle.
Oh, I know it was whisky and rum and youth that made the
heat of me; but there, in that moment, the mad mind of me
resolved, if she spoke to him and yielded to dance with him
first, that I would put both my hands around his throat and
throw him down and under the wahine surf there beside us,
and drown and choke out his life and the obstacle of him
that stood between me and her. For know, that she had never
decided between us, and it was because of him that she was
not already and long since mine.

"She was a grand young woman, with a body generous
as that of a chiefess and more wonderful, as she came upon
us, across the wet sand, in the shimmer of the moonlight.
Even the haole sailormen made pause of silence and with
open mouths stared upon her. Her walk! I have heard you
talk, O Kanaka Oolea, of the woman Helen who caused the
war of Troy. I say of Malia that more men would have
stormed the walls of hell for her than went against that old-
time city of which it is your custom to talk over much and
long when you have drunk too little milk and too much gin.

"Her walk! In the moonlight there, the soft glow fire of
the jellyfishes in the surf like the kerosene-lamp footlights
I have seen in the new haole theater! It was not the walk of
a girl, but a woman. She did not flutter forward like rippling

wavelets on a reef-sheltered, placid beach. There was that in her manner of walk that was big and queenlike, like the motion of the forces of nature, like the rhythmic flow of lava down the slopes of Kau to the sea, like the movement of the huge orderly trade-wind seas, like the rise and fall of the four great tides of the year that may be like music in the eternal ear of God, being too slow of occurrence in time to make a tune for ordinary quick-pulsing, brief-living, swift-dying man.

"Anapuni was nearest. But she looked at me. Have you ever heard a call, Kanaka Oolea, that is without sound, yet is louder than the conches of God? So called she to me across that circle of the drinking. I half arose, for I was not yet full drunken; but Anapuni's arm caught her and drew her, and I sank back on my elbow and watched and raged. He was for making her sit beside him, and I waited. Did she sit, and, next, dance with him, I knew that ere morning Anapuni would be a dead man, choked and drowned by me in the shallow surf.

"Strange, is it not, Kanaka Oolea, all this heat called 'love'? Yet it is not strange. It must be so in the time of one's youth, else would mankind not go on."

"That is why the desire of woman must be greater than the desire of life," Pool concurred. "Else would there be neither man nor woman."

"Yes," said Kumuhana. "But it is many a year now since the last of such heat has gone out of me. I remember it as one remembers an old sunrise—a thing that was. And so one grows old, and cold, and drinks gin, not for madness, but for warmth. And the milk is very nourishing.

"But Malia did not sit beside him. I remember her eyes were wild, her hair down and flying, as she bent over him and whispered in his ear. And her hair covered him about and hid him as she whispered, and the sight of it pounded my heart against my ribs and dizzied my head till scarcely could I half see. And I willed myself with all the will of me that if, in short minutes, she did not come over to me, I would go across the circle and get her.

"It was one of the things never to be. You remember Chief Konukalani? Himself he strode up to the circle. His face was black with anger. He gripped Malia, not by the arm, but by the hair, and dragged her away behind him and was gone. Of that, even now, can I understand not the half. I, who was for slaying Anapuni because of her, raised neither hand nor voice of protest when Konukalani dragged her away by the hair—nor did Anapuni. Of course, we were common men, and he was a chief. That I know. But why should two common men, mad with desire of woman, with desire of woman stronger in them than desire of life, let any one chief, even the highest in the land, drag the woman away by the hair? Desiring her more than life, why should the two men fear to slay then and immediately the one chief? Here is something stronger than life, stronger than woman, but what is it—and why?"

"I will answer you," said Hardman Pool. "It is because most men are fools, and therefore must be taken care of by the few men who are wise. Such is the secret of chiefship. In all the world are chiefs over men. In all the world that has been have there ever been chiefs, who must say to the many fool men: 'Do this; do not do that. Work, and work as we tell you, or your bellies will remain empty and you will perish. Obey the laws we set you or you will be beasts and without place in the world. You would not have been save for the chiefs before you who ordered and regulated for your fathers. No seed of you will come after you, except that we order and regulate for you now. You must be peace-abiding, and decent, and blow your noses. You must be early to bed of nights, and up early in the morning to work if you would have beds to sleep in and not roost in trees like the silly fowls. This is the reason for the yam-planting and you must plant now. We say now, today, and not picnicking and hulaing today and yam-planting tomorrow or some other day of the many careless days. You must not kill one another, and you must leave your neighbors' wives alone. All this is life for you, because you think but one day at a time, while we, your chiefs, think for you all days and far days ahead.' "

"Like a cloud in the mountaintop that comes down and wraps about you and that you dimly see is a cloud, so is your wisdom to me, Kanaka Oolea," Kumuhana murmured. "Yet is it sad that I should be born a common man and live all my days a common man."

"That is because you were of yourself common," Hardman Pool assured him. "When a man is born common, and is by nature uncommon, he rises up and overthrows the chiefs and makes himself chief over the chiefs. Why do you not run my ranch, with its many thousands of cattle, and shift the pastures by the rainfall, and pick the bulls, and arrange the bargaining and the selling of the meat to the sailing ships and war vessels and the people who live in the Honolulu houses, and fight with lawyers, and help make laws, and even tell the King what is wise for him to do and what is dangerous? Why does not any man do this that I do? Any man of all the men who work for me, feed out of my hand, and let me do their thinking for them?—me, who works harder than any of them, who eats no more than any of them, and who can sleep on no more than one lauhala mat at a time like any of them?"

"I am out of the cloud, Kanaka Oolea," said Kumuhana, with a visible brightening of countenance. "More clearly do I see. All my long years have the aliis I was born under thought for me. Ever, when I was hungry, I came to them for food, as I come to your kitchen now. Many people eat in your kitchen, and the days of feasts when you slay fat steers for all of us are understandable. It is why I come to you this day, an old man whose labor of strength is not worth a shilling a week, and ask of you twelve dollars to buy a jackass and a secondhand saddle and bridle. It is why twice ten fool men of us, under these monkeypods half an hour ago, asked of you a dollar or two, or four or five, or ten or twelve. We are the careless ones of the careless days who will not plant the yam in season if our alii does not compel us, who will not think one day for ourselves, and who, when we age to worthlessness, know that our alii will think kow-kow into our bellies and a grass thatch over our heads."

Hardman Pool bowed his appreciation, and urged:

"But the bones of Kahekili. The Chief Konukalani had just dragged away Malia by the hair of her head, and you and Anapuni sat on without protest in the circle of drinking. What was it Malia whispered in Anapuni's ear, bending over him, her hair hiding the face of him?"

"That Kahekili was dead. That was what she whispered to Anapuni. That Kahekili was dead, just dead, and that the chiefs, ordering all within the house to remain within, were debating the disposal of the bones and meat of him before word of his death should get abroad. That the high priest Eoppo was deciding them, and that she had overheard no less than Anapuni and me chosen as the sacrifices to go the way of Kahekili and his bones and to care for him afterward and forever, in the shadowy other world."

"The *moepuu*, the human sacrifice," Pool commented. "Yet it was nine years since the coming of the missionaries."

"And it was the year before their coming that the idols were cast down and the tabu broken," Kumuhana added. "But the chiefs still practiced the old ways, the custom of *hunakele*, and hid the bones of aliis where no man should find them and make fishhooks of their jaws or arrowheads of their long bones for the slaying of little mice in sport. Behold, O Kanaka Oolea!"

The old man thrust out his tongue, and, to Pool's amazement, he saw the surface of that sensitive organ, from root to tip, tattooed in intricate designs.

"That was done after the missionaries came, several years afterward, when Keopuolani died. Also did I knock out four of my front teeth, and half circles did I burn over my body with blazing bark. And whoever ventured out of doors that night was slain by the chiefs. Nor could a light be shown in a house or a whisper of noise be made. Even dogs and hogs that made a noise were slain, nor all that night were the ships' bells of the haoles in the harbor allowed to strike. It was a terrible thing in those days when an alii died.

"But the night that Kahekili died. We sat on in the drinking circle after Konukalani dragged Malia away by the hair. Some of the haole sailors grumbled; but they were few in the land in those days and the Kanakas many. And never was Malia seen of men again. Konukalani alone knew the manner of her slaying, and he never told. And in after years what common men like Anapuni and I should dare to question him!

"Now she had told Anapuni before she was dragged away. But Anapuni's heart was black. Me he did not tell. Worthy he was of the killing I had intended for him. There was a giant harpooner in the circle, whose singing was like the bellowing of bulls; and, gazing on him in amazement while he roared some song of the sea, when next I looked across the circle to Anapuni, Anapuni was gone. He had fled to the high mountains where he could hide with the bird catchers a week of moons. This I learned afterward.

"I? I sat on, ashamed of my desire of woman that had not been so strong as my slave obedience to a chief. And I drowned my shame in large drinks of rum and whisky, till the world went round and round, inside my head and out, and the Southern Cross danced a hula in the sky, and the Koolau Mountains bowed their lofty summits to Waikiki and the surf of Waikiki kissed them on their brows. And the giant harpooner was still roaring, his the last sounds in my ear, as I fell back on the lauhala mat and was to all things for the time as one dead.

"When I awoke was at the faint first beginning of dawn. I was being kicked by a hard naked heel in the ribs. What of the enormousness of the drink I had consumed, the feelings aroused in me by the heel were not pleasant. The Kanakas and wahines of the drinking were gone. I alone remained among the sleeping sailormen, the giant harpooner, snoring like a whale, his head upon my feet.

"More heel kicks, and I sat up and was sick. But the one who kicked was impatient, and demanded to know where was Anapuni. And I did not know, and was kicked, this time from both sides by two impatient men, because I did not know. Nor did I know that Kahekili was dead. Yet did I guess something serious was afoot, for the two men who kicked me were chiefs, and no common men crouched behind them to do their bidding. One was Aimoku, of Kaneohe; the other Humuhumu, of Manoa.

"They commanded me to go with them, and they were not kind in their commanding; and as I uprose, the head of the giant harpooner was rolled off my feet, past the edge of the mat, into the sand. He grunted like a pig, his lips opened, and all of his tongue rolled out of his mouth into the sand. Nor did he draw it back. For the first time I knew how long was a man's tongue. The sight of the sand on it made me sick for the second time. It is a terrible thing, the next day after a night of drinking. I was afire, dry afire, all the inside of me like a burnt cinder, like aa lava, like the harpooner's tongue dry and gritty with sand. I bent for a half-drunk drinking coconut, but Aimoku kicked it out of my shaking fingers, and Humuhumu smote me with the heel of his hand on my neck.

"They walked before me, side by side, their faces solemn and black, and I walked at their heels. My mouth stank of the drink, and my head was sick with the stale fumes of it, and I would have cut off my right hand for a drink of water, one drink, a mouthful even. And, had I had it, I know it would have sizzled in my belly like water spilled on heated stones for the roasting. It is terrible, the next day after the drinking. All the lifetime of many men who died young has passed by me since the last I was able to do such mad drinking of youth when youth knows not capacity and is undeterred.

"But as we went on, I began to know that some alii was dead. No Kanakas lay asleep in the sand, nor stole home from their love-making; and no canoes were abroad after the early fish most catchable then inside the reef at the change of the tide. When we came, past the heiau (temple), to where the Great Kamehameha used to haul out his brigs and schooners, I saw, under the canoe sheds, that the mat thatches of Kahekili's great double canoe had been taken off, and that even then, at low tide, many men were launching it down across the sand into the water. But all these men were chiefs. And, though my eyes swam, and the inside of my head went around and around, and the inside of my body was a cinder athirst, I guessed that the alii who was dead was Kahekili. For he was old, and most likely of the aliis to be dead."

"It was his death, as I have heard it, more than the intercession of Kekuanaoa, that spoiled Governor Boki's rebellion," Hardman Pool observed.

"It was Kahekili's death that spoiled it," Kumuhana confirmed. "All commoners, when the word slipped out that night of his death, fled into the shelter of the grass houses, nor lighted fire nor pipes, nor breathed loudly, being therein and thereby tabu from use for sacrifice. And all Governor Boki's commoners of fighting men, as well as the haole deserters from ships, so fled, so that the brass guns lay unserved and his handful of chiefs of themselves could do nothing.

"Aimoku and Humuhumu made me sit on the sand to the side from the launching of the great double canoe. And when it was afloat, all the chiefs were athirst, not being used to such toil; and I was told to climb the palms beside the canoe sheds and throw down drinking coconuts. They drank and were refreshed, but me they refused to let drink.

"They then bore Kahekili from his house to the canoe in a haole coffin, oiled and varnished and new. It had been made by a ship's carpenter who thought he was making a boat that must not leak. It was very tight, and over, where the face of Kahekili lay, was nothing but thin glass. The chiefs had not screwed on the outside plank to cover the glass. Maybe they did not know the manner of haole coffins; but at any rate I was to be glad they did not know, as you shall see.

" 'There is but one moepuu,' said the priest Eoppo, looking at me where I sat on the coffin in the bottom of the canoe. Already the chiefs were paddling out through the reef.

" 'The other has run into hiding,' Aimoku answered. 'This one was all we could get.'

"And then I knew. I knew everything. I was to be sacrificed. Anapuni had been planned for the other sacrifice. That was what Malia had whispered to Anapuni at the drinking. And she had been dragged away before she could tell me. And in his blackness of heart he had not told me.

" 'There should be two,' said Eoppo. 'It is the law.'

"Aimoku stopped paddling and looked back shoreward as if to return and get a second sacrifice. But several of the chiefs contended no, saying that all commoners were fled to the mountains or were lying tabu in their houses, and that it might take days before they could catch one. In the end Eoppo gave in, though he grumbled from time to time that the law required two moepuus.

"We paddled on, past Diamond Head and abreast of Koko Head, till we were in the midway of the Molokai Channel. There was quite a sea running, though the trade wind was blowing light. The chiefs rested from their paddles, save for the steersmen who kept the canoe's bow on the wind and swell. And, ere they proceeded further in the matter, they opened more coconuts and drank.

" 'I do not mind so much, being the moepuu,' I said to Humuhumu; 'but I should like to have a drink before I am slain.' I got no drink. But I spoke true. I was too sick of the much whisky and rum to be afraid to die. At least my mouth would stink no more, nor my head ache, nor the inside of me be as dry-hot sand. Almost worst of all, I suffered at thought of the harpooner's tongue, as last I had seen it, lying on the sand and covered with sand. O Kanaka Oolea, what animals young men are with the drink! Not until they have grown old, like you and me, do they control their wantonness of thirst and drink sparingly, like you and me."

"Because we have to," Hardman Pool rejoined. "Old stomachs are worn thin and tender, and we drink sparingly because we dare not drink more. We are wise, but the wisdom is bitter."

"The priest Eoppo sang a long mele about Kahekili's mother, and his mother's mother, and all their mothers all the way back to the beginning of time," Kumuhana resumed. "And it seemed I must die of my sand-hot dryness ere he was done. And he called upon all the gods of the underworld, the middle world, and the overworld to care for and cherish the dead alii about to be consigned to them, and to carry out the curses—they were terrible curses—he laid upon all living men and men to live after who might tamper with the bones of Kahekili to use them in sport of vermin slaying.

"Do you know, Kanaka Oolea, the priest talked a language largely different, and I know it was the priest language, the old language. Maui he did not name Maui, but Maui-Tiki-Tiki and Maui-Po-Tiki. And Hina, the goddess mother of Maui, he named Ina. And Maui's godfather he named sometimes Akalana and sometimes Kanaloa. Strange how one about to die and very thirsty could remember such things! And I remember the priest named Hawaii as Vaii, and Lanai as Ngangai."

"Those were the Maori names," Hardman Pool explained, "and the Samoan and Tongan names, that the priests brought with them in their first voyages from the south in the long ago when they found Hawaii and settled to dwell upon it."

"Great is your wisdom, O Kanaka Oolea," the old one accorded solemnly. "Ku, our Supporter of the Heavens, the priest named Tu, and also Ru; and La, our God of the Sun, he named Ra—"

"And Ra was a sun god in Egypt in the long ago," Pool interrupted with a sparkle of interest. "Truly, you Polynesians have traveled far in time and space since first you began. A far cry it is from old Egypt, when Atlantis was still afloat, to young Hawaii in the North Pacific. —But proceed, Kumuhana. Do you remember anything else of what the priest Eoppo sang?"

— "At the very end," Kumuhana went on, "though I was near dead myself, and nearer to die under the priest's knife, he sang what I have remembered every word of. Listen! It was thus."

And in quavering falsetto, with customary broken notes, the old man sang.

"A Maori death chant unmistakably," Pool exclaimed, "sung by a Hawaiian with a tattooed tongue! Repeat it once again, and I shall say it to you in English."

And when it had been repeated, he spoke it slowly in English:

> "But death is nothing new.
> Death is and has been ever since old Maui died.
> Then Pata-tai laughed loud
> And woke the goblin god,
> Who severed him in two, and shut him in,
> So dusk of eve came on."

"And at the last," Kumuhana resumed, "I was not slain. Eoppo, the killing knife in hand and ready to lift the blow, did not lift. And I? How did I feel and think? Often, Kanaka Oolea, have I since laughed at the memory of it. I felt very thirsty. I did not want to die. I wanted a drink of water. I knew I was going to die, and I kept remembering the thousand waterfalls falling to waste down the *palis* (precipices) of the windward Koolau Mountains. I did not think of Anapuni. I was too thirsty. I did not think of Malia. I was too thirsty. But continually, inside my head, I saw the tongue of the harpooner, covered dry with sand, as I had last seen it, lying in the sand. My tongue was like that, too. And in the bottom of the canoe rolled about many drinking nuts. Yet I did not attempt to drink, for these were chiefs and I was a common man.

" 'No,' said Eoppo, commanding the chiefs to throw overboard the coffin. 'There art not two moepuus, therefore there shall be none.'

" 'Slay the one,' the chiefs cried.

"But Eoppo shook his head, and said: 'We cannot send Kahekili on his way with only the tops of the taro.'

" 'Half a fish is better than none,' Aimoku said the old saying.

" 'Not at the burying of an alii,' was the priest's quick reply. 'It is the law. We cannot be niggard with Kahekili and cut his allotment of sacrifice in half.'

"So, for the moment, while the coffin went overside, I was not slain. And it was strange that I was glad immediately that I was to live. And I began to remember Malia, and to begin to plot a vengeance on Anapuni. And with the blood of life thus freshening in me, my thirst multiplied on itself tenfold, and my tongue and mouth and throat seemed as sanded as the tongue of the harpooner. The coffin being overboard, I was sitting in the bottom of the canoe. A coconut rolled between my legs and I closed them on it. But as I picked it up in my hand, Aimoku smote my hand with the paddle edge. Behold!"

He held up the hand, showing two fingers crooked from never having been set.

"I had no time to vex over my pain, for worse things were upon me. All the chiefs were crying out a horror. The coffin, head end up, had not sunk. It bobbed up and down in the sea astern of us. And the canoe, without way on it, bow on to sea and wind, was drifted down by sea and wind upon the coffin. And the glass of it was to us, so that we could see the face and head of Kahekili through the glass; and he grinned at us through the glass and seemed alive already in the other world and angry with us, and, with other-world power, about to wreak his anger upon us. Up and down he bobbed, and the canoe drifted closer upon him.

" 'Kill him!' 'Bleed him!' 'Thrust to the heart of him!' These things the chiefs were crying out to Eoppo in their fear. 'Over with the taro tops!' 'Let the alii have the half of a fish!'

"Eoppo, priest though he was, likewise was afraid, and his reason weakened before the sight of Kahekili in his haole coffin that would not sink. He seized me by the hair, drew me to my feet, and lifted the knife to plunge to my heart. And there was no resistance in me. I knew again only that I was very thirsty, and before my swimming eyes, in mid-air and close up, dangled the sanded tongue of the harpooner.

"But before the knife could fall and drive in, the thing happened that saved me. Akai, half brother to Governor Boki as you will remember, was steersman of the canoe, and, therefore, in the stern, was nearest to the coffin and its dead that would not sink. He was wild with fear, and he thrust out with the point of his paddle to fend off the coffined alii that seemed bent to come on board. The point of the paddle struck the glass. The glass broke—"

"And the coffin immediately sank," Hardman Pool broke in; "the air that floated it escaping through the broken glass."

"The coffin immediately sank, being builded by the ship's carpenter like a boat," Kumuhana confirmed. "And I, who was a moepuu, became a man once more. And I lived, though I died a thousand deaths from thirst before we gained back to the beach at Waikiki.

"And so, O Kanaka Oolea, the bones of Kahekili do not lie in the Royal Mausoleum. They are at the bottom of Molokai Channel, if not, long since, they have become floating dust of slime, or, builded into the bodies of the coral creatures dead and gone, are builded into the coral reef itself. Of men I am the one living one who saw the bones of Kahekili sink into the Molokai Channel."

In the pause that followed, wherein Hardman Pool was deep sunk in meditation, Kumuhana licked his dry lips many times. At the last he broke silence:

"The twelve dollars, Kanaka Oolea, for the jackass and the secondhand saddle and bridle?"

"The twelve dollars would be thine," Pool responded,

passing to the ancient one six dollars and a half, "save that I have in my stable junk the very bridle and saddle for you which I shall give you. These six dollars and a half will buy you the perfectly suitable jackass of the *pake* (Chinese) at Kokako who told me only yesterday that such was the price."

They sat on, Pool meditating, conning over and over to himself the Maori death chant he had heard, and especially the line, "So dusk of eve came on," finding in it an intense satisfaction of beauty; Kumuhana licking his lips and tokening that he waited for something more. At last he broke silence.

"I have talked long, O Kanaka Oolea. There is not the enduring moistness in my mouth that was when I was young. It seems that afresh upon me is the thirst that was mine when tormented by the visioned tongue of the harpooner. The gin and milk is very good, O Kanaka Oolea, for a tongue that is like the harpooner's."

A shadow of a smile flickered across Pool's face. He clapped his hands, and the little maid came running.

"Bring one glass of gin and milk for old Kumuhana," commanded Hardman Pool.

WHEN ALICE TOLD HER SOUL

THIS, OF ALICE AKANA, IS AN AFFAIR OF HAWAII, NOT OF THIS day, but of days recent enough, when Abel Ah Yo preached his famous revival in Honolulu and persuaded Alice Akana to tell her soul. But what Alice told concerned itself with the earlier history of the then surviving generation.

For Alice Akana was fifty years old, had begun life early, and, early and late, lived it spaciously. What she knew went back into the roots and foundations of families, businesses, and plantations. She was the one living repository of accurate information that lawyers sought out, whether the information they required related to land boundaries and land gifts, or to marriages, births, bequests, or scandals. Rarely, because of the tight tongue she kept behind her teeth, did she give them what they asked; and, when she did, it was when equity alone was served and no one could be hurt.

For Alice had lived, from early in her girlhood, a life of flowers and song and wine and dance; and, in her later years, had herself been mistress of these revels by office of mistress of the hula house. In such atmosphere, where mandates of God and man and caution are inhibited, and where woozled tongues will wag, she acquired her historical knowledge of things never otherwise whispered and rarely guessed. Her tight tongue had served her well, so that, while the old-timers knew she must know, none ever heard her gossip of the times of Kalakaua's boathouse, nor the high times of officers of visiting warships, nor of the diplomats and ministers and counsels of the countries of the world.

So, at fifty, loaded with historical dynamite sufficient, if it were ever exploded, to shake the social and commercial life of the Islands, still tight of tongue, Alice Akana was mistress of the hula house, manageress of the dancing girls who hula'd for royalty, for luaus, house parties, poi suppers, and curious tourists. Moreover, at fifty, she was not merely buxom, but short and fat in the Polynesian peasant way, with a constitution and lack of organic weakness that promised incalculable years. But it was, at fifty, that she strayed, quite by chance of time and curiesity, into Abel Ah Yo's revival meeting.

Now Abel Ah Yo, in his theology and word wizardry, was as much mixed a personage as Billy Sunday. In his genealogy he was much more mixed, for he was compounded of one-fourth Portuguese, one-fourth Scotch, one-fourth Hawaiian, and one-fourth Chinese. The pentecostal fire he flamed forth was hotter and more variegated than could any one of the four races of him alone have flamed forth. For in him were gathered together the canniness and the cunning, the wit and the wisdom, the sublety and the rawness, the passion and the philosophy, the agonizing spirit groping and the legs up to the knees in the dung of reality, of the four radically different breeds that contributed to the sum of him. His, also, was the clever self-deceivement of the entire clever compound.

When it came to word wizardry, he had Billy Sunday, master of slang and argot of one language, skinned by miles. For in Abel Ah Yo were the live verbs and nouns and adjectives and metaphors of four living languages. Intermixed and living promiscuously and vitally together, he possessed in these languages a reservoir of expression in which a myriad Billy Sundays could drown. Of no race, a mongrel par excellence, a heterogeneous scrabble, the genius of the admixture was superlatively Abel Ah Yo's. Like a chameleon, he titubated and scintillated grandly between the diverse parts of him, stunning by frontal attack and surprising and confounding by flanking sweeps the mental homogeneity of the more simply constituted souls who came in to his revival to sit under him and flame to his flaming.

Abel Ah Yo believed in himself and his mixedness, as he believed in the mixedness of his weird concept that God looked as much like him as like any man, being no mere tribal god but a world god that must look equally like all races of all the world even if it led to piebaldness. And the concept worked. Chinese, Korean, Japanese, Hawaiian, Puerto Rican, Russian, English, French—members of all races —knelt without friction, side by side, to his revision of deity.

Himself, in his tender youth an apostate to the Church of England, Abel Ah Yo had for years suffered the lively sense of being a Judas sinner. Essentially religious, he had forsworn the Lord. Like Judas therefore he was. Judas was damned. Wherefore he, Abel Ah Yo, was damned; and he did not want to be damned. So, quite after the manner of humans, he squirmed and twisted to escape damnation. The day came when he solved his escape. The doctrine that Judas was damned, he concluded, was a misinterpretation of God, who, above all things, stood for justice. Judas had been God's servant, specially selected to perform a particularly nasty job. Therefore Judas, ever faithful, a betrayer only by divine command, was a saint. Ergo, he, Abel Ah Yo, was a saint by very virtue of his apostasy to a particular sect, and he could have access with clear grace any time to God.

This theory became one of the major tenets of his preaching, and was especially efficacious in cleansing the consciences of the backsliders from all other faiths who else, in the secrecy of their subconscious selves, were being crushed by the weight of the Judas sin. To Abel Ah Yo, God's plan was as clear as if he, Abel Ah Yo, had planned it himself. All would be saved in the end, although some took longer than others and would win only to back seats. Man's place in the ever-fluxing chaos of the world was definite and preordained—if, by no other token, by denial that there was any ever-fluxing chaos. This was a mere bugbear of mankind's addled fancy; and, by stinging audacities of thought and speech, vivid slang that bit home by sheerest intimacy into his listeners' mental processes, he drove the bugbear from their brains, showed them the loving clarity of God's design, and, thereby, induced in them spiritual serenity and calm.

What chance had Alice Akana, herself pure and homogeneous Hawaiian, against his subtle, democratic-tinged, four-race-engendered, slang-munitioned attack? He knew, by contact, almost as much as she about the waywardness of living and sinning—having been singing boy on the passenger ships between Hawaii and California, and, after that, bar boy, afloat and ashore, from San Francisco's Barbary Coast to Heinie's Tavern at Waikiki. In point of fact, he had left his job of Number One Bar Boy at Honolulu's University Club to embark on his great preachment revival.

So, when Alice Akana strayed in to scoff, she remained to pray to Abel Ah Yo's god, who struck her hard-headed mind as the most sensible god of which she had ever heard. She gave money into Abel Ah Yo's collection plate, closed up the hula house and dismissed the hula dancers to more devious ways of earning a livelihood, shed her gala colors and raiments and flower garlands, and bought a Bible.

It was a time of religious excitement in the purlieus of Honolulu. The thing was a democratic movement of the people toward God. Place and caste were invited, but never came. The stupid lowly, and humble lowly, only, went down on its knees at the penitent form, admitted its pathological weight and hurt of sin, eliminated and purged all its bafflements, and walked forth again upright under the sun, childlike and pure, upborne by Abel Ah Yo's god's arm around it. In short, Abel Ah Yo's revival was a clearing house for sin and sickness of spirit, wherein sinners were relieved of their burdens and made light and bright and spiritually healthy again.

But Alice was not happy. She had not been cleared. She bought and dispersed Bibles, contributed more money to the plate, contralto'd gloriously in all the hymns, but would not tell her soul. In vain Abel Ah Yo wrestled with her. She would not go down on her knees at the penitent form and voice the things of tarnish within her—the ill things of good friends of the old days. "You cannot serve two masters," Abel Ah Yo told her. "Hell is full of those who have tried. Single of heart and pure of heart must you make your peace with God. Not until you tell your soul to God right out in meeting will you be ready for redemption. In the meantime you will suffer the canker of sin you carry about within you."

Scientifically, though he did not know it and though he continually jeered at science, Abel Ah Yo was right. Not could she be again as a child and become radiantly clad in God's grace, until she had eliminated from her soul, by telling all the sophistications that had been hers, including those she shared with others. In the Protestant way, she must bare her soul in public, as in the Catholic way it was done in the privacy of the confessional. The result of such baring would be unity, tranquillity, happiness, cleansing, redemption, and immortal life.

"Choose!" thundered Abel Ah Yo. "Loyalty to God or loyalty to man." And Alice could not choose. Too long had she kept her tongue locked with the honor of man. "I will tell all my soul about myself," she contended. "God knows I am tired of my soul and should like to have it clean and shining once again as when I was a little girl at Kaneohe."

"But all the corruption of your soul has been with other souls," was Abel Ah Yo's invariable reply; "when you have a burden, lay it down. You cannot bear a burden and be quit of it at the same time."

"I will pray to God each day, and many times each day," she urged. "I will approach God with humility, with sighs and with tears. I will contribute often to the plate, and I will buy Bibles, Bibles, Bibles without end."

"And God will not smile upon you," God's mouthpiece retorted. "And you will remain weary and heavy laden. For you will not have told all your sin, and not until you have told all will you be rid of any."

"This rebirth is difficult," Alice sighed.

"Rebirth is even more difficult than birth," Abel Ah Yo did anything but comfort her. "Not until you become as a little child. . . .' "

"If ever I tell my soul, it will be a big telling," she confided.

"The bigger the reason to tell it then."

And so the situation remained at deadlock, Abel Ah Yo demanding absolute allegiance to God, and Alice Akana flirting on the fringes of paradise.

"You bet it will be a big telling, if Alice ever begins," the beachcombing and disreputable *kamaainas* (old-timers) gleefully told one another over their Palm Tree gin.

In the clubs the possibility of her telling was of more moment. The younger generation of men announced that they had applied for front seats at the telling, while many of the older generation of men joked hollowly about the conversion of Alice. Further, Alice found herself abruptly popular with friends who had forgotten her existence for twenty years.

One afternoon, as Alice, Bible in hand, was taking the electric streetcar at Hotel and Fort, Cyrus Hodge, sugar factor and magnate, ordered his chauffeur to stop beside her. Willy-nilly, in excess of friendliness, he had her into his limousine beside him and went three quarters of an hour out of his way and time personally to conduct her to her destination.

"Good for sore eyes to see you," he burbled. "How the years fly! You're looking fine. The secret of youth is yours."

Alice smiled and complimented in return in the royal Polynesian way of friendliness.

"My, my," Cyrus Hodge reminisced. "I was such a boy in those days!"

"*Some* boy," she laughed acquiescence.

"But knowing no more than the foolishness of a boy in those long-ago days."

"Remember the night your hack-driver got drunk and left you—"

"S-s-sh!" he cautioned. "That Jap driver is a high-school graduate and knows more English than either of us. Also, I think he is a spy for his government. So why should we tell him anything? Besides, I was so very young. You remember . . . ?"

"Your cheeks were like the peaches we used to grow before the Mediterranean fruit fly got into them," Alice agreed. "I don't think you shaved more than once a week then. You were a pretty boy. Don't you remember the hula we composed in your honor, the—"

"S-s-sh!" he hushed her. "All that's buried and forgotten. May it remain forgotten."

And she was aware that in his eyes was no longer any of the ingenuousness of youth she remembered. Instead, his eyes were keen and speculative, searching into her for some assurance that she would not resurrect his particular portion of that buried past.

"Religion is a good thing for us as we get along into middle age," another old friend told her. He was building a magnificent house on Pacific Heights, had but recently married a second time, and was even then on his way to the steamer to welcome home his two daughters just graduated from Vassar. "We need religion in our old age, Alice. It softens, makes us more tolerant and forgiving of the weaknesses of others; especially the weaknesses of youth of—of others, when they played high and low and didn't know what they were doing."

He waited anxiously.

"Yes," she said. "We are all born to sin, and it is hard to grow out of sin. But I grow. I grow."

"Don't forget, Alice, in those other days I always played square. You and I never had a falling out."

"Not even the night you gave that luau when you were twenty-one and insisted on breaking the glassware after every toast. But of course you paid for it."

"Handsomely," he asserted almost pleadingly.

"Handsomely," she agreed. "I replaced more than double the quantity with what you paid me, so that at the next luau I catered one hundred and twenty plates without having to rent or borrow a dish or glass. Lord Mainweather gave that luau—you remember him."

"I was pigsticking with him at Mana," the other nodded. "We were at a two weeks' house party there. But say, Alice, as you know, I think this religion stuff is all right and better than all right. But don't let it carry you off your feet. And don't get to telling your soul on me. What would my daughters think of that broken glassware!"

"I always did have an *aloha* (warm regard) for you, Alice," a member of the Senate, fat and bald-headed, assured her.

And another, a lawyer and a grandfather: "We were always friends, Alice. And remember, any legal advice or handling of business you may require I'll do for you gladly, and without fees, for the sake of our old-time friendship."

Came a banker to her late Christmas Eve, with formidable, legal-looking envelopes in his hand which he presented to her.

"Quite by chance," he explained, "when my people were looking up land records in Iapio Valley, I found a mortgage of two thousand on your holdings there—that rice land leased to Ah Chin. And my mind drifted back to the past when we were all young together, and wild, a bit wild, to be sure. And my heart warmed with the memory of you, and, so, just as an aloha, here's the whole thing cleared off for you."

Nor was Alice forgotten by her own people. Her house became a Mecca for native men and women, usually performing pilgrimage privily after darkness fell, with presents always in their hands—squid fresh from the reef, *opihis* and *limu*, baskets of alligator pears, roasting corn of the earliest from windward Oahu, mangoes and star apples, taro pink and royal of the finest selection, sucking pigs, banana poi, breadfruit, and crabs caught the very day from Pearl Harbor. Mary Mendaña, wife of the Portuguese consul, remembered her with a five-dollar box of candy and a mandarin coat that would have fetched three quarters of a hundred dollars at a fire sale. And Elvira Miyahara Makaena Yin Gap, the wife of Yin Gap, the wealthy Chinese importer, brought personally

to Alice two entire bolts of piña cloth from the Philippines
and a dozen pairs of silk stockings.

The time passed, and Abel Ah Yo struggled with Alice for
a properly penitent heart, and Alice struggled with herself for
her soul, while half of Honolulu wickedly or apprehensively
hung on the outcome. Carnival Week was over, polo and the
races had come and gone, and the celebration of Fourth of
July was ripening, ere Abel Ah Yo beat down by brutal
psychology the citadel of her reluctance. It was then that he
gave his famous exhortation which might be summed up as
Abel Ah Yo's definition of eternity. Of course, like Billy Sunday on certain occasions, Abel Ah Yo had cribbed the definition. But no one in the Islands knew it, and his rating as a
revivalist uprose a hundred per cent.

So successful was his preaching that night, that he recon-
verted many of his converts, who fell and moaned about the
penitent form and crowded for room amongst scores of new
converts burned by the pentecostal fire, including half a
company of Negro soldiers from the garrisoned Twenty-
fifth Infantry, a dozen troopers from the Fourth Cavalry on
its way to the Philippines, as many drunken man-of-war's
men, divers ladies from Iwilei, and half the riffraff of the
beach.

Abel Ah Yo, subtly sympathetic himself by virtue of his
racial admixture, knowing human nature like a book and
Alice Akana even more so, knew just what he was doing when
he arose that memorable night and exposited God, hell, and
eternity in terms of Alice Akana's comprehension. For, quite
by chance, he had discovered her cardinal weakness. First of
all, like all Polynesians, an ardent lover of nature, he found
that earthquake and volcanic eruption were the things of
which Alice lived in terror. She had been, in the past, on the
Big Island, through cataclysms that had shaken grass houses
down upon her while she slept, and she had beheld Madame
Pele fling red-fluxing lava down the long slopes of Mauna
Loa, destroying fish ponds on the sea brim and licking up
droves of beef cattle, villages, and humans on her fiery way.

The night before, a slight earthquake had shaken Honolulu and given Alice Akana insomnia. And the morning
papers had stated that Mauna Kea had broken into eruption,
while the lava was rising rapidly in the great pit of Kilauea.
So, at the meeting, her mind vexed between the terrors of
this world and the delights of the eternal world to come, Alice
sat down in a front seat in a very definite state of the
"jumps."

And Abel Ah Yo arose and put his finger on the sorest part
of her soul. Sketching the nature of God in the stereotyped
way, but making the stereotyped alive again with his gift of
tongues in pidgin English and pidgin Hawaiian, Abel Ah Yo
described the day when the Lord, even His infinite patience
at an end, would tell Peter to close his day book and ledgers,
command Gabriel to summon all souls to judgment, and cry
out with a voice of thunder: *"Welakahao!"*

This anthropomorphic deity of Abel Ah Yo thundering the
modern Hawaiian-English slang of welakahao at the end of
the world is a fair sample of the revivalists' speech tools of
discourse. Welakahao means literally, "hot iron." It was
coined in the Honolulu Iron Works by the hundreds of
Hawaiian men there employed, who meant by it "to hustle,"
"to get a move on," the iron being hot meaning that the time
had come to strike.

"And the Lord cried 'Welakahao,' and the Day of Judgment began and was over *wikiwiki* (quickly), just like that;
for Peter was a better bookkeeper than any on the Water-
house Trust Company, Limited, and, further, Peter's books
were true."

Swiftly Abel Ah Yo divided the sheep from the goats and
hastened the latter down into hell.

"And now," he demanded, perforce his language on these
pages being properly Englished, "what is hell like? Oh, my
friends, let me describe to you, in a little way, what I have
beheld with my own eyes on earth of the possibilities of hell.
I was a young man, a boy, and I was at Hilo. Morning began
with earthquake. Throughout the day the mighty land con-

tinued to shake and tremble, till strong men became seasick, and women clung to the trees to escape falling, and cattle were thrown down off their feet. Myself I beheld a young calf so thrown. A night of terror indescribable followed. The land was in motion like a canoe in a Kona gale. There was an infant crushed to death by its fond mother stepping upon it whilst fleeing her falling house.

"The heavens were on fire above us. We read our Bibles by the light of the heavens, and the print was fine even for young eyes. Those missionary Bibles were always too small of print. Forty miles away from us, the heart of hell burst from the lofty mountains and gushed red blood of fire-melted rock toward the sea. The heavens in vast conflagration, and the earth hulaing beneath our feet, was a scene too awful and too majestic to be enjoyed. We could think only of the thin bubble skin of earth between us and the everlasting lake of fire and brimstone, and of God to whom we prayed to save us. There were earnest and devout souls who there and then promised their pastors to give not their shaved tithes, but five tenths of their all to the church if only the Lord would let them live to contribute.

"Oh, my friends, God saved us. But first he showed us a foretaste of that hell that will yawn for us on the last day when he cries 'Welakahao!' in a voice of thunder. When the iron is hot! Think of it! When the iron is hot for sinners!

"By the third day, things being much quieter, my friend the preacher and I, being calm in the hand of God, journeyed up Mauna Loa and gazed into the awful pit of Kilauea. We gazed down into the fathomless abyss to the lake of fire far below, roaring and dashing its fiery spray into billows and fountaining hundreds of feet into the air like Fourth of July fireworks you have all seen, and all the while we were suffocating and made dizzy by the immense volumes of smoke and brimstone ascending.

"And I say unto you, no pious person could gaze down upon that scene without recognizing fully the Bible picture of the Pit of Hell. Believe me, the writers of the New Testament had nothing on us. As for me, my eyes were fixed upon the exhibition before me, and I stood mute and trembling under a sense never before so fully realized of the power, the majesty, and terror of Almighty God—the resources of his wrath, and the untold horrors of the finally impenitent who do not tell their souls and make their peace with the Creator.

"But oh, my friends, think you our guides, our native attendants, deep-sunk in heathenism, were affected by such a scene? No. The devil's hand was upon them. Utterly regardless and unimpressed, they were only careful about their supper, chatted about their raw fish, and stretched themselves upon their mats to sleep. Children of the devil they were, insensible to the beauties, the sublimities, and the awfu terror of God's works. But you are not heathen I now address. What is a heathen? He is one who betrays a stupid insensibility to every elevated idea and to every elevated emotion. If you wish to awaken his attention, do not bid him to look down into the Pit of Hell. But present him with a calabash of poi, a raw fish, or invite him to some low, groveling, and sensuous sport. Oh, my friends, how lost are they to all that elevates the immortal soul! But the preacher and I, sad and sick of heart from them, gazed down into hell. Oh, my friends, it *was* hell, the hell of the Scriptures, the hell of eternal torment for the undeserving . . ."

Alice Akana was in an ecstasy or hysteria of terror. She was mumbling incoherently: "O Lord, I will give nine tenths of my all. I will give all. I will give even the two bolts of piña cloth, the mandarin coat, and the entire dozen silk stockings . . ."

By the time she could lend her ear again, Abel Ah Yo was launching out on his famous definition of eternity.

"Eternity is a long time, my friends. God lives, and, therefore, God lives inside eternity. And God is very old. The fires of hell are as old and as everlasting as God. How else could there be everlasting torment for those sinners cast down by God into the Pit on the Last Day to burn forever and forever through all eternity? Oh, my friends, your minds are small—too small to grasp eternity. Yet is it given to me, by God's grace, to convey to you an understanding of a tiny bit of eternity.

"The grains of sand on the beach of Waikiki are as many as the stars, and more. No man may count them. Did he have a million lives in which to count them, he would have to ask for more time. Now let us consider a little, dinky, old myna bird with one broken wing that cannot fly. At Waikiki the myna bird that cannot fly takes one grain of sand in its beak and hops, hops, all day long and for many days, all the way to Pearl Harbor and drops that one grain of sand into the harbor. Then it hops, hops, all day and for many days, all the way back to Waikiki for another grain of sand. And again it hops, hops all the way back to Pearl Harbor. And it continues to do this through the years and centuries and the thousands and thousands of centuries, until, at last, there remains not one grain of sand at Waikiki, and Pearl Harbor is filled up with land and growing coconuts and pineapples. And then, oh my friends, even then, *it would not yet be sunrise in hell!*"

Here, at the smashing impact of so abrupt a climax, unable to withstand the sheer simplicity and objectivity of such artful measurement of a trifle of eternity, Alice Akana's mind broke down and blew up. She uprose, reeled blindly, and stumbled to her knees at the penitent form. Abel Ah Yo had not finished his preaching, but it was his gift to know crowd psychology, and to feel the heat of the pentecostal conflagration that scorched his audience. He called for a rousing revival hymn from his singers, and stepped down to wade among the hallelujah-shouting Negro soldiers to Alice Akana. And, ere the excitement began to ebb, nine tenths of his congregation and all his converts were down on knees and praying and shouting aloud an immensity of contriteness and sin.

Word came, via telephone, almost simultaneously to the Pacific and University Clubs, that at last Alice was telling her soul in meeting; and, by private machine and taxicab, for the first time Abel Ah Yo's revival was invaded by those of caste and place. The firstcomers beheld the curious sight of Hawaiian, Chinese, and all variegated racial mixtures of the smelting pot of Hawaii, men and women, fading out and slinking away through the exits of Abel Ah Yo's tabernacle. But those who were sneaking out were mostly men, while those who remained were avid-faced as they hung on Alice's utterance.

Never was a more fearful and damning community narrative enunciated in the entire Pacific, north and south, than that enunciated by Alice Akana, the penitent Phryne of Honolulu.

"Huh!" the firstcomers heard her saying, having already disposed of most of the venial sins of the lesser ones of her memory. "You think this man, Stephen Makekau, is the son of Moses Makekau and Minnie Ah Ling and has a legal right to the two hundred and eight dollars he draws down each month from Parke Richards Limited for the lease of the fish pond to Bill Kong at Amana. Not so. Stephen Makekau is not the son of Moses. He is the son of Aaron Kama and Tillie Naone. He was given as a present, as a feeding child, to Moses and Minnie by Aaron and Tillie. I know. Moses and Minnie and Aaron and Tillie are dead. Yet I know and can prove it. Old Mrs. Poepoe is still alive. I was present when Stephen was born, and in the nighttime, when he was two months old, I myself carried him as a present to Moses and Minnie, and old Mrs. Poepoe carried the lantern. This secret has been one of my sins. It has kept me from God. Now I am free of it. Young Archie Makekau, who collects bills for the Gas Company and plays baseball in the afternoons, and drinks too much gin, should get that two hundred and eight dollars the first of each month from Parke Richards Limited. He will blow it in on gin and a Ford automobile. Stephen is a good man. Archie is no good. Also he is a liar, and he has served two sentences on the reef, and was in reform school before that. Yet God demands the truth, and Archie will get the money and make a bad use of it."

And in such fashion Alice rambled on through the experiences of her long and full-packed life. And women forgot they were in the tabernacle, and men, too, and faces darkened with passion as they learned for the first time the long-buried secrets of their other halves.

"The lawyers' offices will be crowded tomorrow morning," MacIlwaine, chief of detectives, paused long enough from storing away useful information to lean and mutter in Colonel Stilton's ear.

Colonel Stilton grinned affirmation, although the chief of detectives could not fail to note the ghastliness of the grin.

"There is a banker in Honolulu. You all know his name. He is 'way up, swell society because of his wife. He owns much stock in General Plantations and Interisland."

MacIlwaine recognized the growing portrait and forbore to chuckle.

"His name is Colonel Stilton. Last Christmas Eve he came to my house with big aloha and gave me mortgages on my land in Iapio Valley, all canceled, for two thousand dollars' worth. Now why did he have such big cash aloha for me? I will tell you . . ."

And tell she did, throwing the searchlight on ancient business transactions and political deals, which from their inception had lurked in the dark.

"This," Alice concluded the episode, "has long been a sin upon my conscience and kept my heart from God.

"And Harold Miles was that time president of the senate, and next week he bought three town lots at Pearl Harbor, and painted his Honolulu house, and paid up his back dues in his clubs. Also the Ramsay home at Honokiki was left by will to the people if the government would keep it up. But if the government, after two years, did not begin to keep it up, then would it go to the Ramsay heirs, who old Ramsay hated like poison. Well, it went to the heirs all right. Their lawyer was Charley Middleton, and he had me help fix it with the government men. And their names were—" Six names, from both branches of the legislature, Alice recited, and added: "Maybe they all painted their houses after that. For the first time have I spoken. My heart is mighty lighter and softer. It has been coated with an armor of house paint against the Lord. And there is Harry Werther. He was in the senate that time. Everybody said bad things about him and he was never re-elected. Yet his house was not painted. He was honest. To this day his house is not painted, as everybody knows.

"There is Jim Lokendamper. He has a bad heart. I heard him, only last week, right here before you all, tell his soul. He did not tell all his soul, and he lied to God. I am not lying to God. It is a big telling, but I am telling everything. Now Azalea Akau, sitting right over there, is his wife. But Lizzie Lokendamper is his married wife. A long time ago he had the great aloha for Azalea. You think her uncle who went to California and died left her by will that two thousand five hundred dollars she got. Her uncle did not. I know. Her uncle died broke in California, and Jim Lokendamper sent eighty dollars to California to bury him. Jim Lokendamper had a piece of land in Kohala he got from his mother's aunt. Lizzie, his married wife, did not know this. So he sold it to the Kohala Ditch Company and gave the twenty-five hundred to Azalea Akau—"

Here, Lizzie, the married wife, upstood like a fury long thwarted, and, in lieu of her husband, already fled, flung herself tooth and nail on Azalea.

"Wait, Lizzie Lokendamper!" Alice cried out. "I have much weight of you on my heart, and some house paint, too . . ."

And when she had finished her disclosure of how Lizzie had painted her house, Azalea was up and raging.

"Wait, Azalea Akau. I shall now lighten my heart about you. And it is not house paint. Jim always paid that. It is your new bathtub and modern plumbing that is heavy on me . . ."

Worse, much worse, about many and sundry, did Alice Akana have to say, cutting high in business, financial and social life, as well as low. None was too high nor too low to escape; and not until two in the morning, before an entranced audience that packed the tabernacle to the doors, did she complete her recital of the personal and detailed iniquities she knew of the community in which she had lived intimately all her days. Just as she was finishing, she remembered more.

"Huh!" she sniffed. "I gave last week one lot worth eight hundred dollars cash market price to Abel Ah Yo to pay running expenses and add up in Peter's account books in heaven. Where did I get that lot? You all think Mr. Fleming Jason is a good man. He is more crooked than the entrance was to Pearl Lochs before the United States Government straightened the channel. He has liver disease now; but his sickness is a judgment of God, and he will die crooked. Mr. Fleming Jason gave me that lot twenty-two years ago when its cash market price was thirty-five dollars. Because his aloha for me was big? No. He never had aloha inside of him except for dollars.

"You listen. Mr. Fleming Jason put a great sin upon me. When Frank Lomiloli was at my house, full of gin, for which gin Mr. Fleming Jason paid me in advance five times over, I got Frank Lomiloli to sign his name to the sale paper of his town land for one hundred dollars. It was worth six hundred then. It is worth twenty thousand now. Maybe you want to know where that town land is. I will tell you and remove it off my heart. It is on King Street, where is now the Come Again Saloon, the Japanese Taxicab Company Garage, the Smith & Wilson plumbing shop, and the Ambrosia Ice Cream Parlors, with the two more stories big Addison Lodging House overhead. And it is all wood, and always has been well painted. Yesterday they started painting it again. But that paint will not stand between me and God. There are no more paint pots between me and my path to heaven."

The morning and evening papers of the day following held an unholy hush on the greatest news story of years; but Honolulu was half a-giggle and half aghast at the whispered reports, not always basely exaggerated, that circulated whereever two Honoluluans chanced to meet.

"Our mistake," said Colonel Chilton, at the club, "was that we did not, at the very first, appoint a committee of safety to keep track of Alice's soul."

Bob Cristy, one of the younger islanders, burst into laughter so pointed and so loud that the meaning of it was demanded.

"Oh, nothing much," was his reply. "But I heard, on my way here, that old John Ward had just been run in for drunken and disorderly conduct and for resisting an officer. Now Abel Ah Yo fine-tooth combs the police court. He loves nothing better than soul-snatching a chronic drunkard."

Colonel Chilton looked at Lask Finneston, and both looked at Gary Wilkinson. He returned to them a similar look.

"The old beachcomber!" Lask Finneston cried. "The drunken old reprobate! I'd forgotten he was alive. Wonderful constitution. Never drew a sober breath except when he was shipwrecked, and, when I remember him, into every deviltry afloat. He must be going on eighty."

"He isn't far away from it," Bob Cristy nodded. "Still beachcombs, drinks when he gets the price, and keeps all his senses, though he's not spry and has to use glasses when he reads. And his memory is perfect. Now if Abel Ah Yo catches him . . ."

Gary Wilkinson cleared his throat preliminary to speech.

"Now there's a grand old man," he said. "A leftover from a forgotten age. Few of his type remain. A pioneer. A true kamaaina. Helpless and in the hands of the police in his old age! We should do something for him in recognition of his yeoman work in Hawaii. His old home, I happen to know, is Sag Harbor. He hasn't seen it for over half a century. Now why shouldn't he be surprised tomorrow morning by having his fine paid and by being presented with return tickets to Sag Harbor, and, say, expenses for a year's trip? I move a committee. I appoint Colonel Chilton, Lask Finneston, and, and myself. . . . As for chairman, who more appropriate than Lask Finneston, who knew the old gentleman so well in the early days? Since there is no objection, I hereby appoint Lask Finneston Chairman of the Committee for the Purpose of Raising and Donating Money to Pay the Police-court Fine and Expenses of a Year's Travel for that Noble Pioneer, John Ward, in Recognition of a Lifetime of Devotion of Energy to the Upbuilding of Hawaii."

There was no dissent.

"The Committee will now go into secret session," said Lask Finneston, arising and indicating the way to the library.

SHIN BONES

They have gone down to the pit with their weapons of war, and they have laid their swords under their heads.

"IT WAS A SAD THING TO SEE THE OLD LADY REVERT." PRINCE Akuli shot an apprehensive glance sideward to where, under the shade of a kukui tree, an old wahine was just settling herself to begin on some work in hand.

"Yes," he nodded, half sadly to me, "in her last years Hiwilani went back to the old ways and to the old beliefs—in secret, of course. And, *believe* me, she was some collector herself. You should have seen her bones. She had them all about her bedroom, in big jars, and they constituted most all her relatives, except a half dozen or so that Kanau beat her out of by getting to them first. The way the pair of them used to quarrel about those bones was awe-inspiring. And it gave me the creeps, when I was a boy, to go into that big, forever-twilight room of hers, and know that in this jar was all that remained of my maternal grand-aunt, and that in that jar was my great-grandfather, and that in all the jars were the preserved bone remnants of the shadowy dust of the ancestors whose seed had come down and been incorporated in the living, breathing me. Hiwilani had gone quite native at the last, sleeping on mats on the hard floor—she'd fired out of the room the great, royal, canopied four-poster that had been presented to her grandmother by Lord Byron, who was the cousin of the Don Juan Byron and came here in the frigate *Blonde* in 1825.

"She went back to all native at the last, and I can see her yet, biting a bite of the raw fish ere she tossed them to her women to eat. And she made them finish her poi, or whatever else she did not finish herself. She—"

But he broke off abruptly, and by the sensitive dilation of his nostrils and by the expression of his mobile features I saw that he had read in the air and identified the odor that offended him.

"Deuce take it!" he cried to me. "It stinks to heaven. And I shall be doomed to wear it until we're rescued."

There was no mistaking the object of his abhorrence. The ancient crone was making a dearest-loved lei (wreath) of the fruit of the *hala*, which is the screw pine or pandanus of the South Pacific. She was cutting the many sections or nut envelopes of the fruit into fluted bell shapes preparatory to stringing them on the twisted and tough inner bark of the hau tree. It certainly smelled to heaven, but, to me, a mali-hini, the smell was more wine woody and fruit juicy and not unpleasant.

Prince Akuli's limousine had broken an axle a quarter of a mile away, and he and I had sought shelter from the sun in this veritable bowery of a mountain home. Humble and grass-thatched was the house, but it stood in a treasure garden of begonias that sprayed their delicate blooms a score of feet above our heads, that were like trees, with willowy trunks of trees as thick as a man's arm. Here we refreshed ourselves with drinking coconuts, while a cowboy rode a dozen miles to the nearest telephone and summoned a machine from town. The town itself we could see, the Lakanaii metropolis of Olokona, a smudge of smoke on the shore line, as we looked down across the miles of cane fields, the billow-wreathed reef lines, and the blue haze of ocean to where the island of Oahu shimmered like a dim opal on the horizon.

Maui is the Valley of Hawaii, and Kauai the Garden Isle; but Lakanaii, lying abreast of Oahu, is recognized in the present, and was known of old and always as the Jewel Isle of the group. Not the largest, nor nearly the smallest, Lakanaii is conceded by all to be the wildest, the most wildly beautiful, and, in its size, the richest of all the islands. Its sugar tonnage per acre is the highest, its mountain beef cattle the fattest, its rainfall the most generous without ever being disastrous. It resembles Kauai in that it is the first formed and therefore the oldest island, so that it has had time sufficient to break down its lava rock into the richest of soil, and to erode the canyons between the ancient craters until they are like Grand Canyons of the Colorado, with numberless waterfalls plunging thousands of feet in the sheer or dissipating into veils of vapor and evanescing in mid-air to descend softly and invisibly through a mirage of rainbows, like so much dew or gentle shower, upon the abyss floors.

Yet Lakanaii is easy to describe. But how can one describe Prince Akuli? To know him is to know all Lakanaii most thoroughly. In addition, one must know thoroughly a great deal of the rest of the world. In the first place, Prince Akuli has no recognized nor legal right to be called "Prince." Furthermore, "Akuli" means the "squid." So that Prince Squid could scarcely be the dignified title of the straight descendant of the oldest and highest aliis of Hawaii—an old and exclusive stock, wherein, in the ancient way of the Egyptian Pharaohs, brothers and sisters had even wed on the throne for the reason that they could not marry beneath rank, that in all their known world there was none of higher rank, and that, at every hazard, the dynasty must be perpetuated.

I have heard Prince Akuli's singing historians (inherited from his father) chanting their interminable genealogies, by which they demonstrated that he was the highest alii in all Hawaii. Beginning with Wakea, who is their Adam, and with Papa, their Eve, through as many generations as there are letters in our alphabet they trace down to Nanakaoko, the first ancestor born in Hawaii and whose wife was Kahihiokalani. Later, but always highest, their generations split from the generations of Ua, who was the founder of the two distinct lines of the Kauai and Oahu kings.

In the eleventh century A.D., by the Lakanaii historians, at

the time brothers and sisters mated because none existed to
exceed them, their rank received a boost of new blood of
rank that was next to heaven's door. One Hoikemaha, steer-
ing by the stars and the ancient traditions, arrived in a great
double canoe from Samoa. He married a lesser alii of Lakanaii, and, when his three sons were grown, returned with
them to Samoa to bring back his own youngest brother. But
with him he brought back Kumi, the son of Tui Manua,
which latter's rank was highest in all Polynesia and barely
second to that of the demigods and gods. So the estimable
seed of Kumi, eight centuries before, had entered into the
aliis of Lakanaii and been passed down by them in the un-
deviating line to reposit in Prince Akuli.

Him I first met, talking with an Oxford accent, in the officers' mess of the Black Watch in South Africa. This was just
before that famous regiment was cut to pieces at Magersfon-
tein. He had as much right to be in that mess as he had to
his accent, for he was Oxford-educated and held the Queen's
Commission. With him, as his guest, taking a look at the
war, was Prince Cupid, so nicknamed, but true prince of
all Hawaii, including Lakanaii, whose real and legal title was
Prince Jonah Kuhio Kalanianaole and who might have been
the living King of Hawaii Nei had it not been for the haole
revolution and annexation—this, despite the fact that Prince
Cupid's alii genealogy was lesser to the heaven-boosted genealogy of Prince Akuli. For Prince Akuli might have been
King of Lakanaii, and of all Hawaii, perhaps, had not his
grandfather been soundly thrashed by the first and greatest
of the Kamehamehas.

This had occurred in the year 1810, in the booming days
of the sandalwood trade and in the same year that the King
of Kauai came in and was good and ate out of Kamehameha's
hand. Prince Akuli's grandfather, in that year, had received
his trouncing and subjugating because he was "old school."
He had not imagined island empire in terms of gunpowder
and haole gunners. Kamehameha, farther-visioned, had annexed the service of haoles, including such men as Isaac Davis,

mate and sole survivor of the massacred crew of the schooner *Fair American,* and John Young, captured boatswain of the snow *Eleanor.* And Isaac Davis and John Young and others of their waywardly adventurous ilk, with six-pounder brass carronades from the captured *Iphigenia* and *Fair American,* had destroyed the war canoes and shattered the morale of the King of Lakanaii's land fighters, receiving duly in return from Kamehameha, according to agreement: Isaac Davis, six hundred mature and fat hogs; John Young, five hundred of the same described pork on the hoof that was split.

And so, out of all incests and lusts of the primitive cultures and beast man's gropings toward the stature of manhood, out of all red murders and brute battlings and matings with the younger brothers of the demigods, world-polished, Oxford-accented, twentieth-century to the tick of the second, comes Prince Akuli, Prince Squid, pure-veined Polynesian, a living bridge across the thousand centuries, comrade, friend, and fellow traveler, out of his wrecked seven-thousand-dollar limousine, marooned with me in a begonia paradise fourteen hundred feet above the sea and his island metropolis of Olokona, to tell me of his mother who reverted in her old age to ancientness of religious concept and ancestor worship and collected and surrounded herself with the charnel bones of those who had been her forerunners back in the darkness of time.

"King Kalakaua started this collecting fad, over on Oahu," Prince Akuli continued. "And his queen, Kapiolani, caught the fad from him. They collected everything—old makaloa mats, old *tapas,* old calabashes, old double-canoes, and idols which the priests had saved from the general destruction in 1819. I haven't seen a pearl-shell fishhook in years, but I swear that Kalakaua accumulated ten thousand of them, to say nothing of human jawbone fishhooks, and feather cloaks, and capes and helmets, and stone adzes, and poi pounders of phallic design. When he and Kapiolani made their royal progresses around the islands, their hosts had to hide away their personal relics. For to the king, in theory, belongs all property of his people, and with Kalakaua, when it came to the old things, theory and practice were one.

"From him my father, Kanau, got the collecting bee in his bonnet, and Hiwilani was likewise infected. But father was modern to his finger tips. He believed neither in the gods of the *kahunas* (priests) nor of the missionaries. He didn't believe in anything except sugar stocks, horse breeding, and that his grandfather had been a fool in not collecting a few Isaac Davises and John Youngs and brass carronades before he went to war with Kamehameha. So he collected curios in the pure collector's spirit; but my mother took it seriously. That was why she went in for bones. I remember, too, she had an ugly old stone idol she used to yammer to and crawl around on the floor before. It's in the Deacon Museum now. I sent it there after her death, and her collection of bones to the Royal Mausoleum in Olokona.

"I don't know whether you remember her father was Kaau-kuu. Well, he was, and he was a giant. When they built the Mausoleum, his bones, nicely cleaned and preserved, were dug out of their hiding place and placed in the Mausoleum. Hiwilani had an old retainer, Ahuna. She stole the key from Kanau one night, and made Ahuna go and steal her father's bones out of the Mausoleum. I know. And he must have been a giant. She kept him in one of her big jars. One day, when I was a tidy size of a lad and curious to know if Kaaukuu was as big as tradition had him, I fished his intact lower jaw out of the jar and the wrappings and tried it on. I stuck my head right through it, and it rested around my neck and on my shoulders like a horse collar. And every tooth was in the jaw, whiter than porcelain, without a cavity, the enamel unstained and unchipped. I got the walloping of my life for that offense, although she had to call old Ahuna in to help give it to me. But the incident served me well. It won her confidence in me that I was not afraid of the bones of the dead ones, and it won for me my Oxford education. As you shall see, if that car doesn't arrive first.

"Old Ahuna was one of the real old ones with the hallmark on him and branded into him of faithful born-slave service. He knew more about my mother's family, and my father's, than did both of them put together. And he knew, what no living other knew, the burial place of centuries where were hid the bones of most of her ancestors and of Kanau's. Kanau couldn't worm it out of the old fellow, who looked upon Kanau as an apostate.

"Hiwilani struggled with the old codger for years. How she ever succeeded is beyond me. Of course, on the face of it, she was faithful to the old religion. This might have persuaded Ahuna to loosen up a little. Or she may have jolted fear into him; for she knew a lot of the line of chatter of the old Huni sorcerers, and she could make a noise like being on terms of utmost intimacy with Uli, who is the chiefest god of sorcery of all the sorcerers. She could skin the ordinary *kahuna lanaau* (medicine man) when it came to praying to Lonopuha and Koleamoku; read dreams and visions and signs and omens and indigestions to beat the band; make the practitioners under the medicine god, Maiola, look like thirty cents; pull off a *pule hoe* incantation that would make them dizzy; and she claimed to a practice of *kahuna hoenoho*, which is modern spiritism, second to none. I have myself seen her drink the wind, throw a fit, and prophesy. The *aumakuas* were brothers to her when she slipped offerings to them across the altars of the ruined *heiaus* with a line of prayer that was as unintelligible to me as it was hair-raising. And as for old Ahuna, she could make him get down on the floor and yammer and bite himself when she pulled the real mystery dope on him.

"Nevertheless, my private opinion is that it was the *anaana* stuff that got him. She snipped off a lock of his hair one day with a pair of manicure scissors. This lock of hair was what we call the *maunu*, meaning the bait. And she took jolly good care to let him know she had that bit of his hair. Then she tipped it off to him that she had buried it, and was deeply engaged each night in her offerings and incantations to Uli."

"That was the regular praying-to-death?" I queried in the pause of Prince Akuli's lighting his cigarette.

"Sure thing," he nodded. "And Ahuna fell for it. First he tried to locate the hiding place of the bait of his hair. Failing that, he hired a *pahiuhiu* sorcerer to find it for him. But Hiwilani queered that game by threatening to the sorcerer to practice *apo leo* on him, which is the art of permanently depriving a person of the power of speech without otherwise injuring him.

"Then it was that Ahuna began to pine away and get more like a corpse every day. In desperation he appealed to Kanau. I happened to be present. You have heard what sort of a man my father was.

" 'Pig!' he called Ahuna. 'Swine brains! Stinking fish! Die and be done with it. You are a fool. It is all nonsense. There is nothing in anything. The drunken haole, Howard, can prove the missionaries wrong. Square-face gin proves Howard wrong. The doctors say he won't last six months. Even square-face gin lies. Life is a liar, too. And here are hard times upon us and a slump in sugar. Glanders has got into my brood mares. I wish I could lie down and sleep for a hundred years and wake up to find sugar up a hundred points.'

"Father was something of a philosopher himself, with a bitter wit and a trick of spitting out staccato epigrams. He clapped his hands. 'Bring me a highball,' he commanded; 'no, bring me two highballs.' Then he turned on Ahuna, 'Go and let yourself die, old heathen, survival of darkness, blight of the pit that you are. But don't die on these premises. I desire merriment and laughter, and the sweet tickling of music and the beauty of youthful motion, not the croaking of sick toads and googly-eyed corpses about me still afoot on their shaky legs. I'll be that way soon enough if I live long enough. And it will be my everlasting regret if I don't live long enough. Why in hell did I sink that last twenty thousand into Curtis's plantation? Howard warned me the slump was coming, but I thought it was the square-face making him lie. And Curtis has blown his brains out, and his head *luna* has run away with his daughter, and the sugar chemist has got typhoid, and everything's going to smash.'

"He clapped his hands for his servants, and commanded: 'Bring me my singing boys. And the hula dancers—plenty of them. And send for old Howard. Somebody's got to pay, and I'll shorten his six months of life by a month. But above all, music. Let there be music. It is stronger than drink, and quicker than opium.'

"He with his music druggery! It was his father, the old savage, who was entertained on board a French frigate and for the first time heard an orchestra. When the little concert was over, the captain, to find which piece he liked best, asked which piece he'd like repeated. Well, when grandfather got done describing, what piece do you think it was?"

I gave up, while the prince lighted a fresh cigarette.

"Why, it was the first one, of course. Not the real first one, but the tuning up that preceded it."

I nodded, with eyes and face mirthful of appreciation, and Prince Akuli, with another apprehensive glance at the old wahine and her half-made hala lei, returned to his tale of the bones of his ancestors.

"It was somewhere around this stage of the game that old Ahuna gave in to Hiwilani. He didn't exactly give in. He compromised. That's where I come in. If he would bring her the bones of her mother, and of her grandfather (who was the father of Kaaukuu, and who, by tradition, was rumored to have been even bigger than his giant son), she would return to Ahuna the bait of his hair she was praying him to death with. He, on the other hand, stipulated that he was not to reveal to her the secret burial place of all the alii of Lakanaii all the way back. Nevertheless, he was too old to dare the adventure alone, must be helped by someone who of necessity would come to know the secret, and I was that one. I was the highest alii, besides my father and mother, and they were no higher than I.

"So I came upon the scene, being summoned into the

twilight room to confront those two dubious old ones who dealt with the dead. They were a pair!—Mother fat to despair of helplessness, Ahuna thin as a skeleton and as fragile. Of her one had the impression that if she lay down on her back she could not roll over without the aid of block and tackle; of Ahuna one's impression was that the tooth pickness of him would shatter to splinters if one bumped into him.

"And when they had broached the matter, there was more *pilikia* (trouble). My father's attitude stiffened my resolution. I refused to go on the bone-snatching expedition. I said I didn't care a whoop for the bones of all the aliis of my family and race. You see, I had just discovered Jules Verne, loaned me by old Howard, and was reading my head off. Bones? When there were North Poles, and centers of earths, and hairy comets to ride across space among the stars! Of course I didn't want to go on any bone-snatching expedition. I said my father was able-bodied, and he could go, splitting equally with her whatever bones he brought back. But she said he was only a blamed collector, or words to that effect, only stronger.

" 'I know him,' she assured me. 'He'd bet his mother's bones on a horse race or an ace-full.'

"I stood with Father when it came to modern skepticism, and I told her the whole thing was rubbish. 'Bones?' I said. 'What are bones? Even field mice, and mangy rats, and cockroaches have bones, though the roaches wear their bones outside their meat instead of inside. The difference between man and other animals,' I told her, 'is not bones but brains. Why, a bullock has bigger bones than a man, and more than one fish I've eaten has more bones, while a whale beats creation when it comes to bone.'

"It was frank talk, which is our Hawaiian way, as you have long since learned. In return, equally frank, she regretted she hadn't given me away as a feeding child when I was born. Next she bewailed that she had ever borne me. From that it was only a step to anaana me. She threatened me with it, and I did the bravest thing I have ever done. Old Howard had given me a knife of many blades and corkscrews and screwdrivers and all sorts of contrivances, including a tiny pair of scissors. I proceeded to pare my fingernails.

" 'There,' I said, as I put the parings into her hand. 'Just to show you what I think of it. There's bait and to spare. Go on and anaana me if you can.'

"I have said it was brave. It was. I was only fifteen, and I had lived all my days in the thick of the mystery stuff, while my skepticism, very recently acquired, was only skin deep. I could be a skeptic out in the open in the sunshine. But I was afraid of the dark. And in that twilight room, the bones of the dead all about me in the big jars, why, the old lady had me scared stiff. As we say today, she had my goat. Only I was brave and didn't let on. And I put my bluff across, for my mother flung the parings into my face and burst into tears. Tears in an elderly woman weighing three hundred and twenty pounds are scarcely impressive, and I hardened the brassiness of my bluff.

"She shifted her attack, and proceeded to talk with the dead. Nay, more, she summoned them there, and, though I was all ripe to see but couldn't, Ahuna saw the father of Kaaukuu in the corner and lay down on the floor and yammered. Just the same, although I almost saw the old giant, I didn't quite see him.

" 'Let him talk for himself,' I said. But Hiwilani persisted in doing the talking for him and in laying upon me his solemn injunction that I must go with Ahuna to the burial place and bring back the bones desired by my mother. But I argued that if the dead ones could be invoked to kill living men by wasting sicknesses, and that if the dead ones could transport themselves from their burial crypts into the corner of her room, I couldn't see why they shouldn't leave their bones behind them, there in her room and ready to be jarred, when they said good-by and departed for the middle world, the overworld, or the underworld, or wherever they abided when they weren't paying social calls.

"Whereupon Mother let loose on poor old Ahuna, or let

loose upon him the ghost of Kaaukuu's father supposed to
be crouching there in the corner, who commanded Ahuna
to divulge to her the burial place. I tried to stiffen him up,
telling him to let the old ghost divulge the secret himself,
than whom nobody else knew it better seeing that he had
resided there upwards of a century. But Ahuna was old
school. He possessed no iota of skepticism. The more Hiwilani frightened him, the more he rolled on the floor and the
louder he yammered.

"But when he began to bite himself, I gave in. I felt sorry
for him; but, over and beyond that, I began to admire him.
He was sterling stuff, even if he was a survival of darkness.
Here, with the fear of mystery cruelly upon him, believing
Hiwilani's dope implicitly, he was caught between two fideli-
ties. She was his living alii, his *alii kapo* (sacred chiefess).
He must be faithful to her, yet more faithful must he be to
all the dead-and-gone aliis of her line who depended solely
on him that their bones should not be disturbed.

"I gave in. But I, too, imposed stipulations. Steadfastly had
my father, new school, refused to let me go to England for
my education. That sugar was slumping was reason sufficient
for him. Steadfastly had my mother, old school, refused, her
heathen mind too dark to place any value on education while
it was shrewd enough to discern that education led to un-
belief in all that was old. I wanted to study, to study science,
the arts, philosophy, to study everything old Howard knew,
which enabled him, on the edge of the grave, undauntedly
to sneer at superstition and to give me Jules Verne to read.
He was an Oxford man before he went wild and wrong, and
it was he who had set the Oxford bee buzzing in my noddle.

"In the end Ahuna and I, old school and new school
leagued together, won out. Mother promised that she'd make
Father send me to England, even if she had to pester him
into a prolonged drinking that would make his digestion go
back on him. Also, Howard was to accompany me, so that
I could decently bury him in England. He was a queer one,
old Howard, an individual if there ever was one. Let me

tell you a little story about him. It was when Kalakaua was
starting on his trip around the world. You remember, when
Armstrong and Judd and the drunken valet of a German
baron accompanied him. Kalakaua made the proposition to
Howard—"

But here the long-apprehended calamity fell upon Prince
Akuli. The old wahine had finished her lei hala. Barefooted,
with no adornment of femininity, clad in a shapeless shift
of much-washed cotton, with age-withered face and labor-
gnarled hands, she cringed before him and crooned a *mele* in
his honor, and, still cringing, put the lei around his neck. It
is true, the hala smelled most freshly strong, yet was the act
beautiful to me, and the old woman herself beautiful to
me. My mind leaped into the prince's narrative so that to
Ahuna I could not help likening her.

Oh, truly, to be an alii in Hawaii, even in this second
decade of the twentieth century, is no light thing. The alii,
utterly of the new, must be kindly and kingly to those old
ones absolutely of the old. Nor did the prince without a kingdom, his loved island long since annexed by the United States
and incorporated into a territory along with the rest of the
Hawaiian Islands—nor did the prince betray his repugnance
for the odor of the hala. He bowed his head graciously; and
his royal condescending words of pure Hawaiian I knew
would make the old woman's heart, until she died, warm
with remembrance of the wonderful occasion. The very
grimace he stole to me would not have been made had he
felt any uncertainty of its escaping her.

"And so," Prince Akuli resumed, after the wahine had
tottered away in an ecstasy, "Ahuna and I departed on our
grave-robbing adventure. You know the Iron-bound Coast."

I nodded, knowing full well the spectacle of those lava
leagues of weather coast, truly iron-bound so far as landing
places or anchorages were concerned, great forbidding cliff
walls thousands of feet in height, their summits wreathed
in cloud and rain squall, their knees hammered by the trade-
wind billows into spouting, spuming white, the air, from

sea to rain cloud, spanned by a myriad leaping waterfalls, provocative, in day or night, of countless sun and lunar rainbows. Valleys, so called, but fissures, rather, slit the cyclopean walls here and there, and led away into a lofty and madly vertical back country, most of it inaccessible to the foot of man and trod only by the wild goat.

"Precious little you know of it," Prince Akuli retorted, in reply to my nod. "You've seen it only from the decks of steamers. There are valleys there, inhabited valleys, out of which there is no exit by land, and perilously accessible by canoe only on the selected days of two months in the year. When I was twenty-eight I was over there in one of them on a hunting trip. Bad weather, in the auspicious period, marooned us for three weeks. Then four of my party and myself swam for it out through the surf. Three of us made the canoes waiting for us. The other two were flung back on the sand, each with a broken arm. Save for us, the entire party remained there until the next year ten months afterward. And one of them was Wilson, of Wilson & Wall, the Honolulu sugar factors. And he was engaged to be married.

"I've seen a goat, shot down by a hunter above, land at my feet a thousand yards underneath. *Believe* me, that landscape seemed to rain goats and rocks for ten minutes. One of my canoe men fell off the trail between the two little valleys of Aipio and Luno. He hit first fifteen hundred feet beneath us, and fetched up in a ledge three hundred feet farther down. We didn't bury him. We couldn't get to him, and flying machines had not yet been invented. His bones are there now, and, barring earthquake and volcano, will be there when the Trumps of Judgment sound.

"Goodness me! Only the other day, when our promotion committee, trying to compete with Honolulu for the tourist trade, called in the engineers to estimate what it would cost to build a scenic drive around the Iron-bound Coast, the lowest figures were a quarter of a million dollars a mile!

"And Ahuna and I, an old man and a young boy, started for that stern coast in a canoe paddled by old men! The youngest of them, the steersman, was over sixty, while the rest of them averaged seventy at the very least. There were eight of them, and we started in the nighttime so that none should see us go. Even these old ones, trusted all their lives, knew no more than the fringe of the secret. To the fringe, only, could they take us.

"And the fringe was—I don't mind telling that much— the fringe was Ponuloo Valley. We got there the third afternoon following. The old chaps weren't strong on the paddles. It was a funny expedition into such wild waters, with now one and now another of our ancient-mariner crew collapsing and even fainting. One of them actually died on the second morning out. We buried him overside. It was positively uncanny, the heathen ceremonies those gray ones pulled off in burying their gray brother. And I was only fifteen, alii kapo over them by blood of heathenness and right of hereditary heathen rule, with a penchant for Jules Verne and shortly to sail for England for my education! So one learns. Small wonder my father was a philosopher, in his own lifetime spanning the history of man from human sacrifice and idol worship, through the religions of man's upward striving, to the Medusa of rank atheism at the end of it all. Small wonder that, like old Ecclesiastes, he found vanity in all things and surcease in sugar stocks, singing boys, and hula dancers."

Prince Akuli debated with his soul for an interval.

"Oh, well," he sighed, "I have done some spanning of time myself." He sniffed disgustedly of the odor of the hala lei that stifled him. "It stinks of the ancient," he vouchsafed. "I stink of the modern. My father was right. The sweetest of all is sugar up a hundred points, or four aces in a poker game. If the Big War lasts another year, I shall clean up three quarters of a million over a million. If peace breaks tomorrow, with the consequent slump, I could enumerate a hundred who will lose my direct bounty and go into the old natives' homes my father and I long since endowed for them."

He clapped his hands, and the old wahine tottered toward

him in an excitement of haste to serve. She cringed before him, as he drew pad and pencil from his breast pocket.

"Each month, old woman of our old race," he addressed her, "will you receive, by rural free delivery, a piece of written paper that you can exchange with any storekeeper anywhere for ten dollars gold. This shall be so for as long as you live. Behold! I write the record and the remembrance of it, here and now, with this pencil on this paper. And this is because you are of my race and service, and because you have honored me this day with your mats to sit upon and your thrice-blessed and thrice-delicious lei hala."

He turned to me a weary and skeptical eye, saying:

"And if I die tomorrow, not alone will the lawyers contest my disposition of my property, but they will contest my benefactions and my pensions accorded and the clarity of my mind.

"It was the right weather of the year; but even then, with our old weak ones at the paddles, we did not attempt the landing until we had assembled half the population of Ponuloo Valley down on the steep little beach. Then we counted our waves, selected the best one, and ran in on it. Of course, the canoe was swamped and the outrigger smashed, but the ones on shore dragged us up unharmed beyond the wash.

"Ahuna gave his orders. In the nighttime all must remain within their houses, and the dogs be tied up and have their jaws bound so that there should be no barking. And in the nighttime Ahuna and I stole out on our journey, no one knowing whether we went to the right or left or up the valley toward its head. We carried jerky, and hard poi and dried *aku,* and from the quantity of the food I knew we were to be gone several days. Such a trail! A Jacob's ladder to the sky, truly, for that first pali, almost straight up, was three thousand feet above the sea. And we did it in the dark!

"At the top, beyond the sight of the valley we had left, we slept until daylight on the hard rock in a hollow nook Ahuna knew and that was so small that we were squeezed. And the old fellow, for fear that I might move in the heavy restlessness of lad's sleep, lay on the outside with one arm resting across me. At daybreak, I saw why. Between us and the lip of the cliff scarcely a yard intervened. I crawled to the lip and looked, watching the abyss take on immensity in the growing light and trembling from the fear of height that was upon me. At last I made out the sea, over half a mile straight beneath. And we had done this thing in the dark!

"Down in the next valley, which was a very tiny one, we found evidences of the ancient population, but there were no people. The only way was the crazy footpaths up and down the dizzy valley walls from valley to valley. But lean and aged as Ahuna was, he seemed untirable. In the second valley dwelt an old leper in hiding. He did not know me, and when Ahuna told him who I was, he groveled at my feet, almost clasping them, and mumbled a mele of all my line out of a lipless mouth.

"The next valley proved to be the valley. It was long and so narrow that its floor had caught not sufficient space of soil to grow taro for a single person. Also, it had no beach, the stream that threaded it leaping a *pali* of several hundred feet down to the sea. It was a God-forsaken place of naked eroded lava, to which only rarely could the scant vegetation find roothold. For miles we followed up that winding fissure through the towering walls, far into the chaos of back country that lies behind the Iron-bound Coast. How far that valley penetrated, I do not know, but, from the quantity of water in the stream, I judged it far. We did not go to the valley's head. I could see Ahuna casting glances to all the peaks, and I knew he was taking bearings, known to him alone, from natural objects. When he halted at the last, it was with abrupt certainty. His bearings had crossed. He threw down the portion of food and outfit he had carried. It was the place. I looked on either hand at the hard, implacable walls, naked of vegetation, and could dream of no burial place possible in such bare adamant.

"We ate, then stripped for work. Only did Ahuna permit

me to retain my shoes. IIe stood beside me at the edge of a deep pool, likewise appareled and prodigiously skinny.

" 'You will dive down into the pool at this spot,' he said. 'Search the ruck with your hands as you descend, and, about a fathom and a half down, you will find a hole. Enter it, headfirst but going slowly, for the lava rock is sharp and may cut your head and body.'

" 'And then?' I queried. 'You will find the hole growing larger,' was his answer. 'When you have gone all of eight fathoms along the passage, come up slowly, and you will find your head in the air, above water, in the dark. Wait there then for me. The water is very cold.'

"It didn't sound good to me. I was thinking, not of the cold water and the dark, but of the bones. 'You go first,' I said. But he claimed he could not. 'You are my alii, my prince,' he said. 'It is impossible that I should go before you into the sacred burial place of your kingly ancestors.'

"But the prospect did not please. 'Just cut out this prince stuff,' I told him. 'It isn't what it's cracked up to be. You go first, and I'll never tell on you.' 'Not alone the living must we please,' he admonished, 'but, more so, the dead must we please. Nor can we lie to the dead.'

"We argued it out, and for half an hour it was stalemate. I wouldn't, and he simply couldn't. He tried to buck me up by appealing to my pride. He chanted the heroic deeds of my ancestors; and, I remember especially, he sang to me of Mokomoku, my great-grandfather and the gigantic father of the gigantic Kaaukuu, telling how thrice in battle Mokomoku leaped among his foes, seizing by the neck a warrior in either hand and knocking their heads together until they were dead. But this was not what decided me. I really felt sorry for old Ahuna, he was so beside himself for fear the expedition would come to naught. And I was coming to a great admiration for the old fellow, not least among the reasons being the fact of his lying down to sleep between me and the cliff lip.

"So, with true alii authority of command, saying, 'You

will immediately follow after me,' I dived in. Everything he
had said was correct. I found the entrance to the subterranean
passage, swam carefully through it, cutting my shoulder once
on the lava-sharp roof, and emerged in the darkness and air.
But before I could count thirty, he broke water beside me,
rested his hand on my arm to make sure of me, and directed
me to swim ahead of him for the matter of a hundred feet
or so. Then we touched bottom and climbed out on the
rocks. And still no light, and I remember I was glad that
our altitude was too high for centipedes.

"He had brought with him a coconut calabash, tightly
stoppered, of whale oil that must have been landed on Lahaina beach thirty years before. From his mouth he took a
water-tight arrangement of a match box composed of two
empty rifle cartridges fitted snugly together. He lighted the
wicking that floated on the oil, and I looked about and knew
disappointment. No burial chamber was it, but merely a
lava tube such as occurs on all the islands.

"He put the calabash of light into my hands and started
me ahead of him on the way, which he assured me was long
but not too long. It was long, at least a mile, in my sober
judgment, though at the time it seemed five miles; and it
ascended sharply. When Ahuna, at the last, stopped me, I
knew we were close to our goal. He knelt on his lean old
knees on the sharp lava rock, and clasped my knees with
his skinny arms. My hand that was free of the calabash lamp
he placed on his head. He chanted to me, with his old
cracked, quavering voice, the line of my descent and my
essential high aliiness. And then he said:

" 'Tell neither Kanau nor Hiwilani aught of what you
are about to behold. There is no sacredness in Kanau. His
mind is filled with sugar and the breeding of horses. I do
know that he sold a feather cloak his grandfather had worn
to that English collector for eight thousand dollars, and the
money he lost the next day betting on the polo game between
Maui and Oahu. Hiwilani, your mother, is filled with sacredness. She is too much filled with sacredness. She grows old

and weak-headed, and she traffics overmuch with sorceries.

" 'No,' I made answer. 'I shall tell no one. If I did, then would I have to return to this place again. And I do not want ever to return to this place. I'll try anything once. This I shall never try twice.'

" 'It is well,' he said, and arose, falling behind so that I should enter first. Also, he said: 'Your mother is old. I shall bring her, as promised, the bones of her mother and of her grandfather. These should content her until she dies; and then, if I die before her, it is you who must see to it that all the bones in her family collection are placed in the Royal Mausoleum.'

"I have given all the Islands' museums the once-over," Prince Akuli lapsed back into slang, "and I must say that the totality of the collections cannot touch what I saw in our Lakanaii burial cave. Remember, and with reason and history, we trace back the highest and oldest genealogy in the Islands. Everything that I had ever dreamed or heard of, and much more that I had not, was there. The place was wonderful. Ahuna, sepulchrally muttering prayers and meles, moved about, lighting various whale-oil lamp calabashes. They were all there, the Hawaiian race from the beginning of Hawaiian time. Bundles of bones and bundles of bones, all wrapped decently in tapa, until for all the world it was like the parcel-post department at a post office.

"And everything! Kahilis, which you may know developed out of the fly flapper into symbols of royalty until they became larger than hearse plumes with handles a fathom and a half and over two fathoms in length. And such handles! Of the wood of the *kauila,* inlaid with shell and ivory and bone with a cleverness that had died out among our artificers a century before. It was a centuries-old family attic. For the first time I saw things I had only heard of, such as the *pahoas,* fashioned of whale teeth and suspended by braided human hair, and worn on the breast only by the highest of rank.

"There were tapas and mats of the rarest and oldest; capes and leis and helmets and cloaks, priceless all, except the too ancient ones, of the feathers of the *mamo,* and of the *iiwi* and the *akakane* and the *o-o.* I saw one of the mamo cloaks that was superior to that finest one in the Bishop Museum in Honolulu and that they value at between half a million and a million dollars. Goodness me, I thought at the time, it was lucky Kanau didn't know about it.

"Such a mess of things! Carved gourds and calabashes, shell scrapers, nets of *olona* fiber, a junk of *ie-ie* baskets, and fish-hooks of every bone and spoon of shell. Musical instruments of the forgotten days—*ukekes* and nose flutes, and *kiokios* which are likewise played with one unstopped nostril. Tabu poi bowls and finger bowls, left-handed adzes of the canoe gods, lava-cup lamps, stone mortars and pestles, and poi pounders. And adzes again, a myriad of them, beautiful ones, from an ounce in weight for the finer carvings of idols to fifteen pounds for the felling of trees, and all with the sweetest handles I have ever beheld.

"There were the *kaekeekes*—you know, our ancient drums, hollowed sections of the coconut tree, covered one end with sharkskin. The first kaekeeke of all Hawaii Ahuna pointed out to me and told me the tale. It was manifestly most ancient. He was afraid to touch it for fear the age-rotted wood of it would crumble to dust, the ragged tatters of the shark-skin head of it still attached. 'This is the very oldest and father of all our kaekeekes,' Ahuna told me. 'Kila, the son of Moikeha, brought it back from far Raiatea in the South Pacific. And it was Kila's own son, Kahai, who made that same journey, and was gone ten years, and brought back with him from Tahiti the first breadfruit trees that sprouted and grew on Hawaiian soil.'

"And the bones and bones! The parcel-delivery array of them! Besides the small bundles of the long bones, there were full skeletons, tapa-wrapped, lying in one-man, and two-and three-man canoes of precious *koa* wood, with curved outriggers of *wiliwili* wood, and proper paddles to hand with the *io* projection at the point simulating the continuance of the handle, as if, like a skewer, thrust through the flat

length of the blade. And their war weapons were laid away
by the sides of the lifeless bones that had wielded them—
rusty old horse pistols, derringers, pepper boxes, five-barreled
fantastiques, Kentucky long rifles, muskets handled in trade
by John Company and Hudson's Bay, shark-tooth swords,
wooden stabbing knives, arrows and spears boneheaded of
the fish and the pig and of man, and spears and arrows
wooden-headed and fire-hardened.

"Ahuna put a spear in my hand, headed and pointed finely
with the long shin bone of a man, and told me the tale of
it. But first he unwrapped the long bones, arms, and legs of
two parcels, the bones, under the wrappings, neatly tied like
so many fagots. 'This,' said Ahuna, exhibiting the pitiful
white contents of one parcel, 'is Laulani. She was the wife
of Akaiko, whose bones now placed in your hands, much
larger and malelike as you observe, held up the flesh of a
large man, a three-hundred pounder, seven-footer, three
centuries agone. And this spearhead is made of the shin bone
of Keola, a mighty wrestler and runner of their own time
and place. And he loved Laulani, and she fled with him. But
in a forgotten battle on the sands of Kalini, Akaiko rushed
the lines of the enemy, leading the charge that was successful,
and seized upon Keola, his wife's lover, and threw him to the
ground, and sawed through his neck to the death with a
shark-tooth knife. Thus, in the old days as always, did man
combat with man for woman. And Laulani was beautiful,
that Keola should be made into a spearhead for her! She was
formed like a queen, and her body was a long bowl of sweetness, and her fingers *lomi'd* to slimness and smallness at her
mother's breast. For ten generations have we remembered
her beauty. Your father's singing boys today sing of her
beauty in the hula that is named of her. This is Laulani,
whom you hold in your hands.'

"And, Ahuna done, I could but gaze, with imagination at
the one time sobered and fired. Old drunken Howard had
lent me his Tennyson, and I had mooned long and often
over the 'Idyls of the King.' Here were the three, I thought—

Arthur and Lancelot and Guinevere. This, then, I pondered, was the end of it all, of life and strife and striving and love, the weary spirits of these long-gone ones to be invoked by fat old women and mangy sorcerers, the bones of them to be esteemed of collectors and betted on horse races and ace-fulls or to be sold for cash and invested in sugar stocks.

"For me it was illumination. I learned there in the burial cave the great lesson. And to Ahuna, I said: 'The spear headed with the long bone of Keola I shall take for my own. Never shall I sell it. I shall keep it always.'

" 'And for what purpose?' he demanded. And I replied: 'That the contemplation of it may keep my head sober and my feet on earth with the knowledge that few men are fortunate enough to have as much of a remnant of themselves as will compose a spearhead when they are three centuries dead.'

"And Ahuna bowed his head, and praised my wisdom of judgment. But at that moment the long-rotted olona cord broke and the pitiful woman's bones of Laulani shed from my clasp and clattered on the rocky floor. One shin bone, in some way deflected, fell under the dark shadow of a canoe bow, and I made up my mind that it should be mine. So I hastened to help him in the picking up of the bones and the tying, so that he did not notice its absence.

" 'This,' said Ahuna, introducing me to another of my ancestors, 'is your great-grandfather, Mokomoku, the father of Kaaukuu. Behold the size of his bones. He was a giant. I shall carry him, because of the long spear of Keola that will be difficult for you to carry away. And this is Lelemahoa, your grandmother, the mother of your mother that you shall carry. And day grows short, and we must still swim up through the waters to the sun ere darkness hides the sun from the world.'

"But Ahuna, putting out the various calabashes of light by drowning the wicks in the whale oil, did not observe me

include the shin bone of Laulani with the bones of my grandmother."

The honk of the automobile, sent up from Olokona to
rescue us, broke off the prince's narrative. We said good-by
to the ancient and fresh-pensioned wahine, and departed. A
half mile on our way, Prince Akuli resumed:

"So Ahuna and I returned to Hiwilani, and to her happiness, lasting to her death the year following, two more of
her ancestors abided about her in the jars of her twilight
room. Also, she kept her compact and worried my father into
sending me to England. I took old Howard along, and he
perked up and confuted the doctors so that it was three years
before I buried him restored to the bosom of his family.
Sometimes I think he was the most brilliant man I have ever
known. Not until my return from England did Ahuna die,
the last custodian of our alii secrets. And at his deathbed he
pledged me again never to reveal the location in that name-
less valley and never to go back myself.

"Much else I have forgotten to mention did I see there
in the cave that one time. There were the bones of Kumi, the
near demigod, son of Tui Manua of Samoa, who in the long
before married into my line and heaven-boosted my genealogy. And the bones of my great-grandmother who had slept
in the four-poster presented her by Lord Byron. And Ahuna
hinted tradition that there was reason for that presentation,
as well as for the historically known lingering of the *Blonde*
in Olokona for so long. And I held her poor bones in my
hands—bones once fleshed with sensate beauty, informed
with sparkle and spirit, instinct with love and love warm-
ness of arms around and eyes and lips together, that had
begat me in the end of the generations unborn. It was a good
experience. I am modern, 'tis true. I believe in no mystery
stuff of old time nor the kahunas. And yet I saw in that cave
things which I dare not name to you, and which I, since old
Ahuna died, alone of the living know. I have no children.
With me my long line ceases. This is the twentieth century,
and we stink of gasoline. Nevertheless these other and name-

less things shall die with me. I shall never revisit the burial place. Nor in all time to come will any man gaze upon it through living eyes unless the quakes of earth rend the mountains asunder and spew forth the secrets contained in the hearts of the mountains."

Prince Akuli ceased from speech. With welcome relief on his face, he removed the lei hala from his neck, and, with a sniff and a sigh, tossed it into concealment in the thick lantana by the side of the road.

"But the shin bone of Laulani?" I queried softly.

He remained silent while a mile of pasture land fled by us and yielded to cane land.

"I have it now," he at last said. "And beside it is Keola, slain ere his time and made into a spearhead for love of the woman whose shin bone abides near to him. To them, those poor pathetic bones, I owe more than to aught else. I became possessed of them in the period of my culminating adolescence. I know they changed the entire course of my life and trend of my mind. They gave to me a modesty and a humility in the world from which my father's fortune has ever failed to seduce me.

"And often, when woman was nigh to winning to the empery of my mind over me, I sought Laulani's shin bone. And often, when lusty manhood stung me into feeling over-proud and lusty, I consulted the spearhead remnant of Keola, one-time swift runner, and mighty wrestler and lover, and thief of the wife of a king. The contemplation of them has ever been of profound aid to me, and you might well say that I have founded my religion or practice of living upon them."

THE WATER BABY

I LENT A WEARY EAR TO OLD KOHOKUMU'S INTERMINABLE chanting of the deeds and adventures of Maui, the Promethean demigod of Polynesia who fished up dry land from ocean depths with hooks made fast to heaven, who lifted up the sky whereunder previously men had gone on all fours, not having space to stand erect, and who made the sun with its sixteen snared legs stand still and agree thereafter to traverse the sky more slowly—the sun being evidently a trade-unionist and believing in the six-hour day, while Maui stood for the open shop and the twelve-hour day.

"Now this," said Kohokumu, "is from Queen Liliuokalani's own family mele:

> " 'Maui became restless and fought the sun
> With a noose that he laid.
> And winter won the sun,
> And summer was won by Maui. . . .' "

Born in the islands myself, I know the Hawaiian myths better than this old fisherman, although I possessed not his memorization that enabled him to recite them endless hours.

"And you believe all this?" I demanded in the sweet Hawaiian tongue.

"It was a long time ago," he pondered. "I never saw Maui with my own eyes. But all our old men from all the way back tell us these things, as I, an old man, tell them to my sons and grandsons, who will tell them to their sons and grandsons all the way ahead to come."

"You believe," I persisted, "that whopper of Maui roping the sun like a wild steer, and that other whopper of heaving up the sky from off the earth?"

"I am of little worth, and am not wise, O Lakana," my fisherman made answer. "Yet have I read the Hawaiian Bible the missionaries translated to us, and there have I read that your Big Man of the Beginning made the earth and sky and sun and moon and stars, and all manner of animals from horses to cockroaches and from centipedes and mosquitoes to sea lice and jellyfish, and man and woman and everything, and all in six days. Why, Maui didn't do anything like that much. He didn't *make* anything. He just put things in order, that was all, and it took him a long, long time to make the improvements. And anyway, it is much easier and more reasonable to believe the little whopper than the big whopper."

And what could I reply? He had me on the matter of reasonableness. Besides, my head ached. And the funny thing, as I admitted to myself, was that evolution teaches in no uncertain voice that man did run on all fours ere he came to walk upright, that astronomy states flatly that the speed of the revolution of the earth on its axis has diminished steadily, thus increasing the length of day, and that the seismologists accept that all the islands of Hawaii were elevated from the ocean floor by volcanic action.

Fortunately, I saw a bamboo pole, floating on the surface several hundred feet away, suddenly upend and start a very devil's dance. This was a diversion from the profitless discussion, and Kohokumu and I dipped our paddles and raced the little outrigger canoe to the dancing pole. Kohokumu caught the line that was fast to the butt of the pole and underhanded it in until a two-foot *ukikiki,* battling fiercely to the end, flashed its wet silver in the sun and began beating a tattoo on the inside bottom of the canoe. Kohokumu picked up a squirming, slimy squid, with his teeth bit a chunk of live

bait out of it, attached the bait to the hook, and dropped
line and sinker overside. The stick floated flat on the surface
of the water, and the canoe drifted slowly away. With a sur-
vey of the crescent composed of a score of such sticks all lying
flat, Kohokumu wiped his hands on his naked sides and
lifted the wearisome and centuries-old chant of Kuali:

" 'Oh, the great fishhook of Maui!
    Manai-i-ka-lani—"made fast to the heavens"!
    An earth-twisted cord ties the hook,
    Engulfed from lofty Kauiki!
    Its bait the red-billed alae,
    The bird to Hina sacred!
    It sinks far down to Hawaii,
    Struggling and in pain dying!
    Caught is the land beneath the water,
    Floated up, up to the surface,
    But Hina hid a wing of the bird
    And broke the land beneath the water!
    Below was the bait snatched away
    And eaten at once by the fishes,
    The ulua of the deep muddy places!' "

His aged voice was hoarse and scratchy from the drinking
of too much swipes at a funeral the night before, nothing of
which contributed to make me less irritable. My head ached.
The sun glare on the water made my eyes ache, while I was
suffering more than half a touch of *mal de mer* from the antic
conduct of the outrigger on the blobby sea. The air was stag-
nant. In the lee of Waihee, between the white beach and the
reef, no whisper of breeze eased the still sultriness. I really
think I was too miserable to summon the resolution to give
up the fishing and go in to shore.

Lying back with closed eyes, I lost count of time. I even
forgot that Kohokumu was chanting till reminded of it by
his ceasing. An exclamation made me bare my eyes to the
stab of the sun. He was gazing down through the water glass.

"It's a big one," he said, passing me the device and slipping overside feet-first into the water.

He went under without splash and ripple, turned over, and swam down. I followed his progress through the water glass, which is merely an oblong box a couple of feet long, open at the top, the bottom sealed water-tight with a sheet of ordinary glass.

Now Kohokumu was a bore, and I was squeamishly out of sorts with him for his volubleness, but I could not help admiring him as I watched him go down. Past seventy years of age, lean as a spear, and shriveled like a mummy, he was doing what few young athletes of my race would do or could do. It was forty feet to bottom. There, partly exposed but mostly hidden under the bulge of a coral lump, I could discern his objective. His keen eyes had caught the projecting tentacle of a squid. Even as he swam, the tentacle was lazily withdrawn, so that there was no sign of the creature. But the brief exposure of the portion of one tentacle had advertised its owner as a squid of size.

The pressure at a depth of forty feet is no joke for a young man, yet it did not seem to inconvenience this oldster. I am certain it never crossed his mind to be inconvenienced. Unarmed, bare of body save for a brief *malo* or loincloth, he was undeterred by the formidable creature that constituted his prey. I saw him steady himself with his right hand on the coral lump, and thrust his left arm into the hole to the shoulder. Half a minute elapsed, during which time he seemed to be groping and rooting around with his left hand. Then tentacle after tentacle, myriad-suckered and wildly waving, emerged. Laying hold of his arm, they writhed and coiled about his flesh like so many snakes. With a heave and a jerk appeared the entire squid, a proper devilfish or octopus.

But the old man was in no hurry for his natural element, the air above the water. There, forty feet beneath, wrapped about by an octopus that measured nine feet across from tentacle tip to tentacle tip and that could well drown the stoutest swimmer, he coolly and casually did the one thing that gave to him his empery over the monster. He shoved his lean, hawklike face into the very center of the slimy, squirming mass, and with his several ancient fangs bit into the heart and the life of the matter. This accomplished, he came upward slowly, as a swimmer should who is changing atmospheres from the depths. Alongside the canoe, still in the water and peeling off the grisly clinging thing, the incorrigible old sinner burst into the *pule* of triumph which had been chanted by countless squid-catching generations before him:

> "'O Kanaloa of the taboo nights!
> Stand upright on the solid floor!
> Stand upon the floor where lies the squid!
> Stand up to take the squid of the deep sea!
> Rise up, O Kanaloa!
> Stir up! Stir up! Let the squid awake!
> Let the squid that lies flat awake! Let the
>   squid that lies spread out. . . .'"

I closed my eyes and ears, not offering to lend him a hand, secure in the knowledge that he could climb back unaided into the unstable craft without the slightest risk of upsetting it.

"A very fine squid," he crooned. "It is a wahine squid. I shall now sing to you the song of the cowrie shell, the red cowrie shell that we used as a bait for the squid—"

"You were disgraceful last night at the funeral," I headed him off. "I heard all about it. You made much noise. You sang till everybody was deaf. You insulted the son of the widow. You drank swipes like a pig. Swipes are not good for your extreme age. Some day you will wake up dead. You ought to be a wreck today—"

"Ha!" he chuckled. "And you, who drank no swipes, who was a babe unborn when I was already an old man, who went to bed last night with the sun and the chickens—this day you are a wreck. Explain me that. My ears are as thirsty to listen as was my throat thirsty last night. And here today, behold, I am, as that Englishman who came here in his yacht used to say, I am in fine form, in devilish fine form."

"I give you up," I retorted, shrugging my shoulders. "Only one thing is clear, and that is that the devil doesn't want you. Report of your singing has gone before you."

"No," he pondered the idea carefully. "It is not that. The devil will be glad for my coming, for I have some very fine songs for him, and scandals and old gossips of the high aliis that will make him scratch his sides. So let me explain to you the secret of my birth. The Sea is my mother. I was born in a double canoe, during a Kona gale, in the channel of Kahoolawe. From her, the Sea, my mother, I received my strength. Whenever I return to her arms, as for a breast clasp, as I have returned this day, I grow strong again and immediately. She, to me, is the milk giver, the life source—"

"Shades of Antaeus!" thought I.

"Some day," old Kohokumu rambled on, "when I am really old, I shall be reported of men as drowned in the sea. This will be an idle thought of men. In truth, I shall have returned into the arms of my mother, there to rest under the heart of her breast until the second birth of me, when I shall emerge into the sun a flashing youth of splendor like Maui himself when he was golden young."

"A queer religion," I commented.

"When I was younger I muddled my poor head over queerer religions," old Kohokumu retorted. "But listen, O Young Wise One, to my elderly wisdom. This I know: as I grow old I seek less for the truth from without me, and find more of the truth from within me. Why have I thought this thought of my return to my mother and of my rebirth from my mother into the sun? You do not know. I do not know, save that, without whisper of man's voice or printed word, without prompting from otherwhere, this thought has arisen from within me, from the deeps of me that are as deep as the sea. I am not a god. I do not make things. Therefore I have not made this thought. I do not know its father or its mother. It is of old time before me, and therefore it is true. Man does not make truth. Man, if he be not blind, only recognizes truth when he sees it. Is this thought that I have thought a dream?"

"Perhaps it is that you are a dream," I laughed. "And that I and sky and sea and the iron-hard land are dreams, all dreams."

"I have often thought that," he assured me soberly. "It may be well so. Last night I dreamed I was a lark bird, a beautiful singing lark of the sky like the larks on the upland pastures of Haleakala. And I flew up, up toward the sun, singing, singing, as old Kohokumu never sang. I tell you now that I dreamed I was a lark bird singing in the sky. But may not I, the real I, be the lark bird? And may not the telling of it be the dream that I, the lark bird, am dreaming now? Who are you to tell me aye or no? Dare you tell me I am not a lark bird asleep and dreaming that I am old Kohokumu?"

I shrugged my shoulders, and he continued triumphantly.

"And how do you know but what you are old Maui himself asleep and dreaming that you are John Lakana talking with me in a canoe? And may you not awake, old Maui yourself, and scratch your sides and say that you had a funny dream in which you dreamed you were a haole?"

"I don't know," I admitted. "Besides, you wouldn't believe me."

"There is much more in dreams than we know," he assured me with great solemnity. "Dreams go deep, all the way down, maybe to before the beginning. May not old Maui have only dreamed he pulled Hawaii up from the bottom of the sea? Then would this Hawaii land be a dream, and you and I and the squid there only parts of Maui's dream? And the lark bird, too?"

He sighed and let his head sink on his breast.

"And I worry my old head about the secrets undiscoverable," he resumed, "until I grow tired and want to forget, and so I drink swipes, and go fishing, and sing old songs, and dream I am a lark bird singing in the sky. I like that best of all, and often I dream it when I have drunk much swipes—"

In great dejection of mood he peered down into the lagoon through the water glass.

"There will be no more bites for a while," he announced. "The fish sharks are prowling around, and we shall have to wait until they are gone. And so that the time shall not be heavy, I will sing you the canoe-hauling song to Lono. You remember:

" 'Give to me the trunk of the tree, O Lono!
Give me the tree's main root, O Lono!
Give me the ear of the tree, O Lono!—' "

"For the love of mercy, don't sing!" I cut him short. "I've got a headache, and your singing hurts. You may be in devilish fine form today, but your throat is rotten. I'd rather you talked about dreams, or told me whoppers."

"It is too bad that you are sick, and you so young," he conceded cheerily. "And I shall not sing any more. I shall tell you something you do not know and have never heard; something that is no dream and no whopper, but is what I know to have happened. Not very long ago there lived here, on the beach beside this very lagoon, a young boy whose name was Keikiwai, which, as you know, means Water Baby. He was truly a water baby. His gods were the sea and fish gods, and he was born with knowledge of the language of fishes, which the fishes did not know until the sharks found it out one day when they heard him talk it.

"It happened this way. The word had been brought, and the commands, by swift runners, that the king was making a progress around the island, and that on the next day a luau was to be served him by the dwellers here of Waihee. It was always a hardship, when the king made a progress, for the few dwellers in small places to fill his many stomachs with food. For he came always with his wife and her women, with his priests and sorcerers, his dancers and flute players and

hula singers, and fighting men and servants, and his high
chiefs with their wives, and sorcerers and fighting men and
servants.

"Sometimes, in small places like Waihee, the path of his
journey was marked afterward by leanness and famine. But a
king must be fed, and it is not good to anger a king. So, like
warning in advance of disaster, Waihee heard of his coming,
and all food-getters of field and pond and mountain and sea
were busied with getting food for the feast. And behold,
everything was got, from the choicest of royal taro to sugarcane joints for the roasting, from opihis to limu, from fowl
to wild pigs and poi-fed puppies—everything save one thing.
The fishermen failed to get lobsters.

"Now be it know that the king's favorite food was lobster.
He esteemed it above all kow-kow (food), and his runners,
had made special mention of it. And there were no lobsters,
and it is not good to anger a king in the belly of him. Too
many sharks had come inside the reef. That was the trouble.
A young girl and an old man had been eaten by them. And
of the young men who dared dive for lobsters, one was eaten,
and one lost an arm, and another lost one hand and one foot.

"But there was Keikiwai, the Water Baby, only eleven
years old, but half fish himself and talking the language of
fishes. To his father the head men came, begging him to send
the Water Baby to get lobsters to fill the king's belly and di-
vert his anger.

"Now this, what happened, was known and observed. For
the fishermen and their women, and the taro growers and the
bird catchers, and the head men, and all Waihee, came down
and stood back from the edge of the rock where the Water
Baby stood and looked down at the lobsters far beneath on
the bottom.

"And a shark, looking up with its cat's eyes, observed him,
and sent out the shark call of 'fresh meat' to assemble all the
sharks in the lagoon. For the sharks work thus together,
which is why they are strong. And the sharks answered the
call till there were forty of them, long ones and short ones

and lean ones and round ones, forty of them by count; and
they talked to one another, saying: 'Look at that titbit of a
child, that morsel delicious of human-flesh sweetness without
the salt of the sea in it, of which salt we have too much,
savory and good to eat, melting to delight under our hearts
as our bellies embrace it and extract from it its sweet.'

"Much more they said, saying: 'He has come for the lobsters. When he dives in he is for one of us. Not like the old
man we ate yesterday, tough to dryness with age, nor like the
young men whose members were too hard-muscled, but
tender, so tender that he will melt in our gullets ere our
bellies receive him. When he dives in, we will rush for him,
and the lucky one of us will get him, and, gulp, he will be
gone, one bite and one swallow, into the belly of the luckiest
one of us.'

"And Keikiwai, the Water Baby, heard the conspiracy,
knowing the shark language; and he addressed a prayer, in
the shark language, to the shark god Moku-halii, and the
sharks heard and waved their tails to one another and winked
their cat's eyes in token that they understood his talk. And
then he said: 'I shall now dive for a lobster for the king.
And no hurt shall befall me, because the shark with the
shortest tail is my friend and will protect me.'

"And, so saying, he picked up a chunk of lava rock and
tossed it into the water, with a big splash, twenty feet to one
side. The forty sharks rushed for the splash, while he dived,
and by the time they discovered they had missed him, he had
gone to the bottom and come back and climbed out, within
his hand a fat lobster, a wahine lobster, full of eggs, for the
king.

" 'Ha!' said the sharks, very angry. 'There is among us a
traitor. The titbit of a child, the morsel of sweetness, has
spoken, and has exposed the one among us who has saved
him. Let us now measure the length of our tails!'

"Which they did, in a long row, side by side, the shorter-
tailed ones cheating and stretching to gain length on themselves, the longer-tailed ones cheating and stretching in order

not to be outcheated and outstretched. They were very angry with the one with the shortest tail, and him they rushed upon from every side and devoured till nothing was left of him.

"Again they listened while they waited for the Water Baby to dive in. And again the Water Baby made his prayer in the shark language to Moku-halii, and said: 'The shark with the shortest tail is my friend and will protect me.' And again the Water Baby tossed in a chunk of lava, this time twenty feet away off to the other side. The sharks rushed for the splash, and in their haste ran into one another, and splashed with their tails till the water was all foam and they could see nothing, each thinking some other was swallowing the titbit. And the Water Baby came up and climbed out with another fat lobster for the king.

"And the thirty-nine sharks measured tails, devouring the one with the shortest tail, so that there were only thirty-eight sharks. And the Water Baby continued to do what I have said, and the sharks to do what I have told you, while for each shark that was eaten by his brothers there was another fat lobster laid on the rock for the king. Of course, there was much quarreling and argument among the sharks when it came to measuring tails; but in the end it worked out in rightness and justice, for, when only two sharks were left, they were the two biggest of the original forty.

"And the Water Baby again claimed the shark with the shortest tail was his friend, fooled the two sharks with another lava chunk, and brought up another lobster. The two sharks each claimed the other had the shorter tail, and each fought to eat the other, and the one with the longer tail won—"

"Hold, O Kohokumu!" I interrupted. "Remember that that shark had already—"

"I know just what you are going to say," he snatched his recital back from me. "And you are right. It took him so long to eat the thirty-ninth shark, for inside the thirty-ninth shark were already the nineteen other sharks he had eaten, and inside the fortieth shark were already the nineteen other sharks he had eaten, and he did not have the appetite he had started with. But do not forget he was a very big shark to begin with.

"It took him so long to eat the other shark, and the nineteen sharks inside the other shark, that he was still eating when darkness fell and the people of Waihee went away home with all the lobsters for the king. And didn't they find the last shark on the beach next morning dead and burst wide open with all he had eaten?"

Kohokumu fetched a full stop and held my eyes with his own shrewd ones.

"Hold, O Lakana!" he checked the speech that rushed to my tongue. "I know what next you would say. You would say that with my own eyes I did not see this, and therefore that I do not know what I have been telling you. But I do know, and I can prove it. My father knew the grandson of the Water Baby's father's uncle. Also, there, on the rocky point to which I point my finger now, is where the Water Baby stood and dived. I have dived for lobsters there myself. It is a great place for lobsters. Also, and often, have I seen sharks there. And there, on the bottom, as I should know, for I have seen and counted them, are the thirty-nine lava rocks thrown in by the Water Baby as I have described."

"But—" I began.

"Ha!" he baffled me. "Look! While we have talked the fish have begun again to bite."

He pointed to three of the bamboo poles erect and devil-dancing in token that fish were hooked and struggling on the lines beneath. As he bent to his paddle, he muttered, for my benefit:

"Of course I know. The thirty-nine lava rocks are still there. You can count them any day for yourself. Of course I know, and I know for a fact."

THE TEARS OF AH KIM

THERE WAS A GREAT NOISE AND RACKET, BUT NO SCANDAL, IN Honolulu's Chinatown. Those within hearing distance merely shrugged their shoulders and smiled tolerantly at the disturbance as an affair of accustomed usualness. "What is it?" asked Chin Mo, down with a sharp pleurisy, of his wife, who had paused for a second at the open window to listen. "Only Ah Kim," was her reply. "His mother is beating him again."

The fracas was taking place in the garden, in back of the living rooms that were in back of the store that fronted on the street with the proud sign above: Ah Kim Company, General Merchandise. The garden was a miniature domain, twenty feet square, that somehow cunningly seduced the eye into a sense and seeming of illimitable vastness. There were forests of dwarf pines and oaks, centuries old yet two or three feet in height, and imported at enormous care and expense. A tiny bridge, a pace across, arched over a miniature river that flowed with rapids and cataracts from a miniature lake stocked with myriad-finned, orange-miracled goldfish that in proportion to the lake and landscape were whales. On every side the many windows of the several-storied shack buildings looked down. In the center of the garden, on the narrow graveled walk close beside the lake, Ah Kim was noisily receiving his beating.

No Chinese lad of tender and beatable years was Ah Kim. His was the store of Ah Kim Company, and his was the achievement of building it up through the long years from the shoestring of savings of a contract coolie laborer to a bank account in four figures and a credit that was gilt-edge. An even half century of summers and winters had passed over his head, and, in the passing, fattened him comfortably and smugly. Short of stature, his full front was as rotund as a watermelon seed. His face was moon-faced. His garb was dignified and silken, and his black silk skullcap with the red button atop, now, alas, fallen on the ground, was the skullcap worn by the successful and dignified merchants of his race.

But his appearance, in this moment of the present, was anything but dignified. Dodging and ducking under a rain of blows from a bamboo cane, he was crouched over in a half-doubled posture. When he was rapped on the knuckles and elbows, with which he shielded his face and head, his winces were genuine and involuntary. From the many surrounding windows the neighborhood looked down with placid enjoyment.

And she who wielded the stick so shrewdly from long practice! Seventy-four years old, she looked every minute of her time. Her thin legs were encased in straight-lined pants of linen stiff-textured and shiny black. Her scraggly gray hair was drawn unrelentingly and flatly back from a narrow, unrelenting forehead. Eyebrows she had none, having long since shed them. Her eyes, of pinhole tinyness, were blackest black. She was shockingly cadaverous. Her shriveled forearm, exposed by the loose sleeve, possessed no more of muscle than several taut bowstrings stretched across meager bone under yellow, parchment-like skin. Along this mummy arm jade bracelets shot up and down and clashed with every blow.

"Ah!" she cried out, rhythmically accenting her blows in series of three to each shrill observation. "I forbade you to talk to Li Faa. Today you stopped on the street with her. Not an hour ago. Half an hour by the clock you talked. What is that?"

"It was the thrice accursed telephone," Ah Kim muttered, while she suspended the stick to catch what he said.

"Mrs. Chang Lucy told you. I know she did. I saw her see me. I shall have the telephone taken out. It is of the devil."

"It is a device of all the devils," Mrs. Tai Fu agreed, taking a fresh grip on the stick. "Yet shall the telephone remain. I like to talk with Mrs. Chang Lucy over the telephone."

"She has the eyes of ten thousand cats," quoth Ah Kim, ducking and receiving the stick stingingly on his knuckles. "And the tongues of ten thousand toads," he supplemented ere his next duck.

"She is an impudent-faced and evil-mannered hussy," Mrs. Tai Fu accented.

"Mrs. Chang Lucy was ever that," Ah Kim murmured like the dutiful son he was.

"I speak of Li Faa," his mother corrected with stick emphasis. "She is only half Chinese, as you know. Her mother was a shameless Kanaka. She wore skirts like the degraded haole women—also corsets, as I have seen for myself. Where are her children? Yet has she buried two husbands."

"The one was drowned, the other kicked by a horse," Ah Kim qualified.

"A year of her, unworthy son of a noble father, and you would gladly be going out to get drowned or be kicked by a horse."

Subdued chucklings and laughter from the window audience applauded her point.

"You buried two husbands yourself, revered mother," Ah Kim was stung to retort.

"I had the good taste not to marry a third. Besides, my two husbands died honorably in their beds. They were not kicked by horses nor drowned at sea. What business is it of our neighbors that you should inform them I have had two husbands, or ten, or none? You have made a scandal of me before all our neighbors, and for that I shall now give you a real beating."

Ah Kim endured the staccato rain of blows, and said when his mother paused, breathless and weary:

"Always have I insisted and pleaded, honorable mother,

that you beat me in the house, with the windows and doors closed tight, and not in the open street or the garden open behind the house."

"You have called this unthinkable Li Faa the Silvery Moon Blossom," Mrs. Tai Fu rejoined, quite illogically and femininely, but with utmost success in so far as she deflected her son from continuance of the thrust he had so swiftly driven home.

"Mrs. Chang Lucy told you," he charged.

"I was told over the telephone," his mother evaded. "I do not know all voices that speak to me over that contrivance of all the devils."

Strangely, Ah Kim made no effort to run away from his mother, which he could easily have done. She, on the other hand, found fresh cause for more stick blows.

"Ah! Stubborn one! Why do you not cry? Mule that shameth its ancestors! Never have I made you cry. From the time you were a little boy I have never made you cry. Answer me! Why do you not cry?"

Weak and breathless from her exertions, she dropped the stick and panted and shook as if with a nervous palsy.

"I do not know, except that it is my way," Ah Kim replied, gazing solicitously at his mother. "I shall bring you a chair now, and you will sit down and rest and feel better."

But she flung away from him with a snort and tottered agedly across the garden into the house. Meanwhile recovering his skullcap and smoothing his disordered attire, Ah Kim rubbed his hurts and gazed after her with eyes of devotion. He even smiled, and almost might it appear that he had enjoyed the beating.

Ah Kim had been so beaten ever since he was a boy, when he lived on the high banks of the eleventh cataract of the Yangtze River. Here his father had been born and toiled all his days from young manhood as a towing coolie. When he died, Ah Kim, in his own young manhood, took up the same honorable profession. Farther back than all remembered annals of the family had the males of it been towing coolies. At the time of Christ his direct ancestors had been doing the same thing, meeting the precisely similarly modeled junks below the white water at the foot of the canyon, bending the half mile of rope to each junk, and, according to size, tailing on from a hundred to two hundred coolies of them and by sheer, two-legged man power, bowed forward and down till their hands touched the ground and their faces were sometimes within a foot of it, dragging the junk up through the white water to the head of the canyon.

Apparently, down all the intervening centuries, the payment of the trade had not picked up. His father, his father's father, and himself, Ah Kim, had received the same invariable remuneration—per junk one-fourteenth of a cent, at the rate he had since learned money was valued in Hawaii. On long, lucky, summer days when the waters were easy, the junks many, the hours of daylight sixteen, sixteen hours of such heroic toil would earn over a cent. But in a whole year a towing coolie did not earn more than a dollar and a half. People could and did live on such an income. There were women servants who received a yearly wage of a dollar. The net makers of Ti Wi earned between a dollar and two dollars a year. They lived on such wages, or, at least, they did not die on them. But for the towing coolies there were pickings, which were what made the profession honorable and the guild a close and hereditary corporation or labor union. One junk in five that was dragged up through the rapids or lowered down was wrecked. One junk in every ten was a total loss. The coolies of the towing guild knew the freaks and whims of the currents, and grappled and raked and netted a wet harvest from the river. They of the guild were looked up to by lesser coolies, for they could afford to drink brick tea and eat No. 4 rice every day.

And Ah Kim had been contented and proud until, one bitter spring day of driving sleet and hail, he dragged ashore a drowning Cantonese sailor. It was this wanderer, thawing out by his fire, who first named the magic name Hawaii to him. He himself had never been to that laborer's paradise, said the sailor; but many Chinese had gone there from Canton, and he had heard the talk of their letters written back. In Hawaii was never frost nor famine. The very pigs, never fed, were ever fat of the generous offal disdained by man. A Cantonese or Yangtze family could live on the waste of a Hawaiian coolie. And wages! In gold dollars, ten a month, or, in trade dollars, twenty a month, was what the contract Chinese coolie received from the white-devil sugar kings. In a year the coolie received the prodigious sum of two hundred and forty trade dollars—more than a hundred times what a coolie, toiling ten times as hard, received on the eleventh cataract of the Yangtze. In short, all things considered, a Hawaiian coolie was one hundred times better off, and, when the amount of labor was estimated, a thousand times better off. In addition was the wonderful climate.

When Ah Kim was twenty-four, despite his mother's pleadings and beatings, he resigned from the ancient and honorable guild of the eleventh cataract towing coolies, left his mother to go into a boss coolie's household as a servant for a dollar a year and an annual dress to cost not less than thirty cents, and himself departed down the Yangtze to the great sea. Many were his adventures and severe his toils and hardships ere, as a salt-sea junk sailor, he won to Canton. When he was twenty-six he signed five years of his life and labor away to the Hawaiian sugar kings and departed, one of eight hundred contract coolies, for that far island land, on a festering steamer run by a crazy captain and drunken officers and rejected of Lloyds.

Honorable, among laborers, had Ah Kim's rating been as a towing coolie. In Hawaii, receiving a hundred times more pay, he found himself looked down upon as the lowest of the low—a plantation coolie, than which could be nothing lower. But a coolie whose ancestors had towed junks up the eleventh cataract of the Yangtze since before the birth of Christ inevitably inherits one character in large degree; namely, the character of patience. This patience was Ah Kim's. At the

end of five years, his compulsory servitude over, thin as ever
in body, in bank account he lacked just ten trade dollars of
possessing a thousand trade dollars.

On this sum he could have gone back to the Yangtze and
retired for life a really wealthy man. He would have possessed
a larger sum, had he not, on occasion, conservatively played
che fa and fan-tan, and had he not, for a twelvemonth, toiled
among the centipedes and scorpions of the stifling cane fields
in the semidream of a continuous opium debauch. Why he
had not toiled the whole five years under the spell of opium
was the expensiveness of the habit. He had had no moral
scruples. The drug had cost too much.

But Ah Kim did not return to China. He had observed
the business life of Hawaii and developed a vaulting ambi-
tion. For six months, in order to learn business and English
at the bottom, he clerked in the plantation store. At the
end of this time he knew more about that particular store
than did ever plantation manager know about any plantation
store. When he resigned his position he was receiving forty
gold a month, or eighty trade, and he was beginning to put
on flesh. Also, his attitude toward mere contract coolies had
become distinctively aristocratic. The manager offered to
raise him to sixty gold, which, by the year, would constitute
a fabulous fourteen hundred and forty trade, or seven hundred times his annual earning on the Yangtze as a two-legged
horse at one-fourteenth of a gold cent per junk.

Instead of accepting, Ah Kim departed to Honolulu and
in the big general merchandise store of Fong & Chow Fong
began at the bottom for fifteen gold per month. He worked
a year and a half, and resigned when he was thirty-three, despite the seventy-five gold per month his Chinese employers
were paying him. Then it was that he put up his own sign:
Ah Kim Company, General Merchandise. Also, better fed,
there was about his less meager figure a foreshadowing of
the melon-seed rotundity that was to attach to him in future
years.

With the years he prospered increasingly, so that, when he

was thirty-six, the promise of his figure was fulfilling rapidly, and, himself a member of the exclusive and powerful Hai Gum Tong and of the Chinese Merchants' Association, he was accustomed to sitting as host at dinners that cost him as much as thirty years of towing on the eleventh cataract would have earned him. Two things he missed: a wife, and his mother to lay the stick on him as of yore.

When he was thirty-seven he consulted his bank balance. It stood him three thousand gold. For twenty-five hundred down and an easy mortgage he could buy the three-story shack building and the ground in fee simple on which it stood. But to do this left only five hundred for a wife. Fu Yee Po had a marriageable, properly small-footed daughter whom he was willing to import from China and sell to him for eight hundred gold plus the costs of importation. Further, Fu Yee Po was even willing to take five hundred down and the remainder on note at six per cent.

Ah Kim, thirty-seven years of age, fat and a bachelor, really did want a wife, especially a small-footed wife; for, Chinese born and reared, the immemorial small-footed female had been deeply impressed into his fantasy of woman. But more, even more and far more than a small-footed wife, did he want his mother and his mother's delectable beatings. So he declined Fu Yee Po's easy terms, and at much less cost imported his own mother from servant in a boss coolie's house at a yearly wage of a dollar and a thirty-cent dress to be mistress of his Honolulu three-story shack building with two household servants, three clerks, and a porter of all work under her, to say nothing of ten thousand dollars' worth of dress goods on the shelves that ranged from the cheapest cotton crêpes to the most expensive hand-embroidered silks. For be it known that even in that early day Ah Kim's emporium was beginning to cater to the tourist trade from the States.

For thirteen years Ah Kim had lived tolerably happily with his mother and by her been methodically beaten for causes just or unjust, real or fancied; and at the end of it all he knew as strongly as ever the ache of his heart and head for a wife and of his loins for sons to live after him and carry on the dynasty of Ah Kim Company. Such the dream that has ever vexed men from those early ones who first usurped a hunting right, monopolized a sand bar for a fish trap, or stormed a village and put the males thereof to the sword. Kings, millionaires, and Chinese merchants of Honolulu have this in common, despite that they may praise God for having made them differently and in self-likable images.

And the ideal of woman that Ah Kim at fifty ached for had changed from his ideal at thirty-seven. No small-footed wife did he want now, but a free, natural, out-stepping, normal-footed woman who, somehow, appeared to him in his day-dreams and haunted his night visions in the form of Li Faa, the Silvery Moon Blossom. What if she were twice widowed, the daughter of a Kanaka mother, the wearer of white-devil skirts and corsets and high-heeled slippers? He wanted her. It seemed it was written that she should be joint ancestor with him of the line that would continue the ownership and management through the generations of Ah Kim Company, General Merchandise.

"I will have no half *paké* daughter-in-law," his mother often reiterated to Ah Kim, paké being the Hawaiian word for Chinese. "All paké must my daughter-in-law be, even as you, my son, and as I, your mother. And she must wear trousers, my son, as all the women of our family before her. No woman, in the she-devil skirts and corsets, can pay due reverence to our ancestors. Corsets and reverence do not go together. Such a one is this shameless Li Faa. She is impudent and independent, and will be neither obedient to her husband nor her husband's mother. This brazen-faced Li Faa would believe herself the source of life and the first ancestor, recognizing no ancestors before her. She laughs at our joss sticks and paper prayers and family gods, as I have been well told—"

"Mrs. Chang Lucy," Ah Kim groaned.

"Not alone Mrs. Chang Lucy, O son. I have inquired. At least a dozen have heard her say of our joss house that it is all monkey foolishness. The words are hers—she, who eats raw fish, raw squid, and baked dog. Ours is the foolishness of monkeys. Yet would she marry you, a monkey, because of your store that is a palace and of the wealth that makes you a great man. And she would put shame on me, and on your father before you long honorably dead."

And there was no discussing the matter. As things were, Ah Kim knew his mother was right. Not for nothing had Li Faa been born forty years before of a Chinese father, renegade to all tradition, and of a Kanaka mother whose immediate forebears had broken the tabus, cast down their own Polynesian gods, and weak-heartedly listened to the preaching about the remote and unimageable god of the Christian missionaries. Li Faa, educated, who could read and write English and Hawaiian and a fair measure of Chinese, claimed to believe in nothing, although in her secret heart she feared the kahunas (Hawaiian witch doctors), who she was certain could charm away ill luck or pray one to death. Li Faa would never come into Ah Kim's house, as he thoroughly knew, and kowtow to his mother and be slave to her in the immemorial Chinese way. Li Faa, from the Chinese angle, was a new woman, a feminist, who rode horseback astride, disported immodestly garbed at Waikiki on the surfboards, and at more than one luau had been known to dance the hula with the worst and in excess of the worst to the scandalous delight of all.

Ah Kim himself, a generation younger than his mother, had been bitten by the acid of modernity. The old order held, in so far as he still felt in his subtlest crypts of being the dusty hand of the past resting on him, residing in him; yet he subscribed to heavy policies of fire and life insurance, acted as treasurer for the local Chinese revolutionists that were for turning the Celestial empire into a republic, contributed to the funds of the Hawaii-born Chinese baseball nine that excelled the Yankee nines at their own game, talked theosophy with Katso Suguri, the Japanese Buddhist and silk importer, fell for police graft, played and paid his insidious share in the democratic politics of annexed Hawaii, and was thinking of buying an automobile. Ah Kim never dared bare himself to himself and thresh out and winnow out how much of the old he had ceased to believe in. His mother was of the old, yet he revered her and was happy under her bamboo stick. Li Faa, the Silvery Moon Blossom, was of the new, yet he could never be quite completely happy without her.

For he loved Li Faa. Moon-faced, rotund as a watermelon seed, a canny business man, wise with half a century of living —nevertheless Ah Kim became an artist when he thought of her. He thought of her in poems of names, as woman transmuted into flower terms of beauty and philosophic abstractions of achievement and easement. She was, to him, and alone to him of all men in the world, his Plum Blossom, his Tranquillity of Woman, his Flower of Serenity, his Moon Lily, and his Perfect Rest. And as he murmured these love endearments of namings, it seemed to him that in them were the ripplings of running waters, the tinklings of silver wind bells, and the scents of the oleander and the jasmine. She was his poem of woman, a lyric delight, a three dimensions of flesh and spirit delicious, a fate and a good fortune written, ere the first man and woman were, by the gods whose whim had been to make all men and women for sorrow and for joy.

But his mother put into his hand the ink brush and placed under it, on the table, the writing tablet.

"Paint," said she, "the ideograph of *to marry*."

He obeyed, scarcely wondering, with the deft artistry of his race and training painting the symbolic hieroglyphic.

"Resolve it," commanded his mother.

Ah Kim looked at her, curious, willing to please, unaware of the drift of her intent.

"Of what is it composed?" she persisted. "What are the three originals, the sum of which is it: to marry, marriage, the coming together and wedding of a man and a woman?

Paint them, paint them apart, the three originals, unrelated, so that we may know how the wise men of old wisely built up the ideograph of *to marry*."

And Ah Kim, obeying and painting, saw that what he had painted was three picture signs—the picture signs of a hand, an ear, and a woman.

"Name them," said his mother; and he named them.

"It is true," said she. "It is a great tale. It is the stuff of the painted pictures of marriage. Such marriage was in the beginning; such shall it always be in my house. The hand of the man takes the woman's ear and by it leads her away to his house, where she is to be obedient to him and to his mother. I was taken by the ear, so, by your long honorably dead father. I have looked at your hand. It is not like his hand. Also have I looked at the ear of Li Faa. Never will you lead her by the ear. She has not that kind of an ear. I shall live a long time yet, and I will be mistress in my son's house, after our ancient way, until I die."

"But she is my revered ancestress," Ah Kim explained to Li Faa.

He was timidly unhappy; for Li Faa, having ascertained that Mrs. Tai Fu was at the temple of the Chinese Æsculapius making a food offering of dried duck and prayers for her declining health, had taken advantage of the opportunity to call upon him in his store.

Li Faa pursed her insolent, unpainted lips into the form of a half-opened rosebud, and replied:

"That will do for China. I do not know China. This is Hawaii, and in Hawaii the customs of all foreigners change."

"She is nevertheless my ancestress," Ah Kim protested, "the mother who gave me birth, whether I am in China or Hawaii, O Silvery Moon Blossom that I want for wife."

"I have had two husbands," Li Faa stated placidly. "One was a paké, one was a Portuguese. I learned much from both. Also am I educated. I have been to high school, and I have played the piano in public. And I learned from my two husbands much. The paké makes the best husband. Never again will I marry anything but a paké. But he must not take me by the ear—"

"How do you know of that?" he broke in suspiciously.

"Mrs. Chang Lucy," was the reply. "Mrs. Chang Lucy tells me everything that your mother tells her, and your mother tells her much. So let me tell you that mine is not that kind of an ear."

"Which is what my honored mother has told me," Ah Kim groaned.

"Which is what your honored mother told Mrs. Chang Lucy, which is what Mrs. Chang Lucy told me," Li Faa completed equably. "And I now tell you, O Third Husband To Be, that the man is not born who will lead me by the ear. It is not the way in Hawaii. I will go only hand in hand with my man, side by side, fifty-fifty, as is the haole slang just now. My Portuguese husband thought different. He tried to beat me. I landed him three times in the police court, and each time he worked out his sentence on the reef. After that he got drowned."

"My mother has been my mother for fifty years," Ah Kim declared stoutly.

"And for fifty years has she beaten you," Li Faa giggled. "How my father used to laugh at Yap Ten Shin! Like you, Yap Ten Shin had been born in China, and had brought the Chinese customs with him. His old father was forever beating him with a stick. He loved his father. But his father beat him harder than ever when he became a missionary paké. Every time he went to the missionary services, his father beat him. And every time the missionary heard of it he was harsh in his language to Yap Ten Shin for allowing his father to beat him. And my father laughed and laughed, for my father was a very liberal paké who had changed his customs quicker than most foreigners. And all the trouble was because Yap Ten Shin had a loving heart. He loved his honorable father. He loved the God of Love of the Christian missionary. But in the end, in me, he found the greatest love of all, which is the love of woman. In me he forgot his love for his father and his love for the loving Christ.

"And he offered my father six hundred gold for me—the price was small because my feet were not small. But I was half Kanaka. I said that I was not a slave woman, and that I would be sold to no man. My high-school teacher was a haole old maid who said love of woman was so beyond price that it must never be sold. Perhaps that is why she was an old maid. She was not beautiful. She could not give herself away. My Kanaka mother said it was not the Kanaka way to sell their daughters for a money price. They gave their daughters for love, and she would listen to reason if Yap Ten Shin provided luaus in quantity and quality. My paké father, as I have told you, was liberal. He asked me if I wanted Yap Ten Shin for my husband. And I said yes; and freely, of myself, I went to him. He it was who was kicked by a horse; but he was a very good husband before he was kicked by the horse.

"As for you, Ah Kim, you shall always be honorable and lovable for me, and some day, when it is not necessary for you to take me by the ear, I shall marry you and come here and be with you always, and you will be the happiest paké in all Hawaii; for I have had two husbands, and gone to high school, and am most wise in making a husband happy. But that will be when your mother has ceased to beat you. Mrs. Chang Lucy tells me that she beats you very hard."

"She does," Ah Kim affirmed. "Behold!" He thrust back his loose sleeves, exposing to the elbow his smooth and cherubic forearms. They were mantled with black and blue marks that advertised the weight and number of blows so shielded from his head and face.

"But she has never made me cry," Ah Kim disclaimed hastily. "Never, from the time I was a little boy, has she made me cry."

"So Mrs. Chang Lucy says," Li Faa observed. "She says that your honorable mother often complains to her that she has never made you cry."

A sibilant warning from one of his clerks was too late. Having regained the house by way of the back alley, Mrs. Tai Fu emerged right upon them from out of the living apartments. Never had Ah Kim seen his mother's eyes so blazing furious. She ignored Li Faa, as she screamed at him:

"Now will I make you cry. As never before shall I beat you until you do cry."

"Then let us go into the back rooms, honorable mother," Ah Kim suggested. "We will close the windows and the doors, and there may you beat me."

"No. Here shall you be beaten before all the world and this shameless woman who would with her own hand take you by the ear and call such sacrilege marriage! Stay, shameless woman."

"I am going to stay anyway," said Li Faa. She favored the clerks with a truculent stare. "And I'd like to see anything less than the police put me out of here."

"You will never be my daughter-in-law," Mrs. Tai Fu snapped.

Li Faa nodded her head in agreement.

"But just the same," she added, "shall your son be my third husband."

"You mean when I am dead?" the old mother screamed.

"The sun rises each morning," Li Faa said enigmatically. "All my life have I seen it rise—"

"You are forty, and you wear corsets."

"But I do not dye my hair—that will come later," Li Faa calmly retorted. "As to my age, you are right. I shall be forty-one next Kamehameha Day. For forty years I have seen the sun rise. My father was an old man. Before he died he told me that he had observed no difference in the rising of the sun since when he was a little boy. The world is round. Confucius did not know that, but you will find it in all the geography books. The world is round. Ever it turns over on itself, over and over and around and around. And the times and seasons of weather and life turn with it. What is, has been before. What has been will be again. The time of the breadfruit and the mango ever recurs, and man and woman repeat themselves. The robins nest, and in the springtime the plovers come from the north. Every spring is followed by another spring. The coconut palm rises into the air, ripens its fruit, and departs. But always are there more coconut palms. This is not all my own smart talk. Much of it my father told me. Proceed, honorable Mrs. Tai Fu, and beat your son who is my Third Husband To Be. But I shall laugh. I warn you I shall laugh."

Ah Kim dropped down on his knees so as to give his mother every advantage. And while she rained blows upon him with the bamboo stick, Li Faa smiled and giggled, and finally burst into laughter.

"Harder! O honorable Mrs. Tai Fu!" Li Faa urged between paroxysms of mirth.

Mrs. Tai Fu did her best, which was notably weak, until she observed what made her drop the stick by her side in amazement. Ah Kim was crying. Down both cheeks great round tears were coursing. Li Faa was amazed. So were the gaping clerks. Most amazed of all was Ah Kim, yet he could not help himself; and, although no further blows fell, he cried steadily on.

"But why did you cry?" Li Faa demanded often of Ah Kim. "It was so perfectly foolish a thing to do. She was not even hurting you."

"Wait until we are married," was Ah Kim's invariable reply, "and then, O Moon Lily, will I tell you."

Two years later, one afternoon, more like a watermelon seed in configuration than ever, Ah Kim returned home from a meeting of the Chinese Protective Association to find his mother dead on her couch. Narrower and more unrelenting than ever were the forehead and the brushed-back hair. But on her face was a withered smile. The gods had been kind. She had passed without pain.

He telephoned, first of all to Li Faa's number, but did not

find her until he called up Mrs. Chang Lucy. The news given, the marriage was dated ahead with ten times the brevity of the old-line Chinese custom. And if there be anything analogous to a bridesmaid in a Chinese wedding, Mrs. Chang Lucy was just that.

"Why," Li Faa asked Ah Kim when alone with him on their wedding night, "why did you cry when your mother beat you that day in the store? You were so foolish. She was not even hurting you."

"That is why I cried," answered Ah Kim.

Li Faa looked at him without understanding.

"I cried," he explained, "because I suddenly knew that my mother was nearing her end. There was no weight, no hurt, in her blows. I cried because I knew *she no longer had strength enough to hurt me*. That is why I cried, my Flower of Serenity, my Perfect Rest. That is the only reason why I cried."

THE KANAKA SURF

THE TOURIST WOMEN, UNDER THE HAU-TREE ARBOR THAT LINES
the Moana Hotel beach, gasped when Lee Barton and his
wife Ida emerged from the bathhouse. And as the pair walked
past them and down to the sand, they continued to gasp. Not
that there was anything about Lee Barton provocative of
gasps. The tourist women were not of the sort to gasp at
sight of a mere man's swimming-suited body, no matter with
what swelling splendor of line and muscle such body was
invested. Nevertheless, trainers and conditioners of men
would have drawn deep breaths of satisfaction at contemplation of the physical spectacle of him. But they would not
have gasped in the way the women did, whose gasps were
indicative of moral shock.

Ida Barton was the cause of their perturbation and disapproval. They disapproved, seriously so, at the first instant's
glimpse of her. They thought—such ardent self-deceivers were
they—that they were shocked by her swimming suit. But
Freud has pointed out how persons, where sex is involved,
are prone sincerely to substitute one thing for another thing,
and to agonize over the substituted thing as strenuously as
if it were the real thing.

Ida Barton's swimming suit was a very nice one, as women's
suits go. Of thinnest of firm-woven black wool, with white
trimmings and a white belt line, it was high-throated, short-
sleeved, and brief-skirted. Brief as was the skirt, the leg
tights were no less brief. Yet on the beach in front of the
adjacent Outrigger Club, and entering and leaving the water,

a score of women, not provoking gasping notice, were more daringly garbed. Their men's suits, as brief of leg tights and skirts, fitted them as snugly, but were sleeveless after the way of men's suits, the armholes deeply low cut and in cut, and, by the exposed armpits, advertiseful that the wearers were accustomed to 1916 décolleté.

So it was not Ida Barton's suit, although the women deceived themselves into thinking it was. It was, first of all, say, her legs; or, first of all, say, the totality of her, the sweet and brilliant jewel of her femininity bursting upon them. Dowager, matron, and maid, conserving their soft-fat muscles or protecting their hothouse complexions in the shade of the hau-tree arbor, felt the immediate challenge of her. She was menace as well, an affront of superiority in their own chosen and variously successful game of life.

But they did not say it. They did not permit themselves to think it. They thought it was the suit, and said so to one another, ignoring the twenty women more daringly clad but less perilously beautiful. Could one have winnowed out of the souls of these disapproving ones what lay at bottom of their condemnation of her suit, it would have been found to be the sex-jealous thought: *that no woman, so beautiful as this one, should be permitted to show her beauty.* It was not fair to them. What chance had they in the conquering of males with so dangerous a rival in the foreground?

They were justified. As Stanley Patterson said to his wife, where the two of them lolled wet in the sand by the tiny fresh-water stream that the Bartons waded in order to gain the Outrigger Club beach:

"Lord god of models and marvels, behold them! My dear, did you ever see two such legs on one small woman? Look at the roundness and taperingness. They're boy's legs. I've seen featherweights go into the ring with legs like those. And they're all woman's legs, too. Never mistake them in the world. The arc of the front line of that upper leg! And the balanced adequate fullness at the back! And the way the opposing curves slender in to the knee that *is* a knee! Makes my fingers itch. Wish I had some clay right now."

"It's a true human knee," his wife concurred, no less breathlessly; for, like her husband, she was a sculptor. "Look at the joint of it working under the skin. It's got form, and blessedly is not covered by a bag of fat." She paused to sigh, thinking of her own knees. "It's correct and beautiful and dainty. Charm! If ever I beheld the charm of flesh it is now. I wonder who she is."

Stanley Patterson, gazing ardently, took up his half of the chorus.

"Notice that the round muscle pads on the inner sides which make most women appear knock-kneed are missing? They're boy's legs, firm and sure—"

"And sweet woman's legs, soft and round," his wife hastened to balance. "And look, Stanley! See how she walks on the balls of her feet. It makes her seem light as swan's-down. Each step seems just a little above the earth, and each other step seems just a little higher above until you get the impression she is flying, or just about to rise and begin flying . . ."

So Stanley and Mrs. Patterson. But they were artists, with eyes therefore unlike the next batteries of human eyes Ida Barton was compelled to run, and that laired on the Outrigger lanais (verandas) and in the hau-tree shade of the closely adjoining Seaside. The majority of the Outrigger audience was composed, not of tourist guests, but of club members and old-timers in Hawaii. And even the old-time women gasped.

"It's positively indecent," said Mrs. Hanley Black to her husband, herself a too-stout-in-the-middle matron of forty-five, who had been born in the Hawaiian Islands and who had never heard of Ostend.

Hanley Black surveyed his wife's criminal shapelessness and voluminousness of antediluvian, New England swimming dress with a withering, contemplative eye. They had been married a sufficient number of years for him frankly to utter his judgment:

"That strange woman's suit makes your own look indecent. You appear as a creature shameful, under a grotesqueness of apparel striving to hide some secret awfulness."

"She carries her body like a Spanish dancer," Mrs. Patterson said to her husband, for the pair of them had waded the little stream in pursuit of the vision.

"By George, she does," Stanley Patterson concurred. "Reminds me of Estrellita. Torso just well enough forward, slender waist, not too lean in the stomach, and with muscles like some lad boxer's armoring that stomach to fearlessness. She has to have them to carry herself that way and to balance the back muscles. See that muscled curve of the back! It's Estrellita's."

"How tall would you say?" his wife queried.

"There she deceives," was the appraised answer. "She might be five feet one, or five feet three or four. It's that way she has of walking that you described as almost about to fly."

"Yes, that's it," Mrs. Patterson concurred. "It's her energy, her seemingness of being on tiptoe with rising vitality."

Stanley Patterson considered for a space.

"That's it," he enounced. "She *is* a little thing. I'll give her five two in her stockings. And I'll weigh her a mere one hundred and ten, or eight, or fifteen at the outside."

"She won't weigh a hundred and ten," his wife declared with conviction.

"And with her clothes on, plus her carriage (which is builded of her vitality and will), I'll wager she'd never impress anyone with her smallness."

"I know her type," his wife nodded. "You meet her out and you have the sense that, while not exactly a fine, large woman, she's a whole lot larger than the average. And now, age?"

"I'll give you best, there," he parried.

"She might be twenty-five, she might be thirty-eight . . ."

But Stanley Patterson had impolitely forgotten to listen.

"It's not her legs alone," he cried on enthusiastically. "It's the all of her. Look at the delicacy of that forearm. And the swell of line to the shoulder. And that biceps! It's alive. Dollars to drowned kittens she can flex a respectable knot of it. . . ."

No woman, much less an Ida Barton, could have been unconscious of the effect she was producing along Waikiki Beach. Instead of making her happy in the small vanity way, it irritated her.

"The cats," she laughed to her husband. "And to think I was born here an almost even third of a century ago! But they weren't nasty then. Maybe because there weren't any tourists. Why, Lee, I learned to swim right here on this beach in front of the Outrigger. We used to come out with daddy for vacations and for week-ends and sort of camp out in a grass house that stood right where the Outrigger ladies serve tea now. And centipedes fell out of the thatch on us while we slept, and we all ate poi and opihis and raw *aku,* and nobody wore much of anything for the swimming, and squidding, and there was no real road to town. I remember times of big rain when it was so flooded we had to go in by canoe, out through the reef and in by Honolulu Harbor."

"Remember," Lee Barton added, "it was just about that time that the youngster that became me arrived here for a few weeks' stay on our way around. I must have seen you on the beach at that very time—one of the kiddies that swam like fishes. Why, merciful me, the women here were all riding cross saddle, and that was long before the rest of the social female world outgrew its immodesty and came around to sitting simultaneously on both sides of a horse. I learned to swim on the beach here at that time myself. You and I may even have tried body surfing on the same waves, or I may have splashed a handful of water into your mouth and been rewarded by your sticking out your tongue at me—"

Interrupted by an audible gasp of shock from a spinster-appearing female sunning herself hard by and angularly in the sand in a swimming suit monstrously unbeautiful, Lee Barton was aware of an involuntary and almost perceptible stiffening on the part of his wife.

"I smile with pleasure," he told her. "It serves only to make your valiant little shoulders the more valiant. It may make you self-conscious, but it likewise makes you absurdly self-confident."

For, be it known in advance, Lee Barton was a superman and Ida Barton a superwoman—or at least they were personalities so designated by the cub book reviewers, flat-floor men and women, and scholastically emasculated critics, who, from across the dreary levels of their living, can descry no glorious humans overtopping their horizons. These dreary folk, echoes of the dead past and importunate and self-elected pallbearers for the present and future, proxy livers of life and vicarious sensualists that they are in a eunuch sort of way, insist, since their own selves, environments, and narrow agitations of the quick are mediocre and commonplace, that no man or woman can rise above the mediocre and commonplace.

Lacking gloriousness in themselves, they deny gloriousness to all mankind; too cowardly for whimsy and derring-do, they assert whimsy and derring-do ceased at the very latest no later than the Middle Ages; flickering little tapers themselves, their feeble eyes are dazzled to unseeingness of the flaming conflagrations of other souls that illumine their skies. Possessing power in no greater quantity than is the just due of pygmies, they cannot conceive of power greater in others than in themselves. In those days there were giants; but, as their moldy books tell them, the giants are long since passed and only the bones of them remain. Never having seen the mountains, there are no mountains.

In the mud of their complacently perpetuated barnyard pond, they assert that no bright-browed, bright-appareled, shining figures can be outside of fairy books, old histories, and ancient superstitions. Never having seen the stars, they deny the stars. Never having glimpsed the shining ways nor the mortals that tread them, they deny the existence of the shining ways as well as the existence of the high-bright mortals who adventure along the shining ways. The narrow pupils of their eyes in the center of the universe, they image

the universe in terms of themselves, of their meager personalities make pitiful yardsticks with which to measure the
high-bright souls, saying: "Thus long are all souls, and no
longer; it is impossible that there should exist greater-sta-
tured souls than we are, and our gods know that we are great
of stature."

But all, or nearly all on the beach, forgave Ida Barton her
suit and form when she took the water. A touch of her hand
on her husband's arm, indication and challenge in her laughing face, and the two ran as one for half a dozen paces and
leaped as one from the hard-wet sand of the beach, their
bodies describing flat arches of flight ere the water was
entered.

There are two surfs at Waikiki: the big, bearded-man surf
that roars far out beyond the diving stage; the smaller,
gentler, wahine, or woman, surf that breaks upon the shore
itself. Here is a great shallowness, where one may wade a
hundred or several hundred feet to get beyond depth. Yet,
with a good surf on outside, the wahine surf can break three
or four feet, so that, close in against the shore, the hard-sand
bottom may be three feet or three inches under the welter of
surface foam. To dive from the beach into this, to fly into
the air off racing feet, turn in mid-flight so that heels are up
and head is down, and so to enter the water headfirst, requires
wisdom of waves, timing of waves, and a trained deftness in
entering such unstable depths of water with pretty, unap-
prehensive, headfirst cleavage while at the same time making
the shallowest possible of dives.

It is a sweet and pretty and daring trick, not learned in a
day nor learned at all without many a mild bump on the
bottom or close shave of fractured skull or broken neck. Here,
on the spot where the Bartons so beautifully dived, two days
earlier a Stanford track athlete had broken his neck. His had
been an error in timing the rise and subsidence of a wahine
wave.

"A professional," Mrs. Hanley Black sneered to her husband at Ida Barton's feat.

"Some vaudeville tank girl," was one of the similar remarks with which the women in the shade complacently reassured one another; finding, by way of the weird mental processes of self-illusion, a great satisfaction in the money caste distinction between one who worked for what she ate and themselves who did not work for what they ate.

It was a day of heavy surf on Waikiki. In the wahine surf it was boisterous enough for good swimmers. But out beyond, in the *Kanaka,* or man, surf, no one ventured. Not that the score or more of young surf-riders, loafing on the beach, could not venture there, or were afraid to venture there; but because their biggest outrigger canoes would have been swamped, and their surfboards would have been overwhelmed in the too-immense overtopple and downfall of the thundering monsters. They themselves, most of them, could have swum, for man can swim through breakers which canoes and surfboards cannot surmount; but to ride the backs of the waves, rise out of the foam to stand full length in the air above and with heels winged with the swiftness of horses to fly shoreward, was what made sport for them and brought them out from Honolulu to Waikiki.

The captain of Number Nine canoe, himself a charter member of the Outrigger and a many-times medalist in long-distance swimming, had missed seeing the Bartons take the water and first glimpsed them beyond the last festoon of bathers who clung to the life lines. From then on, from his vantage of the upstairs lanai, he kept his eyes on them. When they continued out past the steel diving stage where a few of the hardiest divers disported, he muttered vexedly under his breath, "damned malihinis!"

Now malihini means newcomer, tenderfoot; and, despite the prettiness of their stroke, he knew that none except malihinis would venture into the racing channel beyond the diving stage. Hence, the vexation of the captain of Number Nine. He descended to the beach, with a low word here and there picked a crew of the strongest surfers, and returned to the lanai with a pair of binoculars. Quite casually, the crew, six of them, carried Number Nine to the water's edge, saw paddles and everything in order for a quick launching, and lolled about carelessly on the sand. They were guilty of not advertising that anything untoward was afoot, although they did steal glances up to their captain straining through the binoculars.

What made the channel was the fresh-water stream. Coral cannot abide fresh water. What made the channel race was the immense shoreward surf-fling of the sea. Unable to remain flung up on the beach, pounded ever back toward the beach by the perpetual shoreward rush of the Kanaka surf, the up-piled water escaped to the sea by way of the channel and in the form of undertow along the bottom under the breakers. Even in the channel the waves broke big, but not with the magnificent bigness of terror as to right and left. So it was that a canoe or a comparatively strong swimmer could dare the channel. But the swimmer must be a strong swimmer indeed who could successfully buck the current in. Wherefore the captain of Number Nine continued his vigil and his muttered damnation of malihinis, disgustedly sure that these two malihinis would compel him to launch Number Nine and go after them when they found the current too strong to swim in against. As for himself, caught in their predicament, he would have veered to the left toward Diamond Head and come in on the shoreward fling of the Kanaka surf. But then, he was no one other than himself, a bronze Hercules of twenty-two, the whitest blood man ever burned to mahogany brown by a subtropic sun, with body and lines and muscles very much resembling the wonderful ones of Duke Kahanamoku. In a hundred yards the world champion could invariably beat him a second flat; but over a distance of miles he could swim circles around the champion.

No one of the many hundreds on the beach, with the exception of the captain and his crew, knew that the Bartons had passed beyond the diving stage. All who had watched them start to swim out had taken for granted that they had joined the others on the stage.

The captain suddenly sprang upon the railing of the lanai, held on to a pillar with one hand, and again picked up the two specks of heads through the glasses. His surmise was verified. The two fools had veered out of the channel toward Diamond Head and were directly seaward of the Kanaka surf. Worse, as he looked, they were starting to come in through the Kanaka surf.

He glanced down quickly to the canoe, and even as he glanced, and as the apparently loafing members quietly arose and took their places by the canoe for the launching, he achieved judgment. Before the canoe could get abreast in the channel, all would be over with the man and woman. And, granted that it could get abreast of them, the moment it ventured into the Kanaka surf it would be swamped, and a sorry chance would the strongest swimmer of them have of rescuing a person pounding to pulp on the bottom under the smashes of the great bearded ones.

The captain saw the first Kanaka wave, large of itself but small among its fellow, lift seaward behind the two speck swimmers. Then he saw them strike a crawl stroke, side by side, faces downward, full lengths outstretched on surface, their feet sculling like propellers and their arms flailing in rapid overhand strokes as they spurted speed to approximate the speed of the overtaking wave, so that, when overtaken, they would become part of the wave and travel with it instead of being left behind it. Thus, if they were coolly skilled enough to ride outstretched on the surface and the forward face of the crest instead of being flung and crumpled or driven headfirst to bottom, they would dash shoreward, not propelled by their own energy but by the energy of the wave into which they had become incorporated.

And they did it! "*Some* swimmers," the captain of Number Nine made announcement to himself under his breath. He continued to gaze eagerly. The best of swimmers could hold such a wave for several hundred feet. But could they? If they

did, they would be a third of the way through the perils they
had challenged. But, not unexpected by him, the woman
failed first, her body not presenting the larger surfaces that
her husband's did. At the end of seventy feet she was overwhelmed, being driven downward and out of sight by the
tons of water in the overtopple. Her husband followed, and
both appeared swimming beyond the wave they had lost.

The captain saw the next wave first. "If they try to body-
surf on that, *good* night," he muttered; for he knew the
swimmer did not live who would tackle it. Beardless itself, it
was father of all bearded ones, a mile long, rising up far out
beyond where the others rose, towering its solid bulk higher
and higher till it blotted out the horizon and was a giant
among its fellows ere its beard began to grow as it thinned
its crest to the overcurl.

But it was evident that the man and woman knew big
water. No racing stroke did they make in advance of the
wave. The captain inwardly applauded as he saw them turn
and face the wave and wait for it. It was a picture that of all
on the beach he alone saw, wonderfully distinct and vivid
in the magnification of the binoculars. The wall of the wave
was truly a wall, mounting, ever mounting, and thinning,
far up, to a transparency of the colors of the setting sun
shooting athwart all the green and blue of it. The green
thinned to lighter green that merged blue even as he looked.
But it was a blue gem brilliant with innumerable sparkle
points of rose and gold flashed through it by the sun. On and
up, to the sprouting beard of growing crest, the color orgy
increased until it was a kaleidoscopic effervescence of trans-
fusing rainbows.

Against the face of the wave showed the heads of the man
and woman like two sheer specks. Specks they were, of the
quick, adventuring among the blind elemental forces, daring
the Titanic buffets of the sea. The weight of the downfall of
that father of waves, even then imminent above their heads,
could stun a man or break the fragile bones of a woman. The
captain of Number Nine was unconscious that he was hold-

ing his breath. He was oblivious of the man. It was the woman. Did she lose her head or courage, or misplay her muscular part for a moment, she could be hurled a hundred feet by that giant buffet and left wrenched, helpless, and breathless to be pulped on the coral bottom and sucked out by the undertow to be battened on by the fish sharks too cowardly to take their human meat alive.

Why didn't they dive deep, and with plenty of time, the captain wanted to know, instead of waiting till the last tick of safety and the first tick of peril were one? He saw the woman turn her head and laugh to the man, and his head turn in response. Above them, overhanging them, as they mounted the body of the wave, the beard, creaming white, then frothing into rose and gold, tossed upward into a spray of jewels. The crisp offshore trade wind caught the beard's fringes and blew them backward and upward yards and yards into the air. It was then, side by side, and six feet apart, that they dived straight under the overcurl even then disintegrating to chaos and falling. Like insects disappearing into the convolutions of some gorgeous, gigantic orchid, so they disappeared, as beard and crest and spray and jewels, in many tons, crashed and thundered down just where they had disappeared the moment before but where they were no longer.

Beyond the wave they had gone through they finally showed, side by side, still six feet apart, swimming shoreward with a steady stroke until the next wave should make them body-surf it or face and pierce it. The captain of Number Nine waved his hand to his crew in dismissal and sat down on the lanai railing, feeling vaguely tired, and still watching the swimmers through his glasses.

"Whoever and whatever they are," he murmured. "they aren't malihinis. They simply can't be malihinis."

Not all days, and only on rare days, is the surf heavy at Waikiki; and, in the days that followed, Ida and Lee Barton, much in evidence on the beach and in the water, continued to arouse disparaging interest in the breasts of the tourist

ladies, although the Outrigger captains ceased from worry-
ing about them in the water. They would watch the pair
swim out and disappear in the blue distance, and they might,
or might not, chance to see them return hours afterward. The
point was that the captains did not bother about their returning because they *knew* they would return.

The reason for this was that they were not malihinis. They
belonged. In other words, or, rather, in the potent Islands
word, they were *kamaaina*. Kamaaina men and women of
forty remembered Lee Barton from their childhood days,
when, in truth, he had been a malihini, though a very young
specimen. Since that time, in the course of various long stays,
he had earned the kamaaina distinction.

As for Ida Barton, young matrons of her own age (privily
wondering how she managed to keep her figure) met her
with arms around and hearty Hawaiian kisses. Grandmothers
must have her to tea and reminiscence in old gardens of
forgotten houses which the tourist never sees. Less than a
week after her arrival, the aged Queen Liliuokalani must
send for her and chide her for neglect. And old men, on cool
and balmy lanais, toothlessly maundered to her about
Grandpa Captain Wilton, of before their time but whose
wild and lusty deeds and pranks, told them by their fathers,
they remembered with gusto—Grandpa Captain Wilton, or
David Wilton, or "All Hands," as the Hawaiians of that remote day had affectionately renamed him—All Hands, ex-
Northwest trader, the godless, beachcombing, clipper-ship-
less, and shipwrecked skipper who had stood on the beach at
Kailua and welcomed the very first of the missionaries, off the
brig *Thaddeus,* in the year 1820, and who, not many years
later, made a scandalous runaway marriage with one of their
daughters, quieted down and served the Kamehamehas long
and conservatively as Minister of the Treasury and Chief of
the Customs, and acted as intercessor and mediator between
the missionaries on one side and the beachcombing crowd,
the trading crowd, and the Hawaiian chiefs on the variously
shifting other side.

Nor was Lee Barton neglected. In the midst of the dinners and lunches, the luaus and poi suppers, and swims and dances in aloha to both of them, his time and inclination were claimed by the crowd of lively youngsters of old Kohala days who had come to know that they possessed digestions and various other internal functions and who had settled down to somewhat of sedateness, who roistered less, and who played bridge much and went to baseball often. Also, similarly oriented, was the old poker crowd of Lee Barton's younger days, which crowd played for more consistent stakes and limits, while it drank mineral water and orange juice and timed the final round of "Jacks" never later than midnight.

Appeared, through all the rout of entertainment, Sonny Grandison, Hawaiian-born, Hawaiian-prominent, who, despite his youthful forty-one years, had declined the proffered governorship of the Territory. Also, he had ducked Ida Barton in the surf at Waikiki a quarter of a century before, and, still earlier, vacationing on his father's great Lakanaii cattle ranch, had hair-raisingly initiated her, and various other tender tots of from five to seven years of age, into his boys' band, "The Cannibal Head-Hunters" or "The Terrors of Lakanaii." Still further, his Grandpa Grandison and her Grandpa Wilton had been business and political comrades in the old days.

Educated at Harvard, he had become for a time a world-wandering scientist and social favorite. After serving in the Philippines, he had accompanied various expeditions through Malaysia, South America, and Africa in the post of official entomologist. At forty-one he still retained his traveling commission from the Smithsonian Institution, while his friends insisted that he knew more about sugar "bugs" than the expert entomologists employed by him and his fellow sugar planters in the Experiment Station. Bulking large at home, he was the best-known representative of Hawaii abroad. It was the axiom among traveled Hawaiian folk that wherever over the world they might mention they were from Hawaii, the invariable first question asked of them was: "And do you know Sonny Grandison?"

In brief, he was a wealthy man's son who had made good. His father's million he inherited he had increased to ten millions, at the same time keeping up his father's benefactions and endowments and overshadowing them with his own.

But there was still more to him. A ten years' widower, without issue, he was the most eligible and most pathetically sought-after marriageable man in all Hawaii. A clean-and-strong-featured brunet, tall, slenderly graceful, with the lean runners' stomach, always fit as a fiddle, a distinguished figure in any group, the graying of hair over his temples (in juxtaposition to his young-textured skin and bright, vital eyes) made him appear even more distinguished. Despite the social demands upon his time, and despite his many committee meetings and meetings of boards of directors and political conferences, he yet found time and space to captain the Lakanaii polo team to more than occasional victory, and on his own island of Lakanaii vied with the Baldwins of Maui in the breeding and importing of polo ponies.

Given a markedly strong and vital man and woman, when a second equally markedly strong and vital man enters the scene, the peril of a markedly strong and vital triangle of tragedy becomes imminent. Indeed, such a triangle of tragedy may be described, in the terminology of the flat-floor folk, as "super" and "impossible." Perhaps, since within himself originated the desire and the daring, it was Sonny Grandison who first was conscious of the situation, although he had to be quick to anticipate the sensing intuition of a woman like Ida Barton. At any rate, and undebatable, the last of the three to attain awareness was Lee Barton, who promptly laughed away what was impossible to laugh away.

His first awareness, he quickly saw, was so belated that half his hosts and hostesses were already aware. Casting back, he realized that for some time any affair to which he and his wife were invited found Sonny Grandison likewise invited.

Wherever the two had been, the three had been. To Kahuku
or to Haleiwa, to Ahuimanu, or to Kaneohe for the coral
gardens, or to Koko Head for a picnicking and a swimming,
somehow it invariable happened that Ida rode in Sonny's
car or that both rode in somebody's car. Dances, luaus, dinners, and outings were all one; the three of them were there.

Having become aware, Lee Barton could not fail to register Ida's note of happiness ever rising when in the same
company with Sonny Grandison, and her willingness to ride
in the same cars with him, to dance with him, or to sit out
dances with him. Most convincing of all was Sonny Grandison himself. Forty-one, strong, experienced, his face could no
more conceal what he felt than could be concealed a lad of
twenty's ordinary lad's love. Despite the control and restraint
of forty years he could no more mask his soul with his face
than could Lee Barton, of equal years, fail to read that soul
through so transparent a face. And often, to other women,
talking, when the topic of Sonny came up, Lee Barton heard
Ida express her fondness for Sonny, or her almost too-elo-
quent appreciation of his polo playing, his work in the world,
and his general all-rightness of achievement.

About Sonny's state of mind and heart, Lee had no doubts.
It was patent enough for the world to read. But how about
Ida, his own dozen years' wife of a glorious love match? He
knew that woman, ever the mysterious sex, was capable any
time of unguessed mystery. Did her frank comradeliness with
Grandison token merely frank comradeliness and childhood
contacts continued and recrudesced into adult years? Or did
it hide, in woman's subtler and more secretive ways, a heat
of heart and return of feeling that might even outbalance
what Sonny's face advertised?

Lee Barton was not happy. A dozen years of utmost and
postnuptial possession of his wife had proved to him, so far
as he was concerned, that she was his one woman in the
world, and that the woman was unborn, much less un-
glimpsed, who could for a moment compete with her in his
heart, his soul, and his brain. Impossible of existence was

the woman who could lure him away from her, much less overbid her in the myriad, continual satisfactions she rendered him.

Was this, then, he asked himself, the dreaded contingency of all fond Benedicts, to be her first "affair"? He tormented himself with the ever iterant query, and, to the astonishment of the reformed Kahala poker crowd of wise and middle-aged youngsters as well as to the reward of the keen scrutiny of the dinner-giving and dinner-attending women, he began to drink King William instead of orange juice, to bully up the poker limit, to drive of nights his own car more than rather recklessly over the Pali and Diamond Head roads, and, ere dinner or lunch or after, to take more than an average man's due of Old Fashioned cocktails and Scotch highs.

All the years of their marriage, she had been ever complaisant toward him in his card playing. This complaisance, to him, had become habitual. But now that doubt had arisen, it seemed to him that he noted an eagerness in her countenancing of his poker parties. Another point he could not avoid noting was that Sonny Grandison was missed by the poker and bridge crowds. He seemed to be too busy. Now where was Sonny, while he, Lee Barton, was playing? Surely not always at committee and boards of directors' meetings. Lee Barton made sure of this. He easily learned that at such times Sonny was more than usually wherever Ida chanced to be—at dances, or dinners, or moonlight swimming parties, or, the very afternoon he had flatly pleaded rush of affairs as an excuse not to join Lee and Langhorne Jones and Jack Holstein in a bridge battle at the Pacific Club—that afternoon he had played bridge at Dora Niles' home with three women, one of whom was Ida.

Returning, once, from an afternoon's inspection of the great dry-dock building at Pearl Harbor, Lee Barton, driving his machine against time in order to have time to dress for dinner, passed Sonny's car; and Sonny's one passenger, whom he was taking home, was Ida. One night, a week later, during which interval he had played no cards, he came home

at eleven from a stag dinner at the University Club, just preceding Ida's return from the Alstone poi supper and dance.
And Sonny had driven her home. Major Franklin and his
wife had first been dropped off by them, they mentioned, at
Fort Shafter, on the other side of town and miles away from
the beach.

Lee Barton, after all, mere human man, as a human man
unfailingly meeting Sonny in all friendliness, suffered poign-
antly in secret. Not even Ida dreamed that he suffered; and
she went her merry, careless, laughing way, secure in her own
heart, although a trifle perplexed at her husband's increase
in number of pre-dinner cocktails.

Apparently, as always, she had access to almost all of him;
but now she did not have access to his unguessable torment
nor to the long parallel columns of mental bookkeeping
running their total balances from moment to moment, day
and night, in his brain. In one column were her undoubtable
spontaneous expressions of her usual love and care for him,
her many acts of comfort-serving and of advice-asking and
advice-obeying. In another column, in which the items increasingly were entered, were her expressions and acts which
he could not but classify as dubious. Were they what they
seemed? Or were they of duplicity compounded, whether deliberately or unconsciously? The third column, longest of all,
totaling most in human heart appraisements, was filled with
items relating directly or indirectly to her and Sonny Grandison. Lee Barton did not deliberately do this bookkeeping. He
could not help it. He would have liked to avoid it. But in his
fairly ordered mind the items of entry, of themselves and
quite beyond will on his part, took their places automatically
in their respective columns.

In his distortion of vision, magnifying apparently trivial
detail which half the time he felt he magnified, he had re-
course to MacIlwaine, to whom he had once rendered a very
considerable service. MacIlwaine was chief of detectives. "Is
Sonny Grandison a womaning man?" Barton had demanded.
MacIlwaine had said nothing. "Then he is a womaning man,"

had been Barton's declaration. And still the chief of detectives had said nothing.

Briefly afterward, ere he destroyed it as so much dynamite, Lee Barton went over the written report. Not bad, not really bad, was the summarization; but not too good after the death of his wife ten years before. That had been a love match almost notorious in Honolulu society because of the completeness of infatuation, not only before, but after marriage, and up to her tragic death when her horse fell with her a thousand feet off Nahiku Trail. And not for a long time afterward, MacIlwaine stated, had Grandison been guilty of interest in any woman. And whatever it was, it had been unvaryingly decent. Never a hint of gossip or scandal; and the entire community had come to accept that he was a one-woman man and would never marry again. What small affairs MacIlwaine had jotted down he insisted that Sonny Grandison did not dream were known by another person outside the principals themselves.

Barton glanced hurriedly, almost shamedly, at the several names and incidents, and knew surprise ere he committed the document to the flames. At any rate, Sonny had been most discreet. As he stared at the ashes, Barton pondered how much of his own younger life, from his bachelor days, resided in old MacIlwaine's keeping. Next, Barton found himself blushing, to himself, at himself. If MacIlwaine knew so much of the private lives of community figures, then had not he, her husband and protector and shielder, planted in MacIlwaine's brain a suspicion of Ida?

"Anything on your mind?" Lee asked his wife that evening, as he stood holding her wrap while she put the last touches to her dressing.

This was in line with their old and successful compact of frankness, and he wondered, while he waited her answer, why he had refrained so long from asking her.

"No," she smiled. "Nothing particular. . . . Afterward . . . perhaps. . . ."

She became absorbed in gazing at herself in the mirror
while she dabbed some powder on her nose and dabbed it
off again.

"You know my way, Lee," she added after the pause. "It
takes me time to gather things together in my own way—
when there are things to gather; but when I do, you always
get them. And often there's nothing in them, after all, I find,
and so you are saved the nuisance of them."

She held out her arms for him to place the wrap about her
—her valiant little arms that were so wise and steellike in
battling with the breakers, and that yet were such just mere
woman's arms, round and warm and white, delicious as a
woman's arms should be, with the canny muscles, masking
under soft roundness of contour and fine, smooth skin, capable of being flexed at will by the will of her.

He pondered her, with a grievous hurt and yearning of appreciation—so delicate she seemed, so porcelain fragile that a
strong man could snap her in the crook of his arm.

"We must hurry!" she cried, as he lingered in the adjust-
ment of the flimsy wrap over her flimsy prettiness of gown.
"We'll be late. And if it showers up Nuuanu, putting the cur-
tains up will make us miss the second dance."

He made a note to observe with whom she danced that
second dance, as she preceded him across the room to the
door; while at the same time he pleasured his eye in what he
had so often named to himself as the spirit-proud, flesh-proud
walk of her.

"You don't feel I'm neglecting you in my too-much poker?"
he tried again, by indirection.

"Mercy, no! You know I just love you to have your card
orgies. They're tonic for you. And you're so much nicer
about them, so much more middle-aged. Why, it's almost
years since you sat up later than one."

It did not shower up Nuuanu, and every overhead star was
out in a clear trade-wind sky. In time at the Inchkeeps for
the second dance, Lee Barton observed that his wife danced
it with Grandison—which, of itself, was nothing unusual, but

which became immediately a registered item in Barton's mental books.

An hour later, depressed and restless, declining to make one of a bridge foursome in the library and escaping from a few young matrons, he strolled out into the generous grounds. Across the lawn, at the far edge, he came upon the hedge of night-blooming cereus. To each flower, opening after dark and fading, wilting, perishing with the dawn, this was its one night of life. The great, cream-white blooms, a foot in diameter and more, lilylike and waxlike, white beacons of attraction in the dark, penetrating and seducing the night with their perfume, were busy and beautiful with their brief glory of living.

But the way along the hedge was populous with humans, two by two, male and female, stealing out between the dances or strolling the dances out while they talked in low, soft voices and gazed upon the wonder of flower love. From the lanai drifted the love-caressing strains of "Hanalei" sung by the singing boys. Vaguely Lee Barton remembered—perhaps it was from some Maupassant story—the abbé, obsessed by the theory that behind all things were the purposes of God and perplexed so to interpret the night, who discovered at the last that the night was ordained for love.

The unanimity of the night, as betrayed by flowers and humans, was a hurt to Barton. He circled back toward the house along a winding path that skirted within the edge of shadow of the monkeypods and algaroba trees. In the obscurity, where his path curved away into the open again, he looked across a space of a few feet where, on another path in the shadow, stood a pair in each other's arms. The impassioned, low tones of the man had caught his ear and drawn his eyes, and at the moment of his glance, aware of his presence, the voice ceased and the two remained immobile, furtive, in each other's arms.

He continued his walk, sombered by the thought that in the gloom of the trees was the next progression from the openness of the sky over those who strolled the night-flower hedge. Oh, he knew the game when of old no shadow was too deep, no ruse of concealment too furtive, to veil a love moment. After all, humans were like flowers, he meditated. Under the radiance from the lighted lanai, ere entering the irritating movement of life again to which he belonged, he paused to stare, scarcely seeing, at a flaunt of display of scarlet double-hibiscus blooms. And abruptly all that he was suffering, all that he had just observed, from the night-blooming hedge and the two-by-two love-murmuring humans to the pair like thieves in each other's arms, crystallized into a parable of life enunciated by the day-blooming hibiscus upon which he gazed, now at the end of its day. Bursting into its bloom after the dawn, snow-white, warming to pink under the hours of sun and quickening to scarlet with the dark from which its beauty and its being would never emerge, it seemed to him that it epitomized man's life and passion.

What further connotations he might have drawn he was never to know; for from behind, in the direction of the algarobas and monkeypods, came Ida's unmistakably serene and merry laugh. He did not look, being too afraid of what he knew he would see, but retreated hastily, almost stumbling, up the steps to the lanai. Despite that he knew what he was to see, when he did turn his head and beheld his wife and Sonny, the pair he had seen thieving in the dark, he went suddenly dizzy and paused, supporting himself with a hand against a pillar and smiling vacuously at the grouped singing boys who were pulsing the sensuous night into richer sensuousness with their "*honi ka ua wikiwiki*" refrain.

The next moment he had wet his lips with his tongue, controlled his face and flesh, and was bantering with Mrs. Inchkeep. But he could not waste time, or he would have to encounter the pair he could hear coming up the steps behind him.

"I feel as if I had just crossed the Great Thirst," he told his hostess, "and that nothing less than a highball will preserve me."

She smiled permission and nodded toward the smoking

lanai, where they found him talking sugar politics with the oldsters when the dance began to break up.

Quite a party of half a dozen machines were starting for Waikiki, and he found himself billeted to drive the Leslies and Burnstons home, though he did not fail to note that Ida sat in the driver's seat with Sonny in Sonny's car. Thus, she was home ahead of him and brushing her hair when he arrived. The parting of bed-going was usual, on the face of it, although he was most rigid in his successful effort for casualness as he remembered whose lips had pressed hers last before his.

Was, then, woman the utterly unmoral creature as depicted by the German pessimists? he asked himself, as he tossed under his reading lamp unable to sleep or read. At the end of an hour he was out of bed and into his medicine case, and took a heavy sleeping-powder. An hour later, afraid of his thoughts and the prospect of a sleepless night, he took another powder. At one-hour intervals he twice repeated the dosage. But so slow was the action of the drug that dawn had broken ere his eyes closed.

At seven he was awake again, dry-mouthed, feeling stupid and drowsy, yet incapable of dozing off for more than several minutes at a time. He abandoned the idea of sleep, ate breakfast in bed, and devoted himself to the morning papers and the magazines. But the drug effect held, and he continued briefly to doze through his eating and reading. It was the same when he showered and dressed, and, though the drug had brought him little forgetfulness during the night, he felt grateful for the dreaming lethargy with which it possessed him through the morning.

It was when his wife arose, her serene and usual self, and came in to him smiling and roguish, delectable in her kimono, that the whim madness of the opium in his system seized upon him. When she had clearly and simply shown that she had nothing to tell him under their ancient compact of frankness, he began building his opium lie. Asked how he had slept, he replied:

"Miserably. Twice I was routed wide awake with cramps in my feet. I was almost too afraid to sleep again. But they didn't come back, though my feet are sorer than blazes."

"Last year you had them," she reminded him.

"Maybe it's going to become a seasonal affliction," he smiled. "They're not serious, but they're horrible to wake up to. They won't come again till tonight, if they come at all, but in the meantime I feel as if I had been bastinadoed."

In the afternoon of the same day, Lee and Ida Barton made their shallow dive from the Outrigger beach, and went on, at a steady stroke, past the diving stage to the big water beyond the Kanaka surf. So quiet was the sea that when, after a couple of hours, they turned and lazily started shoreward through the Kanaka surf they had it all to themselves. The breakers were not large enough to be exciting, and the last languid surfboarders and canoeists had gone in to shore. Suddenly, Lee turned over on his back.

"What is it?" Ida called from twenty feet away.

"My foot—cramp," he answered calmly, though the words were twisted out through clenched jaws of control.

The opium still had its dreamy way with him, and he was without excitement. He watched her swimming toward him with so steady and unperturbed a stroke that he admired her own self-control, although at the same time doubt stabbed him with the thought that it was because she cared so little for him, or, rather, so much immediately more for Grandison.

"Which foot?" she asked, as she dropped her legs down and began treading water beside him.

"The left one—ouch! Now it's both of them."

He doubled his knees, as if involuntarily, raised his head and chest forward out of the water, and sank out of sight in the down wash of a scarcely cresting breaker. Under no more than a brief several seconds, he emerged spluttering and stretched out on his back again.

Almost he grinned, although he managed to turn the grin into a pain grimace, for his simulated cramp had become real. At least in one foot it had, and the muscles convulsed painfully.

"The right is the worst," he muttered, as she evinced her intention of laying hands on his cramp and rubbing it out. "But you'd better keep away. I've had cramps before, and I know I'm liable to grab you if these get any worse."

Instead, she laid her hands on the hard-knotted muscles and began to rub and press and bend.

"Please," he gritted through his teeth. "You must keep away. Just let me lie out here—I'll bend the ankle and toe joints in the opposite ways and make it pass. I've done it before and know how to work it."

She released him, remaining close beside him and easily treading water, her eyes upon his face to judge the progress of his own attempt at remedy. But Lee Barton deliberately bent joints and tensed muscles in the directions that would increase the cramp. In his bout the preceding year with the affliction, he had learned, lying in bed and reading when seized, to relax and bend the cramps away without even disturbing his reading. But now he did the thing in reverse, intensifying the cramp, and, to his startled delight, causing it to leap into his right calf. He cried out with anguish, apparently lost control of himself, attempted to sit up, and was washed under by the next wave.

He came up, spluttered, spread-eagled on the surface, and had his knotted calf gripped by the strong fingers of both Ida's small hands.

"It's all right," she said, while she worked. "No cramp like this lasts very long."

"I didn't know they could be so savage," he groaned. "If only it doesn't go higher! They make one feel so helpless."

He gripped the biceps of both her arms in a sudden spasm, attempting to climb out upon her as a drowning man might try to climb out on an oar and sinking her down under him. In the struggle under water, before he permitted her to wrench clear, her rubber cap was torn off and her hairpins pulled out, so that she came up gasping for air and half blinded by her wet-clinging hair. Also, he was certain he had surprised her into taking in a quantity of water.

"Keep away!" he warned, as he spread-eagled with acted desperateness.

But her fingers were deep into the honest pain wrack of his calf, and in her he could observe no reluctance of fear.

"It's creeping up," he grunted through tight teeth, the grunt itself a half-controlled groan.

He stiffened his whole right leg, as with another spasm, hurting his real minor cramps but flexing the muscles of his upper leg into the seeming hardness of cramp.

The drug still worked in his brain, so that he could play-act cruelly while at the same time he appraised and appreciated her stress of control and will that showed in her drawn face, and the terror of death in her eyes, with beyond it and behind it, in her eyes and through her eyes, the something more of the spirit of courage and higher thought and resolution.

Still further, she did not enunciate so cheap a surrender as, "I'll die with you." Instead, provoking his admiration, she did say quietly: "Relax. Sink until only your lips are out. I'll support your head. There must be a limit to cramp. No man ever died of cramp on land. Then in the water no strong swimmer should die of cramp. It's bound to reach its worst and pass. We're both strong swimmers and cool-headed—"

He distorted his face and deliberately dragged her under. But when they emerged, still beside him, supporting his head as she continued to tread water, she was saying:

"Relax. Take it easy. I'll hold your head up. Endure it. Live through it. Don't fight it. Make yourself slack—slack in your mind; and your body will slack. Yield. Remember how you taught me to yield to the undertow."

An unusually large breaker for so mild a surf curled over-head, and he climbed out on her again sinking both of them under as the wave crest overfell and smashed down.

"Forgive me," he mumbled through pain-clenched teeth,

as they drew in their first air again. "And leave me." He spoke jerkily, with pain-filled pauses between his sentences. "There is no need for both of us to drown. I've got to go. It will be in my stomach at any moment, and then I'll drag you under and be unable to let go of you. Please, please, dear, keep away. One of us is enough. You've plenty to live for."

She looked at him in reproach so deep that the last vestige of the terror of death was gone from her eyes. It was as if she had said, and more than if she had said: "I have only you to live for."

Then Sonny did not count with her as much as he did!— was Barton's exultant conclusion. But he remembered her in Sonny's arms under the monkeypods and determined on further cruelty. Besides, it was the lingering potion in him that suggested this cruelty. Since he had undertaken this acid test, urged the poppy juice, then let it be a real acid test.

He doubled up and went down, emerged, and apparently strove frantically to stretch out in the floating position. And she did not keep away from him.

"It's too much!" he groaned, almost screamed. "I'm losing my grip. I've got to go. You can't save me. Keep away and save yourself."

But she was to him, striving to float his mouth clear of the salt, saying: "It's all right. It's all right. The worst is right now. Just endure it a minute more and it will begin to ease."

He screamed out, doubled, seized her, and took her down with him. And he nearly did drown her, so well did he play-act his own drowning. But never did she lose her head nor succumb to the fear of death so dreadfully imminent. Always, when she got her head out, she strove to support him while she panted and gasped encouragement in terms of: "Relax . . . Relax . . . Slack . . . Slack out . . . At any time . . . now . . . you'll pass . . . the worst . . . No matter how much it hurts . . . it will pass . . . You're easier now . . . aren't you?"

And then he would put her down again, going from bad to worse in his ill-treatment of her; making her swallow pints of salt water, secure in the knowledge that it would not definitely hurt her. Sometimes they came up for brief emergencies, for gasping seconds in the sunshine on the surface, and then were under again, dragged under by him, rolled and tumbled under by the curling breakers.

Although she struggled and tore herself from his grips, in the times he permitted her freedom she did not attempt to swim away from him, but, with fading strength and reeling consciousness, invariably came to him to try to save him. When it was enough, in his judgment, and more than enough, he grew quieter, left her released, and stretched out on the surface.

"A-a-h," he sighed long, almost luxuriously, and spoke with pauses for breath. "It is passing. It seems like heaven. My dear, I'm water-logged, yet the mere absence of that frightful agony makes my present state sheerest bliss."

She tried to gasp a reply, but could not.

"I'm all right," he assured her. "Let us float and rest up. Stretch out, yourself, and get your wind back."

And for half an hour, side by side, on their backs, they floated in the fairly placid Kanaka surf. Ida Barton was the first to announce recovery by speaking first.

"And how do you feel now, man of mine?" she asked.

"I feel as if I'd been run over by a steam-roller," he replied. "And you, poor darling?"

"I feel I'm the happiest woman in the world. I'm so happy I could almost cry, but I'm too happy even for that. You had me horribly frightened for a time. I thought I was going to lose you."

Lee Barton's heart pounded up. Never a mention of losing herself. This, then, was love, and all real love, proved true— the great love that forgot self in the loved one.

"And I'm the proudest man in the world," he told her; "because my wife is the bravest woman in the world."

"Brave!" she repudiated. "I love you. I never knew how much, how really much, I loved you as when I was losing you. And now let's work for shore. I want you all alone with me, your arms around me, while I tell you all you are to me and shall always be to me."

In another half hour, swimming strong and steadily, they landed on the beach and walked up the hard, wet sand among the sand loafers and sun baskers.

"What were the two of you doing out there?" queried one of the Outrigger captains. "Cutting up?"

"Cutting up," Ida Barton answered with a smile.

"We're the village cut-ups, you know," was Lee Barton's assurance.

That evening, the evening's engagement canceled, found the two, in a big chair, in each other's arms.

"Sonny sails tomorrow noon," she announced casually and irrelevant to anything in the conversation. "He's going out to the Malay Coast to inspect what's been done with that lumber and rubber company of his.

"First I've heard of his leaving us," Lee managed to say, despite his surprise.

"I was the first to hear of it," she added. "He told me only last night."

"At the dance?"

She nodded.

"Rather sudden, wasn't it?"

"Very sudden." Ida withdrew herself from her husband's arms and sat up. "And I want to talk to you about Sonny. I've never had a real secret from you before. I didn't intend ever to tell you. But it came to me today, out in the Kanaka surf, that if we passed out it would be something left behind us unsaid."

She paused, and Lee, half anticipating what was coming, did nothing to help her, save to girdle and press her hand in his.

"Sonny rather lost his—his head over me," she faltered. "Of course, you must have noticed it. And—and last night he wanted me to run away with him. Which isn't my confession at all—"

Still Lee Barton waited.

"My confession," she resumed, "is that I wasn't the least bit angry with him—only sorrowful and regretful. My confession is that I rather slightly, only rather more than slightly, lost my own head. That was why I was kind and gentle to him last night. I am no fool. I knew it was due. And—oh, I know, I'm just a feeble female of vanity compounded—I was proud to have such a man swept off his feet by me, by little me. I encouraged him. I have no excuse. Last night would not have happened had I not encouraged him. And I, and not he, was the sinner last night when he asked me. And I told him no, impossible, as you should know why without my repeating it to you. And I was maternal to him, very much maternal. I let him take me in his arms, let myself rest against him, and, for the first time because it was to be the forever last time, let him kiss me and let myself kiss him. You—I know you understand—it was his renunciation. And I didn't love Sonny. I don't love him. I have loved you, and you only, all the time."

She waited, and felt her husband's arm pass around her shoulder and under her own arm, and yielded to his drawing down of her to him.

"You did have me worried more than a bit," he admitted, "until I was afraid I was going to lose you. And—" He broke off in patent embarrassment, then gripped the idea courageously. "Oh, well, you know you're my one woman. Enough said."

She fumbled the match box from his pocket and struck a match to enable him to light his long-extinct cigar.

"Well," he said, as the smoke curled about them, "knowing you as *I* know you, the *all* of you, all I can say is that I'm sorry for Sonny for what he's missed—awfully sorry for him, but equally glad for me. And—one other thing: five years hence I've something to tell you, something rich, something ridiculously rich and all about me and the foolishness of me over you. Five years. Is it a date?"

"I shall keep it if it is fifty years," she sighed, as she nestled closer to him.

Other Writings

A ROYAL SPORT:
SURFING AT WAIKIKI

THAT IS WHAT IT IS, A ROYAL SPORT FOR THE NATURAL KINGS OF earth. The grass grows right down to the water at Waikiki Beach, and within fifty feet of the everlasting sea. The trees also grow down to the salty edge of things, and one sits in their shade and looks seaward at a majestic surf thundering in on the beach to one's very feet. Half a mile out, where is the reef, the white-headed combers thrust suddenly skyward out of the placid turquoise-blue and come rolling in to shore. One after another they come, a mile long, with smoking crests, the white battalions of the infinite army of the sea. And one sits and listens to the perpetual roar, and watches the unending procession, and feels tiny and fragile before this tremendous force expressing itself in fury and foam and sound. Indeed, one feels microscopically small, and the thought that one may wrestle with this sea raises in one's imagination a thrill of apprehension, almost of fear. Why, they are a mile long, these bull-mouthed monsters, and they weigh a thousand tons, and they charge in to shore faster than a man can run. What chance? No chance at all, is the verdict of the shrinking ego; and one sits, and looks and listens, and thinks the grass and the shade are a pretty good place in which to be.

And suddenly, out there where a big smoker lifts skyward, rising like a sea-god from out of the welter of spume and churning white, on the giddy, toppling, overhanging and downfalling, precarious crest appears the dark head of a man. Swiftly he rises through the rushing white. His black shoulders, his chest, his loins, his limbs—all is abruptly projected on one's vision. Where but the moment before was only the wide desolation and invincible roar, is now a man, erect, full-statured, not struggling frantically in that wild movement, not buried and crushed and buffeted by those mighty monsters, but standing above them all, calm and superb, poised on the giddy summit, his feet buried in the churning foam, the salt smoke rising to his knees, and all the rest of him in the free air and flashing sunlight, and he is flying through the air, flying forward, flying fast as the surge on which he stands. He is a Mercury—a brown Mercury. His heels are winged, and in them is the swiftness of the sea. In truth, from out of the sea he has leaped upon the back of the sea, and he is riding the sea that roars and bellows and cannot shake him from its back. But no frantic outreaching and balancing is his. He is impassive, motionless as a statue carved suddenly by some miracle out of the sea's depth from which he rose. And straight on toward shore he flies on his winged heels and the white crest of the breaker. There is a wild burst of foam, a long tumultuous rushing sound as the breaker falls futile and spent on the beach at your feet; and there, at your feet, steps calmly ashore a Kanaka, burnt golden and brown by the tropic sun. Several minutes ago he was a speck a quarter of a mile away. He has "bitted the bull-mouthed breaker" and ridden it in, and the pride in the feat shows in the carriage of his magnificent body as he glances for a moment carelessly at you who sit in the shade of the shore. He is a Kanaka—and more, he is a man, a member of the kingly species that has mastered matter and the brutes and lorded it over creation.

And one sits and thinks of Tristram's last wrestle with the sea on that fatal morning; and one thinks further to the fact that that Kanaka has done what Tristram never did, and that he knows a joy of the sea that Tristram never knew. And still further one thinks. It is all very well, sitting here in cool shade of the beach, but you are a man, one of the kingly species, and what that Kanaka can do, you can do yourself. Go to. Strip off your clothes that are a nuisance in this mellow clime. Get in and wrestle with the sea; wing your heels with the skill and power that reside in you; bit the sea's breakers, master them, and ride upon their backs as a king should.

And that is how it came about that I tackled surf-riding. And now that I have tackled it, more than ever do I hold it to be a royal sport. But first let me explain the physics of it. A wave is a communicated agitation. The water that composes the body of a wave does not move. If it did, when a stone is thrown into a pond and the ripples spread away in an ever widening circle, there would appear at the center an ever increasing hole. No, the water that composes the body of a wave is stationary. Thus, you may watch a particular portion of the ocean's surface and you will see the same water rise and fall a thousand times to the agitation communicated by a thousand successive waves. Now imagine this communicated agitation moving shoreward. As the bottom shoals, the lower portion of the wave strikes land first and is stopped. But water is fluid, and the upper portion has not struck anything, wherefore it keeps on communicating its agitation, keeps on going. And when the top of the wave keeps on going, while the botttom of it lags behind, something is bound to happen. The bottom of the wave drops out from under and the top of the wave falls over, forward, and down, curling and cresting and roaring as it does so. It is the bottom of a wave striking against the top of the land that is the cause of all surfs.

But the transformation from a smooth undulation to a breaker is not abrupt except where the bottom shoals abruptly. Say the bottom shoals gradually for from quarter of a mile to a mile, then an equal distance will be occupied by the transformation. Such a bottom is that off the beach of Waikiki, and it produces a splendid surf-riding surf. One leaps upon the back of a breaker just as it begins to break, and stays on it as it continues to break all the way in to shore.

And now to the particular physics of surf-riding. Get out on a flat board, six feet long, two feet wide, and roughly oval in shape. Lie down upon it like a small boy on a coaster and paddle with your hands out to deep water, where the waves begin to crest. Lie out there quietly on the board. Sea after sea breaks before, behind, and under and over you, and rushes in to shore, leaving you behind. When a wave crests, it gets steeper. Imagine yourself, on your board, on the face of that steep slope. If it stood still, you would slide down just as a boy slides down a hill on his coaster. "But," you object, "the wave doesn't stand still." Very true, but the water composing the wave stands still, and there you have the secret. If ever you start sliding down the face of that wave, you'll keep on sliding and you'll never reach the bottom. Please don't laugh. The face of that wave may be only six feet, yet you can slide down it a quarter of a mile, or half a mile, and not reach the bottom. For, see, since a wave is only a communicated agitation or impetus, and since the water that composes a wave is changing every instant, new water is rising into the wave as fast as the wave travels. You slide down this new water, and yet remain in your old position on the wave, sliding down the still newer water that is rising and forming the wave. You slide precisely as fast as the wave travels. If it travels fifteen miles an hour, you slide fifteen miles an hour. Between you and shore stretches a quarter of mile of water. As the wave travels, this water obligingly heaps itself into the wave, gravity does the rest, and down you go, sliding the whole length of it. If you still cherish the notion, while sliding, that the water is moving with you, thrust your arms into it and attempt to paddle; you will find that you have to be remarkably quick to get a stroke, for that water is dropping astern just as fast as you are rushing ahead.

And now for another phase of the physics of surf-riding. All rules have their exceptions. It is true that the water in a wave does not travel forward. But there is what may be called the send of the sea. The water in the overtoppling crest does move forward, as you will speedily realize if you are slapped in the face by it, or if you are caught under it and are pounded by one mighty blow down under the surface panting and gasping for half a minute. The water in the top of a wave rests upon the water in the bottom of the wave. But when the bottom of the wave strikes the land, it stops, while the top goes on. It no longer has the bottom of the wave to hold it up. Where was solid water beneath it, is now air, and for the first time it feels the grip of gravity, and down it falls, at the same time being torn asunder from the lagging bottom of the wave and flung forward. And it is because of this that riding a surfboard is something more than a mere placid sliding down a hill. In truth, one is caught up and hurled shoreward as by some Titan's hand.

I deserted the cool shade, put on a swimming suit, and got hold of a surfboard. It was too small a board. But I didn't know, and nobody told me. I joined some little Kanaka boys in shallow water, where the breakers were well spent and small—a regular kindergarten school. I watched the little Kanaka boys. When a likely-looking breaker came along, they flopped upon their stomachs on their boards, kicked like mad with their feet, and rode the breaker in to the beach. I tried to emulate them. I watched them, tried to do everything that they did, and failed utterly. The breaker swept past, and I was not on it. I tried again and again. I kicked twice as madly as they did, and failed. Half a dozen would be around. We would all leap on our boards in front of a good breaker. Away our feet would churn like the stern-wheels of river steamboats, and away the little rascals would scoot while I remained in disgrace behind.

I tried for a solid hour, and not one wave could I persuade to boost me shoreward. And then arrived a friend, Alexander Hume Ford, a globe-trotter by profession, bent ever on the pursuit of sensation. And he had found it at Waikiki. Heading for Australia, he had stopped off for a week to find out if there were any thrills in surf-riding, and he had become wedded to it. He had been at it every day for a month and

could not yet see any symptoms of the fascination lessening
on him. He spoke with authority.

"Get off that board," he said. "Chuck it away at once. Look
at the way you're trying to ride it. If ever the nose of that
board hits bottom, you'll be disemboweled. Here, take my
board. It's a man's size."

I am always humble when confronted by knowledge. Ford
knew. He showed me how properly to mount his board. Then
he waited for a good breaker, gave me a shove at the right
moment, and started me in. Ah, delicious moment when
I felt that breaker grip and fling me! On I dashed, a hundred
and fifty feet, and subsided with the breaker on the sand.
From that moment I was lost. I waded back to Ford with his
board. It was a large one, several inches thick, and weighed
all of seventy-five pounds. He gave me advice, much of it. He
had had no one to teach him, and all that he had laboriously
learned in several weeks he communicated to me in half an
hour. I really learned by proxy. And inside of half an hour
I was able to start myself and ride in. I did it time after time,
and Ford applauded and advised. For instance, he told me
to get just so far forward on the board and no farther. But
I must have got some farther, for as I came charging in to
land, that miserable board poked its nose down to bottom,
stopped abruptly, and turned a somersault, at the same time
violently severing our relations. I was tossed through the air
like a chip and buried ignominiously under the downfalling
breaker. And I realized that if it hadn't been for Ford, I'd
have been disemboweled. That particular risk is part of the
sport, Ford says. Maybe he'll have it happen to him before
he leaves Waikiki, and then, I feel confident, his yearning
for sensation will be satisfied for a time.

When all is said and done, it is my steadfast belief that
homicide is worse than suicide, especially if, in the former
case, it is a woman. Ford saved me from being a homicide.
"Imagine your legs are a rudder," he said. "Hold them close
together, and steer with them." A few minutes later I came
charging in on a comber. As I neared the beach, there, in

the water, up to her waist, dead in front of me, appeared a woman. How was I to stop that comber on whose back I was? It looked like a dead woman. The board weighed seventy-five pounds, I weighed a hundred and sixty-five. The added weight had a velocity of fifteen miles per hour. The board and I constituted a projectile. I leave it to the physicists to figure out the force of the impact upon that poor, tender woman. And then I remembered my guardian angel, Ford. "Steer with your legs!" rang through my brain. I steered with my legs, I steered sharply, abruptly, with all my legs and with all my might. The board sheered around broadside on the crest. Many things happened simultaneously. The wave gave me a passing buffet, a light tap as the taps of waves go, but a tap sufficient to knock me off the board and smash me down through the rushing water to bottom, with which I came in violent collision and upon which I was rolled over and over. I got my head out for a breath of air and then gained my feet. There stood the woman before me. I felt like a hero. I had saved her life. And she laughed at me. It was not hysteria. She had never dreamed of her danger. Anyway, I solaced myself, it was not I but Ford that saved her, and I didn't have to feel like a hero. And besides, that leg-steering was great. In a few minutes more of practice I was able to thread my way in and out past several bathers and to remain on top my breaker instead of going under it.

"Tomorrow," Ford said, "I am going to take you out into the blue water."

I looked seaward where he pointed, and saw the great smoking combers that made the breakers I had been riding look like ripples. I don't know what I might have said had I not recollected just then that I was one of a kingly species. So all that I did say was, "All right, I'll tackle them tomorrow."

The water that rolls in on Waikiki Beach is just the same as the water that laves the shores of all the Hawaiian Islands; and in ways, especially from the swimmer's standpoint, it is wonderful water. It is cool enough to be comfortable, while it is warm enough to permit a swimmer to stay in all day without experiencing a chill. Under the sun or the stars, at high noon or at midnight, in midwinter or in midsummer, it does not matter when, it is always the same temperature— not too warm, not too cold, just right. It is wonderful water, salt as old ocean itself, pure and crystal-clear. When the nature of the water is considered, it is not so remarkable after all that the Kanakas are one of the most expert of swimming races.

So it was, next morning, when Ford came along, that I plunged into the wonderful water for a swim of indeterminate length. Astride of our surfboards, or, rather, flat down upon them on our stomachs, we paddled out through the kindergarten where the little Kanaka boys were at play. Soon we were out in deep water where the big smokers came roaring in. The mere struggle with them, facing them and paddling seaward over them and through them, was sport enough in itself. One had to have his wits about him, for it was a battle in which mighty blows were struck, on one side, and in which cunning was used on the other side—a struggle between insensate force and intelligence. I soon learned a bit. When a breaker curled over my head, for a swift instant I could see the light of day through its emerald body; then down would go my head, and I would clutch the board with all my strength. Then would come the blow, and to the onlooker on shore I would be blotted out. In reality the board and I have passed through the crest and emerged in the respite of the other side. I should not recommend those smashing blows to an invalid or delicate person. There is weight behind them, and the impact of the driven water is like a sandblast. Sometimes one passes through half a dozen combers in quick succession, and it is just about that time that he is liable to discover new merits in the stable land and new reasons for being on shore.

Out there in the midst of such a succession of big smoky ones, a third man was added to our party, one Freeth. Shaking the water from my eyes as I emerged from one wave and peered ahead to see what the next one looked like, I saw him tearing in on the back of it, standing upright on his board, carelessly poised, a young god bronzed with sunburn. We went through the wave on the back of which he rode. Ford called to him. He turned an airspring from his wave, rescued his board from its maw, paddled over to us and joined Ford in showing me things. One thing in particular I learned from Freeth, namely, how to encounter the occasional breaker of exceptional size that rolled in. Such breakers were really ferocious, and it was unsafe to meet them on top of the board. But Freeth showed me, so that whenever I saw one of that caliber rolling down on me, I slid off the rear end of the board and dropped down beneath the surface, my arms over my head and holding the board. Thus, if the wave ripped the board out of my hands and tried to strike me with it (a common trick of such waves), there would be a cushion of water a foot or more in depth, between my head and the blow. When the wave passed, I climbed upon the board and paddled on. Many men have been terribly injured, I learn, by being struck by their boards.

The whole method of surf-riding and surf-fighting, I learned, is one of nonresistance. Dodge the blow that is struck at you. Dive through the wave that is trying to slap you in the face. Sink down, feet first, deep under the surface, and let the big smoker that is trying to smash you go by far overhead. Never be rigid. Relax. Yield yourself to the waters that are ripping and tearing at you. When the undertow catches you and drags you seaward along the bottom don't struggle against it. If you do, you are liable to be drowned, for it is stronger than you. Yield yourself to that undertow. Swim with it, not against it, and you will find the pressure removed. And, swimming with it, fooling it so that it does not hold you, swim upward at the same time. It will be no trouble at all to reach the surface.

The man who wants to learn surf-riding must be a strong swimmer, and he must be used to going under the water. After that, fair strength and common sense are all that is required. The force of the big comber is rather unexpected. There are mix-ups in which board and rider are torn apart and separated by several hundred feet. The surf-rider must take care of himself. No matter how many riders swim out with him, he cannot depend upon any of them for aid. The fancied security I had in the presence of Ford and Freeth made me forget that it was my first swim out in deep water among the big ones. I recollected, however, and rather suddenly, for a big wave came in, and away went the two men on its back all the way to shore. I could have been drowned a dozen different ways before they got back to me.

One slides down the face of a breaker on his surfboard, but he has to get started to sliding. Board and rider must be moving shoreward at a good rate before the wave overtakes them. When you see the wave coming that you want to ride in, you turn tail to it and paddle shoreward with all your strength, using what is called the windmill stroke. This is a sort of spurt performed immediately in front of the wave. If the board is going fast enough, the wave accelerates it, and the board begins its quarter-of-a-mile slide.

I shall never forget the first big wave I caught out there in the deep water. I saw it coming, turned my back on it, and paddled for dear life. Faster and faster my board went, till it seemed my arms would drop off. What was happening behind me I could not tell. One cannot look behind and paddle the windmill stroke. I heard the crest of the wave hissing and churning, and then my board was lifted and flung forward. I scarcely knew what happened the first half-minute. Though I kept my eyes open, I could not see anything, for I was buried in the rushing white of the crest. But I did not mind. I was chiefly conscious of ecstatic bliss at having caught the wave. At the end of the half-minute, however, I began to see things, and to breathe. I saw that three feet of the nose of my board was clear out of water and riding on the air. I shifted my weight forward, and made the nose come down. Then I lay, quite at rest in the midst of the wild movement, and watched the shore and the bathers on the beach grow distinct. I didn't cover quite a quarter of a mile on that wave, because, to prevent the board from diving, I shifted my weight back, but shifted it too far and fell down the rear slope of the wave.

It was my second day at surf-riding, and I was quite proud of myself. I stayed out there four hours, and when it was over, I was resolved that on the morrow I'd come in standing up. But that resolution paved a distant place. On the morrow I was in bed. I was not sick, but I was very unhappy, and I was in bed. When describing the wonderful water of Hawaii I forgot to describe the wonderful sun of Hawaii. It is a tropic sun, and, furthermore, in the first part of June, it is an overhead sun. It is also an insidious, deceitful sun. For the first time in my life I was sunburned unawares. My arms, shoulders, and back had been burned many times in the past and were tough; but not so my legs. And for four hours I had exposed the tender backs of my legs, at right angles, to that perpendicular Hawaiian sun. It was not until after I got ashore that I discovered the sun had touched me. Sunburn at first is merely warm; after that it grows intense and the blisters come out. Also, the joints, where the skin wrinkles, refuse to bend. That is why I spent the next day in bed. I couldn't walk. And that is why, today, I am writing this in bed. It is easier to than not to. But tomorrow, ah, tomorrow, I shall be out in that wonderful water, and I shall come in standing up, even as Ford and Freeth. And if I fail tomorrow, I shall do it the next day, or the next. Upon one thing I am resolved: the *Snark* shall not sail from Honolulu until I, too, wing my heels with the swiftness of the sea, and become a sunburned, skin-peeling Mercury.

FROM "MY HAWAIIAN ALOHA"

HAWAII IS THE HOME OF SHANGHAIED MEN AND WOMEN, AND OF the descendants of shanghaied men and women. They never intended to be here at all. Very rarely, since the first whites came, has one, with the deliberate plan of coming to remain, remained. Somehow, the love of the Islands, like the love of a woman, just happens. One cannot determined in advance to love a particular woman, nor can one so determine to love Hawaii. One sees, and one loves or does not love. With Hawaii it seems always to be love at first sight. Those for whom the Islands were made, or who were made for the Islands, are swept off their feet in the first moments of meeting, embrace, and are embraced.

I remember a dear friend who resolved to come to Hawaii and make it his home forever. He packed up his wife, all his belongings including his garden hose and rake and hoe, said, "Good-by, proud California," and departed. Now he was a poet, with an eye and soul for beauty, and it was only to be expected that he would lose his heart to Hawaii as Mark Twain and Stevenson and Stoddard had before him. So he came, with his wife and garden hose and rake and hoe. Heaven alone knows what preconceptions he must have entertained. But the fact remains that he found naught of beauty and charm and delight. His stay in Hawaii, brief as it was, was a hideous nightmare. In no time he was back in California. To this day he speaks with plaintive bitterness of his experience, although he never mentions what became of his garden hose and rake and hoe. Surely the soil could not have proved niggardly to him!

Otherwise was it with Mark Twain, who wrote of Hawaii long after his visit: "No alien land in all the world has any deep, strong charm for me but that one; no other land could so longingly and so beseechingly haunt me, sleeping and waking, through half a lifetime, as that one has done. Other things leave me, but it abides; other things change, but it remains the same. For me its balmy airs are always blowing, its summer seas flashing in the sun; the pulsing of its surf-beat is in my ears; I can see its garlanded crags, its leaping cascades, its plumy palms drowsing by the shore, its remote summits floating like islands above the cloud rack; I can feel the spirit of its woodland solitudes; I can hear the plash of its brooks; in my nostrils still lives the breath of flowers that perished twenty years ago."

One reads of the first Chief Justice under the Kamehamehas, that he was on his way around the Horn to Oregon when he was persuaded to remain in Hawaii. Truly, Hawaii is a woman beautiful and vastly more persuasive and seductive than her sister sirens of the sea.

The sailor boy, Archibald Scott Cleghorn, had no intention of leaving his ship; but he looked upon the Princess Likelike, the Princess Likelike looked on him, and he remained to become the father of the Princess Kaiulani and to dignify a place of honor through long years. He was not the first sailor boy to leave his ship, nor the last. One of the recent ones, whom I know well, arrived several years ago on a yacht in a yacht race from the mainland. So brief was his permitted vacation from his bank cashiership that he had planned to return by fast steamer. He is still here. The outlook is that his children and his grandchildren after him will be here.

Another erstwhile bank cashier is Louis von Tempsky, the son of the last British officer killed in the Maori War. His New Zealand bank gave him a year's vacation. The one place he wanted to see above all others was California. He departed. His ship stopped at Hawaii. It was the same old story. The ship sailed on without him. His New Zealand bank never saw him again, and many years passed ere ever he saw California. But she had no charms for him. And today, his sons and daughters about him, he looks down on half a world and all of Maui from the rolling grasslands of the Haleakala Ranch.

There were the Gays and Robinsons. Scotch pioneers over the world in the good old days when families were large and patriarchal, they had settled in New Zealand. After a time they decided to migrate to British Columbia. Among their possessions was a full-rigged ship, of which one of their sons was master. Like my poet friend from California, they packed all their property on board. But in place of his garden hose and rake and hoe, they took their plows and harrows and all their agricultural machinery. Also, they took their horses and their cattle and their sheep. When they arrived in British Columbia they would be in shape to settle immediately, break the soil, and not miss a harvest. But the ship, as was the custom in the sailing-ship days, stopped at Hawaii for water and fruit and vegetables. The Gays and Robinsons are still here, or, rather, their venerable children, and younger grandchildren and great-grandchildren; for Hawaii, like the Princess Likelike, put her arms around them, and it was love at first sight. They took up land on Kauai and Niihau, the ninety-seven square miles of the latter remaining intact in their possession to this day.

I doubt that not even the missionairies, windjamming around the Horn from New England a century ago, had the remotest thought of living out all their days in Hawaii. This is not the way of missionaries over the world. They have always gone forth to far places with the resolve to devote their lives to the glory of God and the redemption of the heathen, but with the determination, at the end of it all, to return to spend their declining years in their own country. But Hawaii can seduce missionaries just as readily as she

FROM "MY HAWAIIAN ALOHA"

can seduce sailor boys and bank cashiers, and this particular lot of missionaries was so enamored of her charms that
they did not return when old age came upon them. Their
bones lie here in the land they came to love better than their
own; and they, and their sons and daughters after them, have
been, and are, powerful forces in the development of Hawaii.

In missionary annals, such unanimous and eager adoption
of a new land is unique. Yet another thing, equally unique
in missionary history, must be noted in passing. Never did
missionaries, the very first, go out to rescue a heathen land
from its idols, and on arrival find it already rescued, self-
rescued, while they were on the journey. In 1819, all Hawaii
was groaning under the harsh rule of the ancient idols, whose
mouthpieces were the priests and whose utterances were the
frightfully cruel and unjust tabus. In 1819, the first missionaries assembled in Boston and sailed away on the long
voyage around the Horn. In 1819, the Hawaiians, of themselves, without counsel or suggestion, overthrew their idols
and abolished the tabus. In 1820, the missionaries completed their long voyage and landed in Hawaii to find a
country and a people without gods and without religion,
ready, ready and ripe for instruction.

But to return. Hawaii is the home of shanghaied men and
women, who were induced to remain, not by a blow with
a club over the head or a doped bottle of whisky, but by love.
Hawaii and the Hawaiians are a land and a people loving
and lovable. By their language may ye know them, and in
what other land save this one is the commonest form of
greeting, not "Good day," nor "How d'ye do," but "Love"?
That greeting is *Aloha*—love, I love you, my love to you.
Good day—what is it more than an impersonal remark about
the weather? How do you do—it is personal in a merely
casual interrogative sort of a way. But Aloha! It is a positive
affirmation of the warmth of one's own heart-giving. My love
to you! I love you! Aloha!

Well, then, try to imagine a land that is as lovely and loving as such a people. Hawaii is all of this. Not strictly tropical,

but subtropical, rather, in the heel of the northeast trades
(which is a very wine of wind), with altitudes rising from
palm-fronded coral beaches to snow-capped summits fourteen thousand feet in the air; there was never so much climate gathered together in one place on earth. The custom
of the dwellers is as it was of old time, only better, namely:
to have a town house, a seaside house, and a mountain house.
All three homes, by automobile, can be within half an hour's
run of one another; yet, in difference of climate and scenery,
they are the equivalent of a house on Fifth Avenue or the
Riverside Drive, of an Adirondack camp, and of a Florida
winter bungalow, plus a twelve-months' cycle of seasons
crammed into each and every day.

Let me try to make this clearer. The New York dweller
must wait till summer for the Adirondacks, till winter for the
Florida beach. But in Hawaii, say on the island of Oahu,
the Honolulu dweller can decide each day what climate and
what season he desires to spend the day in. It is his to pick
and choose. Yes, and further: he may awake in his Adirondacks, lunch and shop and go to the club in his city, spend
his afternoon and dine at his Palm Beach, and return to
sleep in the shrewd coolness of his Adirondack camp.

And what is true of Oahu, is true of all the other large
islands of the group. Climate and season are to be had for
the picking and choosing, with countless surprising varia-
tions thrown in for good measure. Suppose one be an invalid,
seeking an invalid's climate. A night's run from Honolulu
on a steamer will land him on the leeward coast of the Big
Island of Hawaii. There, amongst the coffee on the slopes
of Kona, a thousand feet above Kailua and the wrinkled sea,
he will find the perfect invalid-climate. It is the land of the
morning calm, the afternoon shower, and the evening tranquillity. Harsh winds never blow. Once in a year or two a
stiff wind of twenty-four to forty-eight hours will blow from
the south. This is the Kona wind. Otherwise there is no wind,
at least no air-drafts of sufficient force to be so dignified.
They are not even breezes. They are air-fans, alternating by

day and by night between the sea and the land. Under the
sun, the land warms and draws to it the mild sea air. In
the night, the land radiating its heat more quickly, the sea
remains the warmer and draws to it the mountain air faintly
drenched with the perfume of flowers.

Such is the climate of Kona, where nobody ever dreams of
looking at a thermometer, where each afternoon there falls
a refreshing spring shower, and where neither frost nor sun-
stroke has ever been known. All of which is made possible
by the towering bulks of Mauna Kea and Mauna Loa. Beyond them, on the windward slopes of the Big Island, along
the Hamakua Coast, the trade wind will as often as not be
blustering at forty miles an hour. Should an Oregon web-
foot become homesick for the habitual wet of his native
clime, he will find easement and a soaking on the windward
coasts of Hawaii and Maui, from Hilo in the south with its
average annual rainfall of one hundred and fifty inches to
the Nahiku country to the north beyond Hana which has
known a downpour of four hundred and twenty inches in
a single twelvemonth. In the matter of rain it is again pick
and choose—from two hundred inches to twenty, or five, or
one. Nay, further, forty miles away from the Nahiku, on the
leeward slopes of the House of the Sun, which is the mightiest
extinct volcano in the world, rain may not fall once in a
dozen years, cattle live their lives without ever seeing a
puddle, and horses brought from that region shy at running
water or try to eat it with their teeth.

One can multiply the foregoing examples indefinitely, and
to the proposition that never was so much climate gathered
together in one place, can be added that never was so much
landscape gathered together in one place. The diversification
is endless, from the lava shores of South Puna to the barking
sands of Kauai. On every island breakneck mountain climbing abounds. One can shiver above timber line on the snow-
caps of Mauna Kea or Mauna Loa, swelter under the banyan
at sleepy old Lahaina, swim in clear ocean water that effer-
vesces like champagne on ten thousand beaches, or sleep

under blankets every night in the upland pastures of the great cattle ranges and awaken each morning to the song of skylarks and the crisp, snappy air of spring. But never, never, go where he will in Hawaii Nei, will he experience a hurricane, a tornado, a blizzard, a fog, or ninety degrees in the shade. Such discomforts are meteorologically impossible, so the meteorologists affirm. When Hawaii was named the Paradise of the Pacific, it was inadequately named. The rest of the Seven Seas and the islands in the midst thereof should have been included along with the Pacific. "See Naples and die"—they spell it differently here: *See Hawaii and live*.

TALES OF THE PACIFIC

JACK LONDON
 Stories of Hawaii $6.95
 South Sea Tales $6.95
 The Mutiny of the "Elsinore" $5.95

HAWAII
 Ancient History of the Hawaiian People to the Times of
  Kamehameha I $7.95
 Kona by Marjorie Sinclair $4.95
 A Hawaiian Reader $6.95
 A Hawaiian Reader, Vol. II $6.95
 Russian Flag Over Hawaii by Darwin Teihet $5.95
 Myths and Legends of Hawaii by W.D. Westervelt $5.95
 Mark Twain in Hawaii $4.95
 The Legends and Myths of Hawaii by Kalakaua $6.95
 Hawaii's Story by Hawaii's Queen $7.95
 Rape in Paradise by Theon Wright $5.95
 The Betrayal of Liliuokalani $7.95
 The Wild Wind by Marjorie Sinclair $5.95
 Hawaii: Fiftieth Star by A. Grove Day $4.95
 Hawaii and Its People by A. Grove Day $4.95
 True Tales of the South Seas ed. by A. Grove Day and Carl
  Stoven $5.95

Orders should be sent to Mutual Publishing Co.
1215 Center Street, Suite 210, Honolulu, HI 96816.
For book rate shipping, add $3.00 for first book, $1.00 for
each additional book (4-6 weeks; in Hawaii, 1-2 weeks);
for first class, add $4.00 for first book, $3.00 for each
additional book (1-2 weeks).